THE LEGEND OF

Con-way®

A HISTORY OF SERVICE, RELIABILITY, INNOVATION, AND GROWTH

THE LEGEND OF

Con·way®

A HISTORY OF SERVICE, RELIABILITY, INNOVATION, AND GROWTH

JEFFREY L. RODENGEN

Edited by Heather Lewin
Design and layout by Sandy Cruz

Dedicated to Johnny Hill ...
the golden coach driver who truly understands the demands of transportation
and has transported Cindy and me to our future together.

Write Stuff Enterprises, Inc.
1001 South Andrews Avenue
Fort Lauderdale, FL 33316
1-800-900-Book (1-800-900-2665)
(954) 462-6657
www.writestuffbooks.com

The publisher has made every effort to identify and locate the source of the photographs included in this edition of *The Legend of Con-way: A History of Service, Reliability, Innovation, and Growth*. Grateful acknowledgment is made to those who have kindly granted permission for the use of their materials in this edition. If there are instances where proper credit was not given, the publisher will gladly make any necessary corrections in subsequent printings.

PUBLISHER'S CATALOGING IN PUBLICATION

(Prepared by The Donohue Group, Inc.)

Rodengen, Jeffrey L.
   The legend of Con-way : a history of service, reliability, innovation, and growth / Jeffrey L. Rodengen ; edited by Heather Lewin ; design and layout by Sandy Cruz ; [foreword by Raymond O'Brien].

      p. : ill. ; cm.

   Includes bibliographical references and index.
   ISBN-13: 978-1-932022-32-2
   ISBN-10: 1-932022-32-5

   1. Con-way (Firm)—History. 2. Trucking—United States—History. I. Lewin, Heather. II. Cruz, Sandy. III. O'Brien, Raymond (Raymond F.) IV. Title. V. Title: Con-way

HE5623.Z7 C66 2008
388.3/24/06573   2008925042

Completely produced in the
United States of America
10 9 8 7 6 5 4 3 2 1

ALSO BY JEFFREY L. RODENGEN

The Legend of Chris-Craft

IRON FIST:
The Lives of Carl Kiekhaefer

Evinrude-Johnson and
The Legend of OMC

Serving the Silent Service:
The Legend of Electric Boat

The Legend of Dr Pepper/Seven-Up

The Legend of Honeywell

The Legend of Briggs & Stratton

The Legend of Ingersoll-Rand

The Legend of Stanley:
150 Years of The Stanley Works

The MicroAge Way

The Legend of Halliburton

The Legend of York International

The Legend of Nucor Corporation

The Legend of Goodyear:
The First 100 Years

The Legend of AMP

The Legend of Cessna

The Legend of VF Corporation

The Spirit of AMD

The Legend of Rowan

New Horizons:
The Story of Ashland Inc.

The History of American Standard

The Legend of Mercury Marine

The Legend of Federal-Mogul

Against the Odds:
Inter-Tel—The First 30 Years

The Legend of Pfizer

State of the Heart: The Practical Guide
to Your Heart and Heart Surgery
with Larry W. Stephenson, M.D.

The Legend of Worthington Industries

The Legend of IBP

The Legend of Trinity Industries, Inc.

The Legend of
Cornelius Vanderbilt Whitney

The Legend of Amdahl

The Legend of Litton Industries

The Legend of Gulfstream

The Legend of Bertram
with David A. Patten

The Legend of Ritchie Bros. Auctioneers

The Legend of ALLTEL
with David A. Patten

The Yes, you can of Invacare Corporation
with Anthony L. Wall

The Ship in the Balloon:
The Story of Boston Scientific and the
Development of Less-Invasive Medicine

The Legend of Day & Zimmermann

The Legend of Noble Drilling

Fifty Years of Innovation: Kulicke & Soffa

Biomet—From Warsaw to the World
with Richard F. Hubbard

NRA: An American Legend

The Heritage and Values of RPM, Inc.

The Marmon Group: The First Fifty Years

The Legend of Grainger

The Legend of The Titan Corporation
with Richard F. Hubbard

The Legend of Discount Tire Co.
with Richard F. Hubbard

The Legend of Polaris
with Richard F. Hubbard

The Legend of La-Z-Boy
with Richard F. Hubbard

The Legend of McCarthy
with Richard F. Hubbard

Intervoice: Twenty Years of Innovation
with Richard F. Hubbard

Jefferson-Pilot Financial:
A Century of Excellence
with Richard F. Hubbard

The Legend of HCA

The Legend of Werner Enterprises
with Richard F. Hubbard

The History of J. F. Shea Co.
with Richard F. Hubbard

True to Our Vision
with Richard F. Hubbard

The Legend of Albert Trostel & Sons
with Richard F. Hubbard

The Legend of Sovereign Bancorp
with Richard F. Hubbard

Innovation is the Best Medicine:
The extraordinary story of Datascope
with Richard F. Hubbard

The Legend of Guardian Industries

The Legend of
Universal Forest Products

Changing the World: Polytechnic
University—The First 150 Years

Nothing is Impossible: The Legend
of Joe Hardy and 84 Lumber

In it for the Long Haul:
The Story of CRST

The Story of Parsons Corporation

Cerner: From Vision to Value

New Horizons:
The Story of Federated Investors

Office Depot: Taking Care of Business—
The First 20 Years

The Legend of General Parts:
Proudly Serving a World in Motion

Bard: Power of the Past,
Force of the Future

Innovation & Integrity:
The Story of Hub Group

Amica: A Century of Service
1907–2007

A Passion for Service:
The Story of ARAMARK

TABLE OF CONTENTS

FOREWORD

BY
RAYMOND O'BRIEN

CHAIRMAN OF THE BOARD, CF INC., 1979–1995
CEO, CF INC., 1977–1988; 1990–1991
PRESIDENT, CF INC., 1975–1980; 1981–1986

EVERY ADVENTURE HAS A BEGINning. Although Con-way traces its long roots to the founding of Consolidated Truck Lines Inc. by Leland James in 1929, Con-way and its operating companies were born through the sale of the Freightliner company by its parent company Consolidated Freightways in 1981.

Freightliner was well established by the time I joined Consolidated Freightways in 1958. Even so, there were daunting challenges to competing in the market. Freightliner had only recently set up its own dealer network, and there were well-entrenched competitors. It became clear to me then that Freightliner would need a lot more money for engineering, marketing, and dealerships.

One day, Don Moffitt and I were considering what to do with Freightliner, and we decided to call on both Volvo and Daimler-Benz to see if a deal was possible. I flew to London, only to find that Volvo had just completed a large acquisition, leaving it somewhat short of cash. Daimler-Benz, however, was very interested. Negotiations dragged on for the better part of a year, but eventually, we received close to $300 million for Freightliner. We then had a portfolio of money that we invested, and the portfolio was probably earning the corporation as much

as our trucking activities. This is where things became interesting.

We hired consultants to advise us on our options to expand the company. They determined that the average length of haul for an LTL shipment of freight was less than 500 miles. Yet, our average length of haul was more than 1,200 miles. So, we said, "We ought to get in that business!" That's where the idea originated. As we thought through the operational model to support that type of business, we realized that you couldn't effectively intermix the long haul and the short haul—at least at that time—because the short haul needed immediate attention and overnight service. You have to get the trucks moving out at about 7 P.M. instead of 10:30 P.M. or 11 P.M. The final piece of the puzzle became labor efficiency. When the trucking industry was regulated, you were able to pass along increases created by inefficiencies to the customer. Then, when deregulation occurred in 1980, vast competition arose that wasn't beholden to traditional labor contracts. We agreed from the start that our new, short-haul business would be high-service and compete with the most productive labor in the market. This created a new environment, where the loyalty of employees was to the company, rather than to a union, and that is one of the secrets of our success.

We formed three autonomous companies; Con-Way Central Express, Con-Way Western Express, and Con-Way Eastern Express. They were located where we thought our greatest opportunities would lie in the short-haul markets. It was a little nerve-wracking at first. During the first night of launching the Con-Way Western Express operation, we were expecting 800 shipments—we received eight. Con-Way Central had similar stories. Some early shipments were sent as luggage on Greyhound buses. We would have delivered shipments in the trunks of salesmen's cars if necessary. Still, I think the idea and culture of excellent service to the customer really paid off from the first shipment.

As you will read, great people, a superior operating model, and a unique culture drove the remarkable growth that ensued. As the company has grown from those fledgling days, I have watched with great pride as the employees of Con-way and Menlo have built their companies into a vibrant and integral part of the U.S. and global economies. As the company matured, it has evolved into a diverse, profitable industry leader that continues to adapt to market conditions.

On the eve of the 25th anniversary of Con-way Freight, the story that got Con-way to this point is a remarkable record of success in an unusually competitive environment. And, it's a testament to the power of the employees and a culture that has always set the industry standard for service and whose employees continue to lead the industry today.

ACKNOWLEDGMENTS

MANY DEDICATED PEOPLE ASSISted in the research, preparation, and publication of *The Legend of Con-way: A History of Service, Reliability, Innovation, and Growth.*

Research Assistant Joseph Cabadas conducted the principal archival research for the book, while Senior Editor Heather Lewin managed the editorial content. Vice President/Creative Director Sandy Cruz brought the story to life.

Several key individuals associated with Con-way provided their assistance in development of the book from its outline to its finished product, including: Ray Halloran, Cathie Hartung, Pat Jannausch, Tara Keezer, Ned Moritz, Crystal Neal, Tom Nightingale, Carmen E. Perkins, Carrie Reese, and Doug Stotlar. A special thank you goes to Raymond O'Brien for contributing the book's foreword.

All of the people interviewed—Con-way employees, retirees, and friends—were generous with their time and insights. Those who shared their memories and thoughts include: Dave Anderson, Jackie Barretta, Bob Bassett, Kay Beher, Bob Bianco, Bob Bull, Wayne Byerley, Ed Conaway, Bob Coon, Hugh "Wes" Cornett, Donna Cottardi, Jerry Detter, Marshall Fulbright, Ray Halloran, John Hickerson, Pat Jannausch, Keith Kennedy, Gary Kowalski, John Labrie, Daryl Lafitte, Rock Magnan, Dave McClimon, Dave Miller, Bryan Millican, Donald Moffitt, Ned Moritz, Tom Nightingale, Raymond O'Brien, Jennifer Pileggi, Kevin Schick, Jim Schlueter, Herb Schmidt, Eb Schmoller, Rick Smith, Tom Smith, Doug Stotlar, Gary Vianueva, and Phil Worthington.

Other individuals who assisted with the collection of historic photographic materials include Stephen Cook, Larry Dumford, David S. Faust, Ken Goudy, George Hamlin, and David Malone, who are collectors of historical photography; Drew Miale from KempGoldberg Strategic Marketing & Communications; and Vicki Wind and Jay Kargula from Smith-Winchester.

Finally, special thanks are extended to the staff at Write Stuff Enterprises, Inc.: Stanimira Stefanova, executive editor; Elizabeth Fernandez and Ann Gossy, senior editors; Elijah Meyer and Ryan Milewicz, graphic designers; Roy Adelman, on-press supervisor; Lynn C. Jones and Martin Schultz, proofreaders; Mary Aaron, transcriptionist; Elliot Linzer, indexer; Amy Major, executive assistant to Jeffrey L. Rodengen; Marianne Roberts, executive vice president, publisher, and chief financial officer; Steven Stahl, director of marketing; and Sherry Pawlirzyn-Hasso, bookkeeper.

CHAPTER ONE
THE BEGINNING
1892–1947

Pack up your cargo in a 10-ton truck
Roll mile on mile
Step on the throttle—give your blues the air
Payloads are worthwhile
There's no time for worrying
Good business is in style
So ... pack up your cargo in a 10-ton truck
And smile—smile—smile.

—Poet unknown, from the
Consolidated Freight Lines scrapbook,
1936–1941

CON-WAY INC.'S HISTORY CAN BE TRACED back to the early 1900s, during the infancy of the transportation industry. William Leland "Lee" James was born on September 10, 1892, to Thomasina Lowry and Captain Alonzo James, who piloted sternwheel steamers, tugboats, and barges on the Columbia River. Lee grew up just outside of Portland, Oregon, in Oregon City, during an era when railroads and ships carried long-haul freight, while horse- and mule-drawn stagecoaches and wagons carried local cargos.

Lee joined river crews during his summer vacations from school, and he landed his first full-time job at 19, driving a truck for the Portland Electric Power Company.[1] He continued his education by taking a correspondence course in law, but was drawn back to life on the road—he was even described as having transportation in his blood.[2,3] In 1913, Lee married Millie Caitlan, a native of Minnesota, and then went into business for himself after purchasing a used 1911 Packard dump truck. The truck was equipped with solid rubber tires; a heavy-duty, wagon-like spring suspension that gave a bone-rattling ride; and wooden wheels powered by a chain drive. With no windshield or overhead protection, Lee hauled sand and gravel around Portland wearing only a duster coat.

It was a job that tested his mettle, as the 1911 Packard was a crude machine, and roads were dusty and rutted during dry weather and muddy quagmires when wet. Roads in the United States had been neglected since the 1850s, and deteriorated as railroads began providing more transcontinental and regional transportation.[4] Many rural roads were simply two ruts running across a prairie or through fenced, private lands. City roads were constructed of brick, cobblestone, wooden planks, asphalt, gravel, and macadam.[5] The wheels of heavily loaded wagons would cut through these surfaces, which would then be torn apart by automobile tires. The lack of acceptable transcontinental roads was a nuisance to automobile enthusiasts, but a major obstacle to the trucking industry.

Above: Leland James, the founder of Consolidated Truck Lines.

Opposite: This collage, as seen in the September 1, 1940 *Journal Sunday*, incorporates elements of the early years of trucking, including railroad transport, which was a challenging and hostile competitor to the nascent industry.

11

THE START OF AN INDUSTRY

In 1916, as World War I raged in Europe, James sold his truck and bought an automotive repair garage. A year later, when the United States was drawn into the war, the U.S. Army ordered hundreds of thousands of transports, stimulating the truck manufacturing industry. When the war ended on November 11, 1918, more than 225,000 of these trucks, which had never been shipped overseas, became available. This surplus allowed the motor freight industry to grow.[6] By 1920, trucks in the Pacific Northwest handled local cartage inside cities or hauled goods to towns within a 50-mile radius.[7]

James hit a major obstacle when his garage burned down in 1921—he persevered, however, and partnered with Jack Fletcher. The two friends started Fletcher & James, which became one of Portland's largest automobile and truck tire retailers.[8] One financial backer was E. W. A. Peake, who had started a savings and loan company.[9]

In 1923, James found an opportunity to reenter the transportation business after the Portland–Tillamook Stage Line, an Oregon intercity bus firm, went bankrupt. Fletcher became the receiver of the bus line, and James and a group of investors bought the company and merged it with Portland–Newberg–McMinnville Stage Line. The combined bus lines were then named the Portland–Newberg–McMinnville–Tillamook Stage Lines Inc. At the time, it was common for bus and truck firms to include main destinations in the company name, while the use of "stage lines" was a carryover from stagecoach days. After purchasing several other bus lines in the Portland area, the intercity bus line company was officially called Pacific Stage Lines.[10]

The success of James' bus line operation caught the attention of the Southern Pacific Railroad, which had started its own bus subsidiary to reclaim lost passenger business. The competition was fierce, and, in 1928, Southern Pacific Railroad bought James' busing operation, merging it into the company that would become Pacific Greyhound Lines. This purchase allowed James the freedom—and the capital—to reenter the motor freight business.[11]

EARLY MOTOR FREIGHT

The trucking industry grew increasingly vital to the United States in the late 1920s, reaching customers that the railroads and riverboats could not. However, the growing industry only attracted small firms that served a few locales and were affected by weather delays, malfunctioning equipment, and road conditions. Although state governments and the Federal Interstate Commerce Commission (ICC) did oversee the industry, there was little government regulation or systematic industry practice, so customers sometimes faced delays, damaged goods, or no service at all.[12]

After the sale of Pacific Stage Lines, James and his stockholders took $110,207 and created the Peerless Investment Company. Gathering like-minded truck operators, the 36-year-old James formed Consolidated Truck Lines Inc., in 1929, as a holding company that was capitalized with $100,000. It had 650 shares of common stock—350 of which were owned by Peerless—and 350 shares of preferred stock. The early stockholders included Peake, the largest shareholder; Roy Swint, who became Consolidated's general auditor; "Jack" Snead, Sr., a Texan whose background included opening a car dealership in California, running a telephone company, auto racing, and founding Reliance Mt. Hood Auto Stages; and LeForest "L. F." McCroskey.[13] James was elected president and general manager, and McCroskey became secretary–treasurer.

Consolidated began on April 1, 1929, by combining the operations of four carriers: Portland–Spokane Auto Freight, East Oregon Fast Freight, Portland–Medford Truck Line, and Portland–Pendleton Truck Line. Within a year, these four carriers were officially dissolved, and their operations were folded into Consolidated.[14] Out of the four truck companies, only the Portland–Medford Truck Line, owned by Joe A. Gritsch, operated in the black. Gritsch's firm owned the route between Medford, Oregon, and San Francisco, California. At the time, coastal steamers could deliver freight between California and Oregon more economically than trucks, so James sold the Medford–San Francisco route back to Gritsch for $30,000 in August 1929—a move that later proved to be a costly mistake.[15] Gritsch operated it as part of a separate trucking firm.

Above: Vice President of Traffic Frederick C. Leibold, working in his office at the far left in 1939, was instrumental in the growth of Consolidated Freightways.

Below right: This new cab-over-engine (COE) six-wheel Fageol was delivered to Consolidated Freight Lines in 1937. Equipped with a Cummins diesel engine, its long body allowed balanced load distribution over its rear wheels.

Consolidated offered overnight delivery service to many communities within a 375-mile radius of Portland, including Spokane, Washington. By May 1929, the Washington Department of Public Works granted Portland–Spokane Auto Freight authorization to provide intrastate service between Spokane and Yakima, Washington. The company's initial fleet consisted of 22 trucks—a motley collection of four-wheel models, including Fageol, Federal, GMC, Kenworth, Sterling, and White. Some had open-air cabs; some needed candles on dashboards to defrost windshields and a kerosene lantern to provide heat during cold weather. Most of the company's 18 trailers did not have brakes. The fleet was painted in bright green and red, which became Consolidated's trademark image.[16]

The company's first headquarters was housed in a 20-by-30-foot office on the upper floor of the East Side Truck Terminal in Portland. Working side by side with other trucking operators, it only used two of the terminal's loading doors and had a small swath of floor space. Its other terminals were less spacious and had fewer staff members. Spokane, for example, had two trucks, but only one employee.

The original employees, who called themselves "Consolidators," worked hard to keep the company going. Drivers, supplemented by terminal managers, took to the roads at night and loaded and unloaded trucks. The entire operation grew to 80 employees and a payroll of $200,000 by the end of the first year. Frederick C. Leibold, the first traffic manager, handled all of Portland's traffic, as well as making sales trips.[17] Leibold was described as meticulous and a gentleman, and his department handled claims for lost or damaged freight.[18]

THE GREAT DEPRESSION

As Consolidated grew, the United States was entering the Great Depression. Throughout 1929, there was an escalating trend of personal and corporate bankruptcies and foreclosures. The stock market crashed that October, signaling a devastating economic downturn.

Despite the onset of the Depression, Consolidated added new, six-wheel trucks to its fleet, mostly Fageols made by the Fageol Truck and Coach Co. of Oakland, California. Consolidated touted the Fageols with signage on the sides of its trucks that claimed they were "Easy on the highways—fast—and surefooted when the going is rough."

At first, the winter weather proved more detrimental to the company than the stock market collapse. Horace H. "Babe" Nash, one of Consolidated's

drivers, claimed that 1929 had the "worst and coldest" winter he had ever experienced.[19] A night run to Roseburg from Portland, which normally took six hours, became a 19-hour ordeal. There was a foot of snow on the ground when it began raining, and temperatures dropped below the freezing point.

"Before the freeze, the rigs made deep ruts in the snow, and after it froze you couldn't get out of them," Nash said. Truckers dug up fence posts to gain access to dirt, which they used to thaw the snow.[20]

Other formidable obstacles that James' company faced included a shortage of well-paved roads and bridges. Some rivers could only be crossed by ferries, while some mountain roads were so narrow that only one truck could pass at a time. Financially, Consolidated also suffered from a lack of backhaul from far-flung areas.

To resolve its backhaul problems, Consolidated shipped regular loads of agricultural goods from farm and cattle ranches in eastern Oregon and Washington to ports on the West Coast. "Anything That Will Go into a Truck" became the Consolidated slogan as it transported cargos, including bulk wheat, cattle, packed goods, furniture, oil drums, salted peanuts, dressmaker's dummies, glassware, and barroom chairs. Despite the Depression, by the end of 1929, Consolidated's revenues for its nine months in operation totaled $397,763.[21]

Above: "Anything That Will Go into a Truck" was the byword of Consolidated Freightways. The photograph shows part of a 30,000-pound shipment of bulk wheat from Maupin, Oregon, to Vancouver, Washington.

Below left: Snowy scenes were common along the Cascade Mountain passes traversed by Consolidated Freightways trucks, as high snowbanks created obstacles for drivers and their trucks.

In 1930, Consolidated had 85 units in its fleet. It acquired four other carriers: Associated Truck Lines, which expanded its reach in Oregon; Portland–Boise Auto Freight, which served Oregon to western Idaho; Old Timers Transfer and Storage (renamed as Idaho Consolidated Truck Lines), which served Oregon to southern Idaho; and Red Arrow. When the Ford car and truck assembly plant in Portland needed a quicker, more dependable freight carrier to deliver automobiles to its dealers, James organized a subsidiary called Consolidated Convoy.

As its expanding business outstripped the rented Portland dock space, Consolidated obtained a $70,000 loan and built a 16-door terminal and shop. At the end of 1930, Consolidated's routes totaled 1,836 miles, and its revenues were $902,000. It had become one of the largest motor freight carriers in the Western states.

DEPRESSION, DEBTS, AND DEALS

By 1931, the Depression had deepened, with the number of bank failures increasing and millions of jobless citizens searching for work. Thousands of lumbermen and agricultural workers traveled to Portland and Seattle looking for work, but instead they found local residents facing their own difficulties with unemployment and foreclosures. Shantytowns, nicknamed "Hoovervilles" after President Hoover, sprung up, and Portland was subjected to curfews, while police arrested the jobless.[22] The railroad companies, which were the main rivals to truckers, also felt the economic collapse as tonnages and revenues plunged by half.

Southern Pacific Railroad's earnings plummeted from $165 million annually to $72 million during 1931. Truckers, such as Consolidated, were filling the freight transport void by picking up the less-than-truckload (LTL) loads the railroads couldn't—or wouldn't—serve. To stem its losses, Southern Pacific Railroad placed a freight car on its fast-moving Portland–Medford passenger train that same year. This experimental concept was the freight-delivery system that James would encounter once again later in the decade.[23]

Although Consolidated had nearly $250,000 in debts, stemming from the purchase of real estate, trucks, tires, and fuel, James merged his operations with A. E. "Jack" Birum's Federal Auto Freight Company on January 20, 1931. Birum had established his company, which consisted of three trucks and three trailers, in 1920, and he drove a four-cylinder, 3½-ton Federal truck.[24] The Federal didn't have a windshield, cab, or a body, and his experiences in early trucking were similar to those of James. Birum explained:

The freight was loaded on "stake racks" and covered with canvas during bad weather. The driver sat on a hard seat with the steering wheel post coming up between his legs like the brake wheel of a boxcar. ... On a rough road, the driver took a good grip on the steering wheel, and each time he came down on the seat managed to brace himself sufficiently to jerk the wheel a little and head the truck toward the middle of the road before he, again, took to the air.[25]

The deal needed the approval of George Youell, Birum's major stockholder.[26] Youell and his sons, Tom and John, were owners of a Seattle fruit and produce company. Their influence had gained Birum a contract to deliver Northern Pacific Railway's freight in the Yakima Valley. George, however, was concerned about Consolidated's debts and arranged a reverse merger. James' operation became part of Federal Auto Freight Company and was renamed Consolidated Freight Lines Inc. (CF).

James' original stockholders received 1,725 shares of preferred stock and 7,469 shares of common stock, while Federal's shareholders

This advertisement describes Consolidated's "transcontinental" network, which linked the Pacific Coast to Chicago. It appeared in *Traffic World* magazine on May 8, 1937.

obtained 1,030 preferred shares and 2,777 common shares. The Youells became CF's major stockholders, while Peake held the second-largest number of shares.[27] James was elected president; John Youell, vice president; Birum, secretary; and McCroskey, treasurer. The number of stockholders increased to 25 and included James, McCroskey, and the owners of the smaller firms previously acquired by Consolidated.

LEGISLATIVE OBSTACLES

While CF was growing, state and federal legislatures—lobbied heavily by the railroads—dealt a blow to the trucking industry by imposing different truck and trailer length and weight limitations among Western states. This caused considerable difficulty in navigating interstate transports.

Between 1917 and 1931, the federal government's permissible gross load on a combination of vehicles was 44,000 pounds. In 1931, this federal limit was increased to 49,000 pounds; four years later it was raised to 54,000 pounds. States in the west also passed laws governing size and weight. In an effort to unify state regulations, Consolidated and other trucking firms lobbied for axle-weight restrictions where no axle of a vehicle could bear a weight greater than 18,000 pounds. They also lobbied for a vehicle height of 12 feet, 6 inches; width at 8 feet; and a maximum truck-trailer combination of 60 feet.[28]

California and Washington adopted truck-trailer length limits of 60 feet, with a maximum gross weight of 68,000 pounds. In 1931, Oregon's legislature, however, set a 50-foot length maximum and limited gross weight to 54,000 pounds.[29] To transport goods in and out of Oregon, truckers created "break-up" points at state borders, where larger trucks halted and reloaded cargo into smaller units to enter Oregon.[30] James and other CF officers regularly explained to the press that the industry needed "rubber trucks" that could be stretched or squeezed as they crossed Oregon's state lines and emphasized that the mishmash of regulations added costs.

INDUSTRY STABILIZATION

During the summer of 1932, the Depression worsened, cutting into CF's finances. To keep the

This editorial cartoon, criticizing efforts to increase truck-trailer size and weight limits, appeared in the February 6, 1937, edition of *The Oregonian* newspaper. *(Illustration courtesy of The Oregonian.)*

company afloat, portions of employee's checks—starting with James—were held back until cash flow issues were resolved.[31] The Youell family assumed payments on some new truck contracts, while James' close friend, Peake, also assisted the struggling company. Standard Oil and other major creditors accepted CF stock instead of cash payments. Other creditors, including General Tire and Kenworth, accepted discounts and debt reductions to ensure Consolidated did not file for bankruptcy. George Youell also attempted to replace James during a board meeting that year, but Peake intervened, siding with the company founder.[32]

James wanted to bring stability to his workforce—he was driven by the ideals of corporate paternalism, which meant that employers were responsible for employees' welfare. In return, employees remained loyal to the company. He invited Portland Teamsters Local 162 and the Seattle Local 174 to organize CF's workforce. Although the company had only been in existence for less than three years, it had always been nonunion, and it paid its drivers per trip. At a safety meeting in late 1932, that would change. James made clear what he believed: "If men belonged to unions, they would be able to better their position."[33] Shortly thereafter, Jack Snead, Sr., was assigned to negotiate a contract with the International Brotherhood of Teamsters, signing a deal that included the drivers and dockworkers in Portland and Seattle.

The reasoning behind this change of culture was that by negotiating with a union instead of individuals, the company could offer numerous workers one contract and reduce the possibility of unauthorized strikes by meeting a collective need. Since unions standardized wages across the industry, it meant that Consolidated could compete for customers based on service performance rather than price (competing for business based on price resulted in reduced wages for workers, causing worker unrest). On the other hand, a union also meant higher wages and less flexibility with workers' schedules and duties. The Teamsters prohibited drivers from performing dock work, so cargos had to be loaded and unloaded at terminals. Drivers would no longer pick up freight directly at wholesalers' warehouses before delivering it to stores and plants.[34]

Another facet to the difficulty of the industry was the emergence of "gypsy truckers." During the Depression, shipping tonnage dropped, and there was a fierce price war among trucking companies and the rate-cutting, nonunion truckers. A 1937 article in *Western Advertising* magazine explained:

The infant trucking business, uncertain of its future, immature in its outlook, consisted of thousands of small operators so busy chiseling each other that they were hard put to eke out decent existences for themselves and their employees.[35]

The notoriously bad service and poor road manners of cut-rate truckers tarnished the motor freight industry. It was the perfect time for the railroads, again, to lobby state and federal governments for stricter regulations on trucking companies.

James supported incoming President Franklin D. Roosevelt's "New Deal" programs created under the National Industrial Recovery Act (NIRA). Industrial associations were established to create operating

IDEAS OF THE INDUSTRY

"The farmer, who must use motor transportation to move his crops to market, is directly penalized when shortsided legal restrictions require two trucks on the highway where one larger piece of equipment would serve the same purpose. This added cost is uneconomical."

LELAND JAMES, President,
Consolidated Freightways,
Portland

(Third in a series of individual messages on questions of the day from trucking operators, representing all shades of opinion.)

Leland James explained how differing vehicle length and weight requirements caused economic and logistical challenges for truckers and farmers alike in the August 1940 issue of the *Pacific Tradesman*.

standards, which James hoped would counteract the railroads' agenda and the intrusion of the cut-rate operations, but the NIRA also introduced a bloated federal bureaucracy. Before the U.S. Supreme Court declared the NIRA unconstitutional in 1935, James and other trucking company owners successfully lobbied Congress to pass the Motor Carrier Act of 1935. This act gave the ICC greater authority to regulate trucking firms, but created confusing tariff bureaus—similar to how railroads operated. The legislation imposed stricter controls on who could enter the trucking industry or expand established routes. New operators had to provide route-specific evidence that an existing trucking company was providing inadequate service on a particular route to gain that business. Although the act limited competition, it offered an additional sense of stability to a tumultuous industry.

Consolidated Freightways pioneered tire recapping when it set up its own plant in Seattle, Washington. The company averaged less than 20 flats daily in 62,000 miles of travel, which was equivalent to about two-and-a-half trips around the globe.

OPERATOR TRAINING AND SAFETY

CF developed the reputation of being a progressive operation, as James was always searching for better business practices.[36] In 1935, the company opened training schools for its drivers, mechanics, shop and service foremen, and sales personnel. James F. Morrell was hired to help run the schools. These duties soon expanded as Morrell became James' assistant, oversaw Consolidated's public relations and personnel departments, and published the company newsletter.[37]

To address an increasing rate of accidents, the company conducted a safety campaign between August 1, 1935, and August 1, 1936, establishing monthly accident prevention and safety meetings. Expert speakers were brought in from the state police and fire departments. According to E. B. Ogden, Consolidated's shop foreman in Spokane, Washington, suggestions by drivers and loaders also helped reduce accident rates. Ideas that were discussed ranged from the improper placement of fire extinguishers in trucks—which caused some drivers difficulty while shifting gears—to the dangers of carbon monoxide, to the need for first aid kits and trouble lamps.

"We have learned a lot from the men," Ogden said. "They have given us many good ideas by checking in places where supervisors or officials could not."[38]

Utilizing this valuable information from employees, accidents dropped by 60 percent even though Consolidated's operating mileage had increased 20 percent when compared to the same period a year earlier.

CF began using its shops to construct larger, more robust braking systems to provide better handling on mountain roads. The company also started a tire recapping program and custom-built, specialized equipment, such as refrigerated trucks and trailers, for its fleet. It was also one of the first trucking companies to experiment with diesel engines. Consolidated replaced the gasoline engines on two of its trucks with Cummins diesel engines in 1931. By 1936, it had switched 90 percent of its fleet to diesel engines—mostly 1,970-pound, six-cylinder Cummins HB6s that produced 125 horsepower. The new power plants allowed CF to cut its fuel bills nearly in half, resulting in a savings of about $202,478 in 1935. Maintenance costs for Cummins were also lower than for gasoline engines.[39]

ACQUISITIONS AND GROWTH

Throughout the 1930s, CF expanded through the purchase of carriers, the creation of subsidiaries, and by partnering with independent trucking firms that served Chicago and the East Coast. In 1932, CF created Shaver Forwarding (later called

Tidewater–Shaver Barge Lines), as a subsidiary. Trucks picked up wheat from central Washington and transported it to the Columbia River where it was loaded onto Shaver boats and barges. These traveled to Portland; bulk petroleum products were brought upriver as backhaul.

In 1934, CF reentered the California market when it opened a 700-mile run between Twin Falls, Idaho, and San Francisco. This "Golden Market Special" route climbed 7,000 feet over the Sierra Mountains, offering second-morning delivery to Idaho cities and third-morning delivery to Montana. This increased the company's total route mileage to 4,273.[40]

Another initiative Consolidated undertook was to boost its revenues during its traditional "winter slump." During the winter of 1934–1935, for instance, CF's revenues declined $36,000. The company's advertising campaign to boost revenues was called the "Payload Drive," and advertisements were placed in 55 newspapers. Posters were affixed to the sides of its trucks.[41] Despite setbacks such as a West Coast dock strike and fierce winter weather, CF officials declared the campaign a success when financial results were "vastly better" than the year before.[42]

By early 1936, CF offered sixth-morning delivery service from Chicago to the West Coast, as well as "transcontinental service" as its lines reached Minneapolis. At the time, transcontinental meant stretching from the West Coast to the Mississippi River. By this time, CF employed 850 people and had 450 pieces of automotive equipment.

DESIGNING THE TRUCKS

Because the Oregon legislature did not raise weight and length limits for trucks and trailers, CF effectively used two fleets of vehicles—one for Oregon and one for other Western states. To add cargo space, CF modified several trucks, creating experimental cab-over-engine (COE) designs. CF also purchased several new COE six-wheelers powered by Cummins engines. Called the "Consolidator," these models had a longer body than other trucks.[43]

CF drivers had to scan nine separate gauges on the dashboard, as well as manipulate 22 levers, pedals, switches, and buttons while driving 30 mph, according to Ed Oddson, a CF driver. He was interviewed in a 1937 article for the *Wilbur (Wash.) Reporter*, which may have been part of an ongoing public relations campaign to improve the trucker's image.[44]

Trucks were equipped with a "stool pigeon"— an automatic time registration device that recorded a truck's every stop and start. According to Oddson, all CF drivers were instructed to stop to render assistance to motorists in trouble. Trucks were equipped with first-aid kits, fire extinguishers, flashlights, tow chains, shovels, and hydraulic jacks. Oddson noted that he had hauled everything from live "Grand Coulee rattlesnakes" to dead bodies, from pinball games to apple washers. Other cargo included pencil sharpeners, airplane components, rowboats, bathtubs, shotgun shells, and soup nuts.

COMPETITION RISING

CF had grown throughout the decade from serving few locations with 85 employees and a handful of trucks along its 938 miles of routes, to supporting trucks and trailers that traveled more than 60,000 miles each day. By 1939, the company

In July 1940, Seattle's Lake Washington pontoon bridge opened, and a new Consolidated Freightways' Freightliner truck-trailer combination became the first commercial vehicle to cross the span.

ROAD SERVICE FOR ALL

ONSOLIDATED FREIGHTWAYS DEMANDED THAT its drivers stop and help all stranded motorists. The quality of courtesy was seen not as a virtue, but as a responsibility to help others when they needed it. These two letters from appreciative motorists were published in the December 1943 edition of the company newsletter, the *Consolidated Freighter*.

Dear Consolidated Freightways,

On Saturday August 29 I was returning to Wadena from Mandan, North Dakota, where I had a flat tire.

I had no more than got nicely started to change tires when one of your truck drivers came by, stopped and changed the tire for me.

I did not learn the gentleman's name. He was on his way to Bismarck, but I want your firm to know that I certainly appreciated his act of kindness.

I asked the driver how it happened that he stopped. He said he had been at a company meeting and that you had stressed courtesy to be exercised by your employees. I want your company to know that you have one truck driver who attended your meeting, who listened, heard and put into practice what his employer told him to.

Sincerely,

Madell Motriff

Madell Motriff

Dear Consolidated Freightways,

My hat is off to your organization for the training it gives its employees! My hat is off especially to your worthy man, Bill Gunderson of Billings!

I want you to know, in my appreciation, what Bill did me for me yesterday, in the pouring-down rain, courteously, willingly, in spite of personal delay, discomfort and convenience.

My car was nose down at the bottom of a ditch just north of Warm Springs, Montana, at about 5:00 p.m. Helpless under its own power, having arrived there through the medium of a combination of loose, wet gravel at the shoulder, a greasy-slick bituminous pavement and loss of control because the sudden jerk, oddly enough, threw my arm against the gear shift, knocking it out of gear. Lady Luck must have been sitting in my lap because neither I nor my car were injured in any way.

Along came Bill with his highway freight train and its Power personified. In spite of the sheets of rain, he stopped, set out his signals, uncoupled the trailer, backed up and hitched a chain to my rear spring shackle. With never a jerk nor a tremble he had my car back on the highway as easy as if it had been a baby buggy. In hardly as much time as it takes to tell it, we were both organized again and on our way.

For all the soaking he got, the inconvenience to which he was put, the invaluable service rendered me, Bill was adamant in his refusal to accept anything but a thank you! Can you beat a man like that? Hence this is the only other way I could think of by which to show my appreciation.

God bless the Bill Gundersons of this world and especially Bill of Billings!

Sincerely yours,

D. A. Roberts

D. A. Roberts

had expanded to 7,700 miles of routes, serving 1,500 points in 17 western states, with nearly 1,000 employees. During its first 10 years, it paid more than $8 million in wages, earned a total of $20 million in revenues, and hauled about a billion pounds of freight.[45] CF maintained overnight delivery service within a 350-mile radius from the originating point throughout its entire system.

Consolidated also had a number of firsts in the 1930s. One of its trucks was the first commercial vehicle to cross the $77 million San Francisco–Oakland Bridge when it opened on November 12, 1936.[46] Similarly, when the 6,620-foot-long Lake Washington Floating Bridge, built on 25 reinforced concrete pontoons, was completed in July 1940, a new CF truck-trailer unit was the first commercial vehicle to cross the span.[47]

On April 1, 1939, which was CF's 10th anniversary, the company unveiled a new name to describe its "freight-over-the-highways operation"—Consolidated Freightways Inc.[48] That same year, James launched two significant initiatives. He founded a confederation of non-competing independent trucking companies called "Freightways," as well as a manufacturing operation to custom build trucks.

The confederation launched on October 1, 1939, and totaled six member companies including CF. All added "Freightways" to their names, but still retained separate identities.[49] This intercarrier cooperative was intended to increase interline business and the number of locations each line served. The five other participating companies were Interstate Motor Lines of Salt Lake City; Garrett Transfer & Storage Co., headquartered in Pocatello, Idaho; Canadian Freightways of Lethbridge, Alberta; L. J. Russell Transportation Co. of Douglas, Wyoming; and Salt Creek Transportation Co. of Casper, Wyoming.

The Freightways-affiliated firms attempted to standardize operations and practices. Shippers using the Freightways system were given a single bill regardless of which member carriers participated in the transfer of a shipment. Cargos were moved swiftly among the companies, and all divided the revenues. Freightways' main operating office was in Salt Lake City, but its headquarters was located in San Francisco.

By 1940, the trucking industry was seen as a nuisance to long-haul railroads. Although trucks only carried 5 percent of the country's commerce—railroads carried 66 percent—the trucking industry was vital to the country.[50] It employed nearly 1 million people and exclusively served two out of five cities, villages, or towns across the United States.

Freightways began to compete directly with the railroads, offering a sixth-day delivery service from the Mississippi River to the West Coast. By 1940, 26 railroad companies were running

This advertisement that appeared in the October 1937 issue of *Traffic World* magazine assured shippers that their cargos would be delivered from the Great Lakes to the Pacific Coast in six days. At the time, motor freight carriers were going head-to-head against railroad delivery service.

6 DAY SERVICE

FROM THE GREAT LAKES TO THE PACIFIC COAST

Shippers via Consolidated are now assured of daily 6-day delivery service between The Great Lakes and the Pacific Coast. Fast, dependable service. Competitive tariffs.

CONSOLIDATED FREIGHT LINES, Inc.
2029 N.W. Quimby Street, Portland, Oregon

the same service. Yet James had a surprising and unexpected announcement the following year: Freightways would offer fifth-day delivery service along the same route.[51]

James also sought to establish a direct route between California and Oregon after ocean steamer traffic declined. This created a conflict with former colleague Gritsch, who refused to join the Freightways group. CF applied to the ICC to extend service from Oregon to San Francisco. In a counter-move, Gritsch applied to extend his service northward from Medford, Oregon. Although both James and Gritsch agreed not to contest each other's application, a third company, Pierce Auto Freight Lines, objected to both proposals. The approval process slowed to a crawl, and each began to incur additional legal expenses.[52]

Ultimately, the organization began falling apart in the 1940s because of intercarrier rival-

ries, and a federal antitrust lawsuit finally brought the organization to a halt. Although the lawsuit was settled in 1943, the courts declared Freightways illegal, and the cooperative was officially dissolved.

TRUCK MANUFACTURING

CF turned its attention to manufacturing with Freightways Manufacturing Company, and it experienced more success than it had with its Freightways cooperative. The first truck was a COE design and debuted in 1940. According to the trade newspaper *Automotive News*, the truck's name was not immediately known—it was soon revealed as the "Freight-Liner" before being renamed as the "Freightliner"—but it was equipped with a 200-horsepower diesel engine and "22 balloon tires," making it a 22 wheeler instead of an 18 wheeler. According to an advertisement released later in the year, it was "the easiest riding transport on the road today."[53]

The first Freightliners were designed to maximize cargo space, and they were constructed with aluminum and lightweight, high-tensile steel to trim net vehicle weight. The goal was to keep the trucks within Oregon's legal weight and length restrictions. Freightliner truck bodies were insulated and 22 feet long, and its trailers were 28 feet long.

Freightliner established an assembly plant in Salt Lake City, although most of the precision machining, axle and brake assembly, and truck cabs were produced at another site in Portland. One difficulty the company encountered was a misunderstanding by its suppliers. Many refused to offer original equipment manufacturer (OEM) prices, as Freightliner was seen as a scheme by Consolidated to buy its own spare parts at a lower cost.[54] In August 1942, the truck manufacturer's name was changed to Freightliner Corporation—although the effects of World War II in Europe would soon put it out of business.

This November 1940 advertisement in *Transportation Topics* was the first to give the CF-built trucks their now iconic name. The hyphen between "Freight" and "Liner" was later dropped.

THE INFLUENCE OF WORLD WAR II

With the outbreak of war in Europe and fears of Japanese aggression in the Pacific, in 1940 the Roosevelt administration began preparing for the possibility of United States' entry into the conflict. Various war material plants were constructed around the United States, and a peacetime draft bolstered the Armed Services. War spending stimulated the economy, and many industries, including railroads and trucking firms, benefited from the increased government spending.

In 1941, CF sold Tidewater–Shaver Barge Lines, eliminating its first effort at coordinating truck and ship transportation, but the company developed a division to handle large and heavy loads.[55] That August, the ICC approved CF's $45,000 purchase of Volks Bros., a trucking firm that had lines in Minnesota and Wisconsin, as well as a direct route to Chicago. The deal gave CF the right to deliver to intermediate and off-route points in those states.[56]

After the December 7, 1941, Japanese attack on the U.S. Pacific Fleet at Pearl Harbor, the United States fully mobilized for war, and CF faced many challenges. The Roosevelt administration created— or enlarged—a number of government agencies

The second annual Freightways Sales Conference was held in Salt Lake City, Utah, on April 13, 1941. Promoting the company's cooperative nature, a banner reads, "Let's Pull Together" over the seated attendees.

including the War Production Board, the Office of Defense Transportation (ODT), and the Office of Price Administration. Directives from these wartime agencies affected CF in a number of ways. The ODT encouraged trucking firms to become more efficient, to pool resources—similar to the Freightways concept—and also to conserve tires, as civilian tires were rationed. Conservation methods included restricting truck speeds to no more than 40 mph to save fuel; the government later imposed a 35 mph speed limit.

CF responded immediately, and its slogan became "War Freight First." Military shipments had priority over civilian cargo. CF played a critical role in transporting ice and supplies to army troops training in central Oregon, although the drivers never knew the ultimate location. They would drive the trucks to a dispatch site and then receive additional directions, haul ice to the location, and sometimes even unload it without seeing a single soldier. The company also moved more than 300 field huts—used as temporary shelter—to Dawson Creek, British Columbia, for soldiers training in subzero weather. CF provided transport of wartime supplies and construction supplies for the nuclear facility built near Richland, Washington.

The federal government, aside from creating a draft that depleted most companies of their employees, also imposed wartime wage and price freezes. Labor strikes prompted the government to lift the wage freeze on truckers' pay, but, unfortunately, prevented carriers from increasing rates to compensate for the additional costs. More than 20 percent of the company's experienced drivers and executives were eventually drafted or enlisted.[57] CF's accident rate grew as drivers with less experience began filling the ranks of its dwindling workforce. These factors combined to cause a net loss in 1944, despite increased wartime revenues. One positive note was that the ODT removed many differing weight and length truck-trailer barriers that had hampered the trucking industry. Many states, including Oregon, also raised length and weight limits.[58]

The Freightliner subsidiary was also negatively affected by the war. In 1942, the War Production Board commandeered the company's aluminum sheet metal, which was a key element in reducing the weight of vehicles, and limited the production of civilian heavy-duty trucks. Freightliner was effectively out of the manufacturing business for the rest of the war and instead became a parts supplier for CF.

Above: In 1943, there were 33 drivers who reached the five-year mark of driving without a chargeable accident. All were given National Safety Council Certificates; some were also given a blanket or a watch. David Cadwell, center, receives his watch during a presentation. From left to right: John Youell; E. R. Gibney, Portland Division superintendent; Cadwell; K. R. Field, safety engineer; and Leland James.

Below: Part of the Consolidated Freightways fleet is lined up near the dispatch office in "the Bend" of Oregon. The drivers await orders from the Army regulating officer before driving supplies into the desert for troops on training maneuvers.

REBUILDING AFTER THE WAR

After the war ended, CF launched a program to rebuild its well-worn equipment, while returning soldiers slowly rejoined the company. The overall annual revenues for CF more than doubled to $8 million in 1945. With 87 trucks and 99 trailers, it was now the

Northwest's leading trucking company serving routes covering nearly 12,000 miles in 11 Western states.

In 1945, CF and Northwest Airlines signed an agreement for the trucking firm to haul supplies. Northwest, in turn, carried rush deliveries for CF and also transported Consolidated personnel. By 1947, CF had also begun pickup and delivery service for Western Airlines and United Airlines in some western cities.

James was leery of expanding farther east with its cutthroat competition and established Teamster presence. It was a difficult market to crack, as the unions already in the area were extremely well organized and aggressively territorial. The company instead concentrated on improving its coverage in the western United States and western Canada, and advertising began to describe the company as "The Friendly Western Line."

The company faced more financial challenges in 1947. In need of additional financing, CF approached Bank of America for a line of credit. At the same time, Tom and John Youell were feeling pressure to sell their CF stock because of gov-ernment estate taxes—their father, George, had died in 1943. Before his death, George had made it known he wanted to retain control over the company. John submitted his name for company president, but was denied.[59] The Youell brothers then sold their company stock and instead bought Consolidated Convoy, CF's automotive hauling unit. When stories surfaced years later in the company's magazine about the James–Youell struggle, John wrote a letter denying the conflict and added that the eventual parting with "Lee" had been friendly.[60]

Peake acquired the Youells' shares. He now owned about 40 percent of CF's stock and was given the title of chairman of the board, a position he held until 1955.[61] Peake's main focus was to revive Freightliner, which was reincorporated in 1947. He built a small 10,000-square-foot plant in Portland and began manufacturing custom-built trucks and tractors.

With solid financial backing, and a vibrant post-World War II economy, CF was ready for additional growth. James was looking toward diversifying his company further and expanding routes in the West.

CHAPTER TWO

A RUSH TO GROW

1948–1960

I was committed to making Consolidated Freightways national.

—Jack Snead Jr.[1]

AFTER WORLD WAR II, MILLIONS OF soldiers returned to the United States, searching for employment, starting families, and rebuilding a nation that had experienced both rationing and a changing workforce. Most industries were prepared to ramp up production to meet the needs of returning GIs and the resultant "baby boom."

J. L. S. "Jack" Snead Jr., son of the Consolidated Freightways' (CF) cofounder, was one of the soldiers. He had begun working at Consolidated at age 18 in the parts room, and later became an equipment engineer, maintenance engineer, and operations and maintenance manager. He was eventually promoted to vice president, operations and maintenance.[2] Snead also codesigned CF's refrigerated trucks in the late 1930s.[3] While a lieutenant colonel in 1944, Snead was given command of the Army's Highway and Highway Transportation Division and worked in occupied Germany for two years.[4]

When Snead returned to Consolidated, the company was in the process of rebuilding and repairing its worn-out fleet. All conventional trucks were rebuilt into Freightliner cab-over-engine (COE) designs, while trailers were rebuilt to 28-foot lengths with six wheels.[5] In the western states, the company used full truck and trailer combinations, but other state regulations required tractors with 35-foot semitractor trailers.

Fixed costs were rising, while shipping rates and freight tonnage dropped from wartime levels. CF looked toward diversification, and Leland James, CF's president, was intent on expanding the company's western beginnings.

THE FRIENDLY WESTERN LINE

The first important post–World War II decision for the company was the opening of a T-shaped terminal in Portland, Oregon, in 1947. The structure covered a city block and included offices, a 400-foot-long dock with doors on both sides, and an overhead chain conveyor to move freight. By 1953, the company spent $5 million to replace or remodel 49 of its terminals, many of which were acquired during its earlier expansion phase.[6]

The new, large terminals featured one of two designs. Some were constructed with doors on both sides and an overhead conveyor, such as the one

---

Above: This 1953 White Freightliner was the first model to have four-wheel drive.

Opposite: The cab-over-engine design, popular during the early 1950s, was used in CF's East Coast operations. This model was built in 1950. *(Photos courtesy of the National Automotive History Collection, Detroit Public Library.)*

built in 1949 in Oakland, California. Others were given in-floor conveyor chains, such those in Minneapolis and Salt Lake City in 1952, and Los Angeles in 1953. Floor space in the smaller terminals was simply narrowed to reduce the time needed to move freight in cross-dock operations.

The company's reliance on business in the Pacific Northwest caused great difficulty when severe winter weather interfered with many routes in late 1948 and early 1949. However, James did not want to expand east of the Mississippi River because of the Teamsters' aggressive reputation and its supposed ties to the mob. This was epitomized by the growing influence of James Riddle "Jimmy" Hoffa in Detroit, cutthroat competition among trucking firms, low rates, and traffic congestion. Instead, James wanted to improve service and coverage in the company's existing markets.

"We can have an ideal company if we just stay in the West and develop. ... That's a big enough slice of the pie," James told his employees.[7]

"His idea was that we would be a western company," explained Ray Doherty, a CF general sales manager. "He wanted to fully develop the area west of Chicago."[8]

The company began marketing itself as "The Friendly Western Line" to stress regional coverage and exemplary customer service. That meant strengthening the weaker links in the CF system—the route to Chicago and the route to Los Angeles. The solution would be found through a series of acquisitions.

In 1950, CF purchased the operating rights between Bozeman, Montana, and St. Anthony, Idaho, and three years later added the segment between St. Anthony and Idaho Falls. These acquisitions trimmed many miles from Chicago and Minneapolis to California. In 1952, CF began serving most of the Pacific Coast when it gained a route into Los Angeles through the purchase of Hills Transportation.

Route expansion also meant that staff increased, and CF's office facilities—including the new Portland terminal—were no longer able to accommodate all its employees. Soon, CF office departments were located throughout a number of facilities, and even James worked out of a "private dwelling."[9]

In 1950, CF purchased both a two- and a four-story building adjacent to its Portland terminal from the Oregon Casket Company for $300,000.[10] The buildings were renovated to include direct wire service to connect to 55 locations in 11 states (at the time it was the largest system in the world), IBM tabulating machines to handle payroll functions, and one of the first semi-automatic teletypewriter systems.[11] The grand reopening took place in 1951, and the General Office building was soon nicknamed Peake Block after CF's influential chairman, E. W. A. "Will" Peake.

EXECUTIVE TRANSITIONS

Peake, after assuming the new office of chairman, had became CF's largest stockholder with a 40 percent stake.[12] Peake had enormous influence on CF and ties to the Bank of America, which became a major lender to the company for capital to purchase new equipment and upgrade facilities. Peake's influence ensured a $1.6 million line of credit, which was much larger than any of its competitors.[13]

Yet there was growing concern about who would eventually succeed James. The company's founder had been diagnosed with Parkinson's disease in the 1940s, and his health began to deteriorate significantly after 1951.

At the July 1949 stockholders' meeting, James chose Snead as executive vice president, although he also considered two other executives, Lester Kassebaum and Ray Doherty, for the position. Kassebaum was a former Ford Motor Company executive in charge of CF's purchasing department in 1940, and he handled a number of wartime parts shortages. Doherty began his career at CF in 1934 as a dockworker and was one of the first employees to enter the company's driver training program. He eventually became terminal manager for the Pendleton, Oregon, facility. Doherty was instead promoted to vice president, personnel; Kassebaum to vice president, purchases and maintenance; and Frederick C. Leibold was given an expanded role in charge of traffic.

Despite his health difficulties and shyness, James was elected president of the American Trucking Associations (ATA), serving a term from 1950 to 1951. Afterward, he became chairman of the ATA's Board of Governors, served on the ATA's Regular Common Carrier Conference, and was a trustee of the ATA Foundation.

Leland James, who was given the title of Founder–Chairman of CF, retired in 1957 due to a worsening case of Parkinson's disease. He stands next to the grille of a Freightliner in 1951. *(Photo courtesy of www.Daimler-TrucksNorthAmerica.com.)*

"As president, he had to travel all over the country and make speeches in every state in the union on behalf of the industry," recalled Tom Taylor, who had joined CF as a part-time clerk in 1934. "I know he hated it, but he did it because he was dedicated to the business and the industry."[14]

James faced several tough challenges as ATA president. The Interstate Commerce Commission (ICC) and state legislatures were imposing new restrictions on the trucking industry. The railroads were again lobbying in an attempt to reduce competition. The railroads controlled about 50 percent of intercity freight traffic, but their importance in the transportation industry was decreasing as the trucking industry grew.[15] Following the beginning of the Korean War, the U.S. government was poised to reinstate many of the same regulations on the trucking industry as it had during World War II. The steel and automotive industries, for example, faced renewed federal rationing. The railroads continued to lobby state legislatures to increase taxes on trucking companies, while convincing the ICC to keep the number of interstate trucking operators low.

In an effort to illustrate the importance of the trucking industry, especially during the Cold War, James addressed the National Defense Transportation Association in October 1950. In the event of a nuclear attack, James said trucks would be needed "to evacuate whole cities and transport food and medical supplies to displaced citizens." He also explained that highways needed improvement, and state laws needed to allow truckers more flexibility.[16]

In 1952, the Teamsters had elected David Beck, the former president of Seattle Local 174, as head of the international union. Beck defeated Detroit rival Hoffa and had once said that CF had developed "the very finest kind of labor relations."[17] By May 1955, however, the Teamsters went on strike when Consolidated and other western motor carriers refused its demand to create a union-controlled pension fund. Although the companies feared the union was trying to create a strike war chest, they eventually capitulated after a month. The strike showed the truckers' vulnerability to the union.

In spite of the difficulties, there was one trend working in favor of the trucking industry—the push by the automobile industry and motorists for better cross-country roads.

REBUILDING FREIGHTLINER

After Freightliner's truck production was halted during World War II, the company instead became CF's Rebuild Shop. It repaired and upgraded existing equipment and built new cabs for the old trucks. Many conventional trucks were rebuilt into cab-over-engines (COEs) while substandard trailers were rebuilt to the 28-foot, six-wheeler Freightliner standard. James, who was ambivalent about reviving the manufacturing operation, turned Freightliner over to Taylor in 1946, who was a returning

veteran who had helped run the U.S. Navy's West Coast truck fleet.

"We have what's left of Freightliner in a tin shed over on East Portland," James told Taylor. "If you want to see what you can do with it, why, that's your job."[18]

Taylor would eventually oversee the accounting and personnel operations for the Portland office. He also worked on interline accounts during the years that Freightways, the confederation of independent carriers, was operating. Taylor had an ally in Peake, who kept Freightliner alive during the mid- to late-1940s through several personal loans of $20,000 to $40,000.[19]

In 1947, Freightliner was reincorporated, and a new 10,000-square-foot truck production plant was built in Portland.[20] Taylor became Freightliner's general manager, and Kassebaum was named president.[21, 22] A former Idaho farm boy, Kenneth Self was appointed production manager and began producing 30 tractors a year.[23] Self began at CF's Spokane, Washington, shop in 1940 when the first Freightliners were constructed, and during the war, he

Above: When the company's manufacturing operations were stalled by government restrictions imposed during World War II, Freightliner became a de facto "rebuild shop" for the parent company. It put new cabs on its older trucks, including this unit from the mid-1940s.

Below: In 1950, Freightliner introduced this Series 32 tractor, which included a sleeper cab and was used on the West Coast. (Photos courtesy of the National Automotive History Collection, Detroit Public Library.)

hunted junkyards for spare parts to repair the aging Fageol trucks.[24]

In 1948, Self, Taylor, and a small group of designers created a short-wheel COE tractor to haul double trailers. To meet the stringent length requirements of some states, the tractor's nose, bumper, and cab front were pushed backward, but the steering gear remained in place creating an external "bump" in the nose. To remedy the uneven exterior, the designers constructed a matching bump solely for aesthetic purposes on the other side of the nose. Known as the Model B-42, this tractor design was dubbed the "Mae West" after the blond movie actress.[25]

Freightliner sold its first full truck and trailer combination in 1948. Vince Graziano, a produce hauler who leased equipment from Consolidated, wanted a vehicle that would carry more freight yet stay within Oregon's 60-foot length limits.[26] The L-89 model was the lightest-weight truck for its size and had a 275-horsepower engine. Graziano, who purchased the truck that October, would later join CF, becoming its vice president of purchasing.

By 1949, Freightliner introduced the Model 900, which was its first sleeper cab.

DRIVING TOWARD SUCCESS

Freightliner gained great strides as a truck manufacturer when the Hyster Company of Portland became the first private carrier to purchase a transcontinental COE tractor in 1950. This particular tractor logged more than 4 million miles during its lifetime before Freightliner repurchased it in 1976, restored it, and donated it to the Smithsonian Institution's Museum of History and Technology in Washington, D.C.[27]

The "Hyster truck" incorporated a number of design firsts for Freightliner, including a 10-speed transmission; an electric sander for traction on slippery roads; an integral sleeper unit; and a standard 19.5-inch main driveline, which was the shortest on any tractor in the early 1950s.[28] Word spread quickly of this new "Western truck," sparking an increased interest in Freightliner tractors from other carriers. Unfortunately, the manufacturer did not have a distribution network.

To expand sales, Freightliner signed an agreement with White Motor Corporation of Ohio in 1951. White began selling Freightliner trucks—renamed

The Hyster Company of Portland became the first private carrier to purchase a transcontinental COE tractor in 1950. This particular tractor logged more than 4 million miles during its lifetime. Freightliner repurchased it in 1976, restored it, and donated it to the Smithsonian Institution's Museum of History and Technology in Washington, D.C. (Photo courtesy of www.Daimler-TrucksNorthAmerica.com.)

White Freightliner—through its dealerships. The partnership proved successful, and Freightliner returned a profit to CF as sales rose from $4.7 million in 1951 to $5.1 million in 1952, climbing to $5.5 million the following year.[29] Production grew, and the company obtained discounted parts from suppliers, with output increasing from 116 vehicles per year in 1950, to 931 in 1960.[30] CF also had access to new trucks at the lowest possible cost.

Due to its increasing sales, CF supported the expansion of Freightliner. In 1952, a new $280,000 truck factory opened in east Portland, near the World War II–era Swan Island shipyard.[31] The total cost of the Swan Island plant also included the price of manufacturing tooling, which ran into the millions of dollars. Kassebaum became Freightliner's chairman, Taylor was promoted to president and general manager, and Self joined the manufacturer's board of directors.

With the increased output of trucks, additional repair and rebuilding services became necessary. In 1952, Factory Motor Company was acquired to provide these services to Freightliner customers. Two years later, Plasti-Glas Inc. was formed in Portland to develop and construct fiberglass racks, bodies, and other truck and trailer parts.[32]

BACK TO THE DRAWING BOARD

Freightliner also helped its parent company solve a vexing problem. In western states, CF's basic line-haul combination had been a full truck and trailer, but some states east of Montana had stricter weight and length regulations, so the company used a tractor and 35-foot trailer.[33] In the late 1940s and early 1950s, however, costs and inflation were on the rise, while trucking rates and cargo tonnage fell. CF could not afford to maintain the status quo and survive.

A believer in utilizing truck size to carry as much freight as possible, James promoted a tractor and double trailers, also called "dubs." In 1951, Consolidated operated its first three sets of dubs on California highways, which concerned many state legislatures that did not believe a tractor could pull two trailers over mountain roads. James turned to Ken Self to create an engineering team to develop a four-wheel-drive (4WD) COE, especially to meet Montana's requirements that trucks needed two drive axles.[34, 35]

Working long hours—even at Self's dining room table—he and Norm Chew, an engineer, developed

This 1953 White Freightliner allowed CF to utilize "dubs," a tractor with double trailers, to haul more freight. (Photo courtesy of the National Automotive History Collection, Detroit Public Library.)

the blueprints for the 4WD truck. Four months later, in early 1954, Freightliner revealed the WF5844T, also called the Mountaineer, which was designed to pull twin trailers over mountain passes, providing enough traction for ice and snow. The state legislatures in Idaho, Montana, and Washington approved the Mountaineer, and CF began using doubles from the Pacific Coast eastward in 1955. That same year, Self became vice president of manufacturing, while nine western states approved the 65-foot dubs.[36]

Also under development in the early 1950s was the Freightliner Spacemaker Model WF4864. This truck included the industry's first 48-inch cab for truck and trailer operators in states that permitted 60-foot lengths and was introduced in 1953. It had a pancake-style Cummins engine mounted horizontally under the frame to create the compact design.[37]

SPECIALIZED SERVICES AND DIVERSIFICATION

CF began expanding into other types of cartage, diversifying its operations. CF entered the bulk petroleum business by purchasing Howard R. Williams Inc. in 1950. The company delivered gasoline, refined oil, and crude oil throughout the Pacific Northwest.[38] With the motto, "If it pours, we'll haul it," CF's stainless steel tanker fleet hauled liquids and semi solids, including brine, whiskey, liquid sugar, liquid wax, paint, and insecticide.

By 1950, Graziano had sold most of his rigs to CF and joined the firm to launch an exempt commodities operation (cargo that was not regulated by the federal government). It hauled agricultural produce from the Sunbelt during the winter, which helped to mitigate CF's traditional winter financial slump.

When the U.S. Post Office switched to private carriers to haul mail in 1952, CF was awarded the Seattle–Portland run. The company-owned moving vans were adapted to carry mail. Other diversification efforts included resuming livestock hauling to cut empty mileage in routes from Montana to Minneapolis and Chicago. Consolidated had ceased this practice during the war.

Twinway, a CF moving service, created a fleet of specialized moving vans while the Heavy Hauling Division had winch-equipped tractors, cranes, and flat and low beds. The Heavy Hauling Division transported extreme freight, such as a 122-foot, 49-ton bridge girder on two trailers to a bridge construction site in central Washington.

In February 1953, the company expanded its routes by acquiring Karst, which had a Montana to Idaho line.[39]

TAKING CF PUBLIC

In the summer of 1951, Peake called Snead from Portland to his home in Palm Springs, California, to tell Snead that he intended on giv-

This 1949 Freightliner was driven in CF's Heavy Hauling Division, which used winch-equipped tractors, cranes, and flat and low beds. For example, the division hauled a 122-foot, 49-ton bridge girder on two trailers to a bridge construction site in central Washington. (*Photo courtesy of the National Automotive History Collection, Detroit Public Library.*)

TRANSCONTINENTAL TRAVEL

EISENHOWER INTERSTATE SYSTEM

THE TWO- AND FOUR-LANE WIDE "SUPER-highways" were built during the 1920s and 1930s, to improve transcontinental travel. Even before they were completed, however, motorists realized that the roads had drawbacks.

In 1941, an article in the *Oregon Journal* claimed:

> *When the superhighway constructed between Oregon City and Portland was built, it was expected to be the fastest road in the state. Development of service stations and hot dog stands along the highway converted it into one of the state's most dangerous roads. Courts held that owners of property abutting highways cannot be denied ingress and egress.*[1]

There were also newspaper articles in the late 1930s and early 1940s that claimed future highways would be wide with gentle turns so as not to impede traffic. Other ideas were under development before World War II, such as separated grade freeways where vehicles used bridges or tunnels to cross highways. One experimental access control freeway was completed in 1935, in Newton, Massachusetts.[2]

At the 1939 New York World's Fair, General Motors' "Futurama" exhibit offered a prediction of what cities would look like 20 years in the future. A model featuring 50,000 moving model cars, a million trees to scale, and a half-million miniature structures demonstrated elevated expressways where vehicles could travel in excess of 100 mph.[3]

The world's first limited access highway opened on January 31, 1943. The 11.5 mile-long, four-lane-wide Willow Run Expressway in Michigan linked Detroit with Ford Motor Company's Willow Run bomber plant. The $5 million expressway, funded by the federal government, allowed workers the option of commuting long distances rather than moving into Michigan's rural Washtenaw County.[4] Similar wartime expressways were built around the country.

President Franklin D. Roosevelt's National Interregional Highway Committee issued a report in 1944 that called for the creation of 33,900 miles of interregional highways, along with 5,000 miles of additional roads.[5] Congress passed the Federal-Aid Highway Act of 1944 to designate a National System of Interstate Highways to serve the National Defense, but road-building efforts were stalled as funds were not readily available.

With the onset of the Cold War, the United States again looked at creating a series of interconnecting freeways to assist with the transportation of war materials.[6] With the passage of the Federal-Aid Highway Act of 1952, the federal government authorized a token $25 million for the construction of an interstate system, but the transcontinental interstate system was placed on hold due to squabbling within the road-building industry, between rural and urban advocates, and apportionment disagreements among the states themselves.[7]

During World War II, General Dwight D. Eisenhower recognized that the autobahns in Germany were utilized for the quick movement of resources, men, and equipment, and that the United States was in need of a similar system. In 1956, after Eisenhower became president, he signed legislation to establish the National System of Interstate and Defense Highways, which proposed creating 41,000 miles of interconnected freeways.[8] The U.S. Department of Defense monitored the construction of the interstate system and identified important highway routes.

The Highway Revenue Act of 1956 created the Highway Trust Fund, which was funded by gasoline and other automotive taxes. The pay-as-you-go, self-financing program provided a dependable source of income for the construction of interstate freeways.[9]

Once completed nearly three decades later, the interconnecting, multilane highways permit-ted high-speed, cross-country travel for motor freight as well as passenger cars. Truckers became an indispensable part of the transportation industry, while the use of railroads, which had overbuilt their systems as far back as the late 19th century, declined.

In 1994, the American Society of Civil Engineers designated President Eisenhower's interstate highway plan as one of the Seven Wonders of the United States, which also included the Hoover Dam, the Golden Gate Bridge, and the Panama Canal.[10]

Hailed by the American Society of Civil Engineers as one of the Seven Wonders of the United States, President Eisenhower's network of interconnecting, multilane highways permitted high-speed, cross-country travel for motor freight and passenger cars.

ON TO OREGON

AS PART OF OREGON'S CENTENNIAL EXPOSITION IN 1959, there was a re-creation of the settlers' journeys along the historic Oregon Trail. CF participated in the "On to Oregon" cavalcade by providing transportation and backup services.[1] The company transported six covered wagons from Oregon to Independence, Missouri, after the railroads had withdrawn from the event.

CF driver Millard F. "Robbie" Roberts was behind the wheel of a 40-foot semi-tractor trailer that accompanied the wagon train, sponsored by the Oregon Trucking Association. The trailer served as a rolling barn and supply shed for the cavalcade. Traveling an average of 20 miles a day, the caravan took 130 days to cover the 2,000-mile route that included fields, prairie land, and dirt tracks. When Roberts reached Oregon, the truck was covered with signatures from visitors at the wagon train's campsites.

ing his 40 percent share of stock to a school for the blind. Peake's donation could pose a potential problem, as the charity might demand dividend payments, which had been suspended during the previous decade so profits could be plowed into the trucking firm's expansion. If the company's profits were distributed as dividends, further expansion efforts could be severely hampered. CF's ability to obtain credit might be adversely affected as most banks were not lending substantial sums to truckers.[40]

Already responsible for most of CF's operations, Snead realized that one solution would be to sell Consolidated's stock directly to the public. This would dilute Peake's power and the threat of losing control over CF. Snead explained to Peake that if CF went public, he could sell his shares on the market and donate the cash. Peake accepted the proposal.

Until 1951, CF had 15,000 shares of outstanding common stock. Ninety percent of the company was owned by employees and management, including James' 27 percent stake and Peake's 40 percent share.[41] Because CF had paid some debts with stock in lieu of cash during the Depression, Standard Oil and General Motors also owned stock. The U.S. Department of Justice ordered Standard Oil to sell 2,000 shares of common stock and 1,000 shares of preferred stock back to CF in 1949. These shares were offered to employees through a payroll deduction plan—one share of preferred stock for two shares of common. The common stocks split 10 for one, so employees could acquire 20 shares of common for every share of preferred stock.

At the time, only three other trucking firms—U.S. Truck Lines, Associated Transport, and Interstate Motor Freight System—had gone public.[42] After receiving the approval of the board of directors, Snead put together a plan with the San Francisco underwriting firm of Blyth and Company Inc. There was one major stipulation by Charles Blyth.

"I don't finance peanut stands," Blyth told Snead. "You give me your word you will take this company national, and I'll underwrite it for you."

Snead accepted Blyth's conditions, which would profoundly influence his well-meaning but misguided plans to expand the company later in the decade.

Consolidated's stock debuted on Wall Street in November 1951, and its first 100,000 shares quickly sold out. Additional stock offerings occurred in 1952, 1954, and 1955.[43]

TWENTY-FIVE YEAR MILESTONE

As CF matured as a company, its management began transitioning from its seasoned veteran employees to younger, more contemporary employees. Leibold announced his resignation from vice president of traffic and sales at the July 1953 board meeting. The board also voted to purchase a small trucking firm based in Wenatchee, Washington, for $5,000, a decision in which James had cast a "no" vote.[44] The board approved the acquisition despite the founder's wishes, demonstrating that the company was moving in a new direction.

Consolidated was on sound financial ground when it reached its 25th anniversary in 1954. It was the nation's second-largest motor carrier in terms of revenue at $36.2 million. It operated nearly 20,000 miles of regular and alternate routes in 15 western states and employed about 4,000 people.[45]

Since nine of the western states had approved the 65-foot tractor and double trailer combinations, CF spent $5.5 million in 1954 and $8 million in 1955 to purchase new equipment as it began switching its truck-trailer fleet to dubs.[46] The company also began using two-way radios in 1954 on its delivery trucks in Chicago as well as Oakland and San Francisco, California. Radio dispatching allowed for quicker pickups, and reduced backtracking and "dead mileage."[47]

In 1955, James' health had deteriorated further, and he relinquished his official day-to-day operating duties. At 63 years of age, James replaced Peake as chairman of the board. Snead was elected president. Two years later, James retired from active participation in the company and received the title of Founder–Chairman.

At the same time Snead became president, CF's red-and-green emblem changed. Doherty and Bill Grant, CF director of advertising and public relations, asked Simeon and Smith, the company's advertising firm, to design a new trademark. The firm's Account Executive Chan Clarkson and Artist Loyd Allen created a flattened and elongated "CF" with the company name italicized on the "F" crossbar.[48] This logo was used in advertisements by early 1955 and added to CF's trailers before the end of the decade.

Simeon and Smith, an advertising firm hired by Consolidated Freightways, was asked to design a new trademark. The result was a flattened and elongated "CF" with the company name italicized on the "F" crossbar. By early 1955, the logo was used in advertisements—by the end of the decade, it was added to CF's trailers.

EXPANSION THROUGH ACQUISITION

Snead, although only 43 when he became president, had 25 years of experience and a thorough knowledge of Consolidated's history. Although CF had a few long routes reaching the upper Midwest and California by the mid-1950s, it remained a predominantly Pacific Northwest motor carrier. Snead's vision was to create a nationwide transportation company. He wanted to reduce CF's dependence on a limited region or industries where an unexpected decrease in business, such as those industries affected by weather, would affect the carrier negatively. The company acquired more than 50 organizations via cash or stock swaps during the next six years, entering Eastern markets and establishing numerous local networks.[49]

One of the first acquisitions was a small carrier serving points in Alberta, Saskatchewan, British Columbia, and Montana. Canadian Freightways, which was part of James' short-lived Freightways intercarrier alliance in 1941, had remained partially under CF's wings. In 1955, CF exchanged shares of its own stock as well as cash to buy the remaining shares of Canadian Freightways. It intended to make the struggling company profitable.

CF also expanded by purchasing carriers or operating rights. Its acquisitions in the West included Arizona Express, with operating routes between Los Angeles and southern Arizona; Gallagher Freight Lines, with operating routes in Billings (Montana), Denver, and Salt Lake City; Sea-Van Express to Vancouver, British Columbia; and Utah–Arizona Freight Lines, with its Salt Lake City to Phoenix route. It also acquired the authority to operate between Fargo, North Dakota, and Winnipeg, Manitoba.

In the Midwest, CF purchased Clipper Transit, serving points between Chicago and eastern Wisconsin and Foster Freight Lines, serving Chicago; Dayton, Ohio; Cincinnati; Indianapolis; Louisville; and St. Louis. Another Midwest purchase was Wheeler Transportation, which held routes from Wisconsin to Minneapolis. CF also acquired Motor Cargo and Liberty Freight Lines in 1960, which served points from the Midwest to the East Coast, and was able to reach many northern cities in the United States from the Pacific to the Atlantic.

Each CF acquisition required ICC approval, and this process took years, hampered by protests from competing trucking firms, railroads, and Congressional investigations. By the end of the decade, however, the company had annexed 53 motor carriers. Yet, the expansion effort and Snead's other ambitions were tempered by economic recessions.

BREAKING TRADITION

In a change from its Northwestern regional roots, in July 1956, Snead relocated CF's corporate headquarters from Portland to Burgess Drive in Menlo Park, California, a suburb 45 miles south of San Francisco. This placed the company's executives near its major creditors, including the Bank of America and Blyth and Company Inc.[50] Snead thought the move to a major metropolitan area would elevate CF's prestige. The location also gave executives access to a busy international airport, facilitating travel to the East Coast where the company was expanding its operations.

Snead also embarked on a plan to decentralize CF's management structure. Snead was inspired by the success of General Motors, which grew during the 1920s and surpassed Ford to become the leading automaker by the 1950s. Longtime General Motors President, CEO, and eventual Chairman Alfred P. Sloan had created a corporate structure in which each division acted as an independent company while corporate "line staff" provided guidance.[51] As part of the divisionalization, Taylor stepped down from Freightliner to become senior vice president for the parent company. Self replaced him as the truck manufacturer's general manager; three years later he became Freightliner's president.[52] Doherty refused to go to California, however, and became vice president of sales for the western region.[53]

Unfortunately, this movement toward divisionalization bloated CF's bureaucracy and greatly slowed the exchange of information sharing among executives. The time in which decisions were made became sluggish, which increased costs as executives couldn't react promptly to fluctuating market conditions. Yet, CF's board of directors did not reject Snead's plan in 1956—the company had reached gross revenues of $63 million for the year. Consolidated had become the nation's largest motor carrier, making $11 million more than Associated Transport, its nearest competitor.[54]

Among those critical of divisionalization, however, was Raymond F. O'Brien, who joined the company as a region controller in 1958. O'Brien had worked as an accountant for Riss & Company, a privately owned trucking carrier in Kansas City.

"My first impression was that CF is a fine company. Later, I got to thinking they were nuts," O'Brien said. "They were talking about divisionalization, and it just didn't make any sense to me."[55]

When planning this decentralized corporate culture, each CF division was allotted its own accounting office. Instead, O'Brien; Joseph J. Schoen Jr., who was CF eastern regional auditor for Indianapolis; and Donald E. Moffitt, formerly Foster's manager of revenue and accounting, sought a solution to save money and reduce bureaucracy.[56, 57] The answer was found through the use of an IBM computer, as Consolidated was one of the first trucking firms to use the technology.

"We decided we could do all of that accounting by simply coding the IBM [computer] cards. It saved them a lot of money," O'Brien said.[58]

The company relocated its headquarters again in 1958 to an executive building at 175 Linfield Drive in Menlo Park.[59]

NEW VENTURES

Although Snead's quest to become a national carrier was realized, the sheer number of mergers and acquisitions proved unwieldy when attempting to create a cohesive corporate culture. There were also challenges with the organization of both drivers and equipment.

Consolidated had used the "relay" system to transport freight along its routes, but this resulted in costly delays as drivers and trucks waited for connecting shipments.[60] Using two-man driver teams, CF instituted a nonstop sleeper operation called Daysaver Service for major cities. The teams drove straight through from Chicago or the Twin Cities to the Pacific Coast.

Despite the increase in total route mileage, the number of intercity general freight hauls dropped from 1955. Snead wanted a balance between long and short hauls, cautioning that much of CF's volume and profits were "derived from long-haul and full-load traffic, which is vulnerable to rail and private cartage." The solution, according to Snead, was to increase the number of shorter, local hauls. CF purchased a number of small operators including J.A. Clark Draying Co., in San Francisco and Los Angeles, and Inland Transportation Corporation, which ran points between Los Angeles and San Diego.

Snead believed the railroads could transport long-haul freight more economically than trucks. He foresaw the need for intermodal freight transportation where truck service would be combined with railroads, ships, pipelines, aircraft, and barge operations to transport cargo fast and economically. Under his guidance, CF adopted the trucking industry's most cooperative attitude toward the railroads, including Southern Pacific. This "piggyback" system, where containers were moved from truck to railroad, transported, and then picked up by truck

OPERATION REINDEER

ONE OF CONSOLIDATED FREIGHTWAY'S PUBLIC efforts at demonstrating the feasibility of inter-modal business was "Operation Reindeer" in December 1958. When Alaska was on the verge of becoming the 49th state of the union, the territory governor gave President Dwight D. Eisenhower and the citizens of the "lower 48" a goodwill present: a herd of reindeer.[1] CF agreed to transport the 14 reindeer and caribou to the White House for the Christmas Pageant of Peace.[2]

The animals came from the Alaska tundra, just outside the community of Kotzebue, which is 33 miles north of the Arctic Circle. The U.S. Air Force's Alaska Air Command shuttled the animals by plane to Anchorage where Garrison Fast Freight (an intermodal carrier that CF acquired for $1.5 million in 1957) took the herd to the Alaska Railroad. The railroad carried the animals to the Seward docks. From the port, an Alaska Steamship liner transported the reindeer (eight were pregnant) and caribou 1,400 miles to Seattle where CF employees loaded them into a specially modified cattle trailer.[3, 4]

Two teams of drivers relayed the animals, who fed on lichen moss and alfalfa hay, from Seattle to Washington, D.C. After the event, the animals took up residence at the National Zoo in Washington, D.C. Alaska was granted statehood on January 3, 1959.

CF became the first trucking company to transport wild reindeer successfully on a transcontinental trek.[5]

In December 1958, the territory of Alaska presented President Eisenhower with a herd of reindeer and caribou. CF transported the animals safely to the White House for the Christmas Pageant of Peace.

for final delivery, eventually became popular during the 1950s.

But first CF needed the cooperation of the railroads. To test this new, coordinated transportation, CF sent 20 sets of double trailers loaded with exempt commodities aboard the *Coast Progress*, a ship. The ship traveled from Portland to Long Beach, California; Graziano, who was then general manager of CF's Western Region, oversaw the operation. Nicknamed a "fishyback" operation, the successful experiment convinced the railroads that CF could use ships to transport cargo. According to Graziano, Southern Pacific realized the potential income and offered CF low rates for piggybacking.

Trailers with wheels were loaded onto lowbed railcars in 1956. Starting in December 1958, Consolidated began using container vans without wheels that allowed the use of standard railroad flatcars. The containers were transferred to flatbed trucks and trailers at railroad terminals for final delivery via CF trucks.

WITH SUCCESS, FAILURE

CF invested heavily in its piggyback segment by purchasing attachments to fasten its containers to railroad flatcars—the attachments failed, costing the trucking company time and money. Additionally, the railcars tended to sit in rail yards for six to 48 hours before they were unloaded, possibly because the railcars were more difficult to maneuver when unloading goods than trucks were. This meant CF's piggyback service was nearly two days slower than other long-haul trucking firms, and the company suffered significant losses.[61]

To expand its fishyback business, CF acquired Trans-Ocean Van Lines in November 1957. This specialized operation moved household goods in aluminum containers to U.S. military bases in the Pacific and also to the states.[62] Trans-Ocean Van Lines proved to be moderately profitable as it expanded its routes from Alaska to the Far East and even to Europe.[63]

Although this operation initially showed promise, Consolidated made a disastrous investment in another company. CF wanted to establish a foothold in Hawaii before it became a state and was subject to the ICC's jurisdiction.[64] In 1959, CF acquired a majority interest in a marine company it renamed

Hawaiian Marine Freightways.[65] CF also purchased a Hawaiian trucking operation, but it faced an entrenched competitor—Matson Navigation Company—and suffered from a lack of backhaul cargo from Hawaii to the West Coast.[66] Within a year, Consolidated lost $9 million on the venture and closed both Hawaiian Marine Freightways and Trans-Ocean Van Lines.

Snead's concept of intermodal operations, although ahead of its time, was not successful. There was resistance on all sides to this new mode of transportation, from both the railroads and the ships, as well as within CF. Ultimately, the piggyback and fishyback operations added costs rather than savings to the trucking company, as well as caused shipment delays.

CF expanded its truck lines and acquired new manufacturing subsidiaries for Freightliner during 1959. The parent company was reincorporated that year in Delaware as Consolidated Freightways Corporation of Delaware (CFCD). CF Corp. became the holding company's name. Its subsidiaries included Freightliner and its motor freight business, which took on the CFCD name.[67] This move gave the corporation greater freedom to seek financing and expand its non-carrier operations while reducing interference from the ICC. Its sales had more than doubled during Snead's five-year tenure, hitting the $146 million mark in 1959. As the country's largest common motor carrier, CF employed nearly 11,000 people and operated 13,800 pieces of equipment in 34 states and Canada.[68]

Under Snead's direction, CF enlarged its truck-air-truck intermodal activities in 1957 in a deal with United Airlines. At the end of World War II, CF had signed agreements with Northwest Airlines, Western Airlines, and United Airlines for a number of western cities. The companies provided joint freight delivery service to more than 900 communities in 16 states. By 1959, Consolidated also was working with Flying Tigers and American Airlines.[69]

Yet, all was not well elsewhere in the company— with overexpansion came a huge price.

THE END OF AN ERA

In 1957, the nation fell into a recession. This, combined with a Teamsters' strike, hurt CF's bottom line as operating income dropped 35 percent.[70] About the time CF made peace with its union, a 116-day strike in the steel industry began, crippling the automotive industry. Then the nation slipped into another recession in 1960.

The ICC and U.S. Department of Justice had stalled the approval process for a number of CF's acquisitions. Not only were there complaints by rival carriers and the railroads to CF's expansion plans, but Congressional hearings about large corporate mergers made the ICC overly cautious.[71]

The lengthy ICC proceedings cost the company in a number of ways. It had to shuttle its executives between California and Washington, D.C., but also had to endure the departure of some experienced personnel who sought employment in other companies they viewed as more stable. There was a level of uncertainty held by CF staff and those working for the companies it wanted to acquire. According to Snead, the whole situation was "very demanding emotionally on everybody involved."

"In a business in which over 50 percent of your total gross revenue is payroll, that kind of frozen fear and aspiration combination is very hard to deal with," Snead said.[72]

With all of the acquisitions, CF found itself with duplicate or mismatched equipment and staffing. However, because of Snead's insistence on divisionalization and the James-era policy of avoiding firings, the company could not streamline its operations quick enough, which added to expenses.[73]

A previous decision made with positive intentions was now having negative consequences. The emphasis on intercity hauls, which was initiated to offset the number of long-haul routes, caused CF's once profitable long-haul business to suffer. By 1958, the company was dispatching only one full trailer per day, on average, westbound over its transcontinental routes.[74] Divisionalization had made it impossible to maintain the long-haul business effectively. Snead learned that Ray Halloran, who had joined CF in 1958 to run its Foster Freight Lines division, was offering service from Portland to San Francisco. He threatened to fire the executive because he wasn't following company policy. Halloran, however, continued this transcontinental service because his customers wanted it.[75]

The losses and write-offs from the discontinued Hawaiian and overseas operations, along with other failed acquisitions and ventures, hurt the company's bottom line.[76] In 1959, CF purchased Youngstown Steel Car Corporation, a manufacturer of railcar components, but the business failed and was discontinued the following year. Freightliner's Plasti-Glas subsidiary, a fiberglass components manufacturer that had changed its name to Techni-Glas, was also discontinued.

Adding to the company's woes was its numerous stock offerings. Investors were growing increasingly restless as CF's stock plunged during the late 1950s. CF's outstanding shares had more than doubled from 1.1 million in 1955 to 2.3 million shares by 1960. CF's earnings per share had been $1.88 in 1955, but the ratio plunged to $1.14 per share in 1958 and only rallied back to $1.35 a year later.[77]

After a 1960 report from a consultant revealed a sense of "serious unease" among executives at corporation headquarters, Snead asked for the resignation of every officer at CFCD. He eventually reappointed most of the executives, but Taylor was demoted from senior vice president to vice president—Taylor quit soon afterward. Snead turned to William G. White, a former railroad executive whom Snead had met during World War II, to replace Taylor and revive CF's intermodal business.[78]

From mid-1959 to 1960, CF rapidly burned through its cash and credit lines. By the summer of 1960, the corporation was on the brink of bankruptcy.[79] It racked up a $2.7 million loss by the year's end and suspended its dividend payments. In a rare move, CF's board of directors appointed a committee to analyze the trucking firm's financial crisis. The committee reported that Snead's divisionalization efforts—and his management style—were key problems.

The board of directors requested Snead's resignation on July 6, 1960. He complied, ending his career at CF. Ironically, the board then turned to White—whom Snead specifically hired to turn the intermodal business around—to revive the entire corporation.[80]

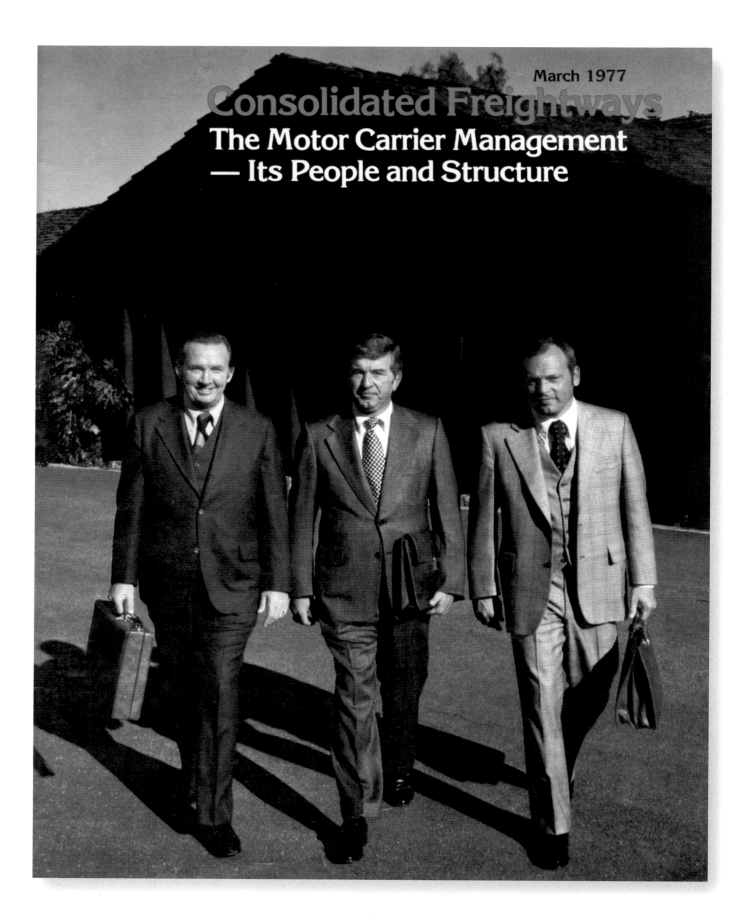

March 1977

Consolidated Freightways

The Motor Carrier Management
— Its People and Structure

CHAPTER THREE

CONSOLIDATED FREIGHTWAYS' GOLDEN AGE

1961–1978

I've had a full life, and I've enjoyed it, and part of my greatest enjoyment was working for Consolidated Freightways. Period. I was very fortunate.

—Ray Halloran, retired executive vice president
of marketing and sales, Consolidated Freightways[1]

ONSOLIDATED FREIGHTWAYS (CF) WAS in a financial crisis as the 1960s began, and its fate rested in the hands of a virtual outsider and a railroad man—William G. White.

Having been recruited by Jack Snead Jr. about three months before Snead's pro forma resignation on July 7, 1960, White became CF's new president. By the end of 1960, CF was the largest trucking company in the nation.[2] Serving 34 states and five Canadian provinces, it had thousands of miles of routes, more than 13,800 pieces of equipment, and employed 10,000 people. Despite generating revenue of $152 million for 1960, the company posted its first major losses of $2 million (with write-offs it totaled nearly $3.5 million).[3] Consolidated's troubles were caused by an economic recession that slowed motor freight traffic and the costs of the failed Hawaiian shipping and piggyback operations.

FIXING THE PAST

White was a seasoned executive with 25 years of railroad transportation experience. Prior to joining the trucking company, he had been vice president of operations for the Delaware, Lackawanna & Western Railroad.[4] Six feet tall and soft-spoken, White usually wore three-piece suits, with a railroader's watch and chain and a hat. According to CF executive Ray Halloran, one of White's favorite expressions

when facing a difficult problem was: "You know what I'd do? I'd put on my hat and go out and solve it."[5]

White launched a drastic program to integrate acquisitions and improve or sell poorly performing divisions. Rumors of bankruptcy threatened relationships with potential customers, and White visited bankers to keep the company's lines of credit open. Negotiations with Bank of America were successful, and he obtained short-term financing needed for upgrades.

Consolidated needed to pay for two of its largest purchases, which occurred during the Snead era—Motor Cargo and Liberty Freight Lines. Both trucking firms operated from the Midwest to the Atlantic Seaboard. At the time of its purchase in 1960, Motor Cargo was CF's largest single acquisition. It was still profitable when the Interstate Commerce Commission (ICC) finally offered approval of the purchase.[6] Liberty Freight Lines, on the other hand, was failing

---

Above: William G. White, chairman of CF Inc., in 1972.

Opposite: On the cover of this March 1977 special edition of the CF employees' magazine, executives (from left to right) Ray Halloran, Ronald E. Burbank, and Lary Scott walked in front of the motor carrier's headquarters in Menlo Park, California.

by 1960 when the agency approved the deal. When CF applied to purchase Liberty Freight Lines in 1956, the carrier had been thriving, but years of doubt surrounding the outcome of the ICC's decision had harmed its operations and sapped employee morale.[7]

White moved cautiously and thoughtfully as he and his executive staff wrestled with the company's financial problems. Holding weekly meetings and traveling the country to visit CF's widespread operations, White not only familiarized himself with the company, but also identified the executives and managers he wanted to tap for promotion.

White halted Snead's divisionalization efforts and centralized the accounting and operating divisions. The company refined its traffic routes and created new financial controls. Within three weeks of his appointment, White cut Menlo Park's executive staff, ordered the sale of company cars, and began closing and selling duplicate terminal facilities, including those in Chicago where CF reduced its number of terminals from five to one by 1963.[8]

Concentrating on CF's less-than-truckload (LTL) business, White sold a number of manufacturing and noncore companies, including Transcontinental Transport, a piggyback leasing company CF Inc., purchased in October 1958 at Snead's insistence, and a household goods moving service to Greyhound in 1963.[9] By 1962, White withdrew from nine of Snead's acquisition deals and instead chose four strategic acquisitions, including Knaus Truck Lines, which operated between Kansas City and Denver.[10, 11]

Within a year, CF's revenues rose, and the company showed a small profit in 1961. Dividend payments were restored by 1962 as net operating income rose to $2 million.[12]

NEW MANAGEMENT

After firing executives he felt were not capable of reversing CF's downward spiral, White looked to fill the vacancies. Halloran, a Cincinnati native, was promoted to western area vice president. Prior to World War II, Halloran had worked at the Rock Island Railroad. During the war, he was an Army Air Force B-29 bomber navigator, and he spent the last months of the war interned in a Japanese prison camp after his plane was shot down over Tokyo in 1945.[13]

Ray Halloran was promoted to western area vice president as a part of William G. White's efforts to reinvigorate Consolidated Freightways.

Upon his return to the United States, Halloran gained experience in the transportation industry by working briefly at a Cincinnati railroad and a small Detroit-based trucking firm. In 1958, CF was operating Indianapolis-based Foster Freight Lines under temporary authority from the ICC as it waited for approval to complete the acquisition. During the 1950s, Foster provided overnight, nonstop delivery service between Chicago and Indianapolis, which it called the "Foster 500" hotshot. Halloran was hired by CF to manage the company.

Shortly after joining CF, Halloran told his wife that he thought he had made a terrible mistake because divisionalization had compromised the corporation's structure. But, he added, "I think there's an opportunity here. My motto is if you're going to go with somebody, go with somebody that's really in trouble where the chances of improvement are that great."[14]

Halloran met with Donald E. Moffitt—who had joined Foster Freight Lines as a clerk, but quickly advanced and was supervising 25 general office employees—soon after the company celebrated its 25th anniversary. On Thanksgiving Day in 1958, Moffitt helped Halloran fill out expenditure forms, called M14s, which detailed Foster's "return on capital," among other financial measures. When CF took over Foster, Moffitt became the carrier's manager of revenue accounting.[15]

Moffitt and several other young CF managers—including Raymond F. O'Brien, the eastern regional controller in Indianapolis, who was hired in 1958—were working in the East. These young executives believed in the company's potential and wanted to improve its operations.

"Ray O'Brien and I, and maybe three other guys were about the same stage as Ray [Halloran]," Moffitt said. "We were starting to become friends. ... Now this bunch of guys wound up as senior vice presidents and presidents."[16]

ACCOUNTING PERSONNEL

In 1960, CF's eastern regional accounting office moved from Indianapolis to the former headquarters of Motor Cargo Inc. in Akron, Ohio. Among the personnel that were also moved were O'Brien, Moffitt, Brian Henry, Joseph Schoen, and James Schlueter. O'Brien used his management and accounting skills to encourage Motor Cargo employees that CF was a company that could be turned around.[17]

The following year, the eastern and western accounting offices were combined. Moffitt and nearly a dozen other accountants left Ohio and moved to Portland. White, however, tapped O'Brien to become CF's controller, and he moved to Menlo Park instead.

"Bill [White] was a great guy," O'Brien said. "You couldn't find a guy more ethical, number one. Number two, once he made a decision, he stuck to it until I could talk him out of it."[18]

O'Brien admitted White was demanding.

"But he was good," O'Brien added. "He didn't want to spend any money, didn't like to give raises. He didn't take any big raises for himself, and that was killing us all down below him."

O'Brien's father worked as a railroad brakeman during the Depression. O'Brien worked three jobs to support his family after his father died and also took night classes at a business college. During World War II, he was a bombardier in Europe. He earned a business administration degree from the University of Missouri after the war and worked as an accountant and auditor for a trucking firm before joining CF.

When O'Brien became CF's controller in late 1961, he also became White's protégé. O'Brien was promoted within two years to vice president and treasurer, and the company posted a slim profit of $400,000 in 1962. The carrier's operations were then realigned into three geographic regions—Western, Central, and Eastern (a fourth region, Southern, was added in 1969).[19]

With this restructuring, White expanded the use of sleeper units, eliminating much of CF's relay system. All western line-haul runs were converted into sleeper operations beginning in 1962. A team of two drivers drove the route with one tractor and trailer; one driver slept while the other drove. Although this operation placed an enormous strain on drivers, who had to develop trust with partners and tolerate the discomfort of life on the road, it offered greater flexibility and quicker delivery times. The Teamsters also increased pay scales for drivers on sleeper long-haul duty.[20]

MANUFACTURING SUCCESS

Even as its parent company restructured, Freightliner expanded its manufacturing capacity as demand for its vehicles increased to more than 600 trucks annually by the end of the 1950s.[21] New production plants opened in 1960 in Pomona, California; in 1961 in Vancouver, British Columbia (at a service stall at a White dealership); and in 1966 in Indianapolis. The Canadian "factory" was created to placate the country's content laws (national content laws, which the United States, Canada, and other nations have had, force manufacturers that attempt to avoid tariffs and other import duties or fees by establishing a presence in a foreign country to conduct at least part of their business locally).[22] But uncertainty remained for the truck manufacturer.

"We didn't know what was going to happen to Freightliner," said Kenneth Self, president of the manufacturing subsidiary. "I figured they'd dump us."[23]

Instead, CF invested in Freightliner and expanded the Portland plant three times between 1960 and 1964 as 96 percent of its sales went to outside customers.[24] Freightliner's profitability aided CF's financial turnaround. The manufacturer's share of overall CF sales was between 25 and 40 percent from 1963 until the mid-1970s.[25]

This is an interior of a Freightliner assembly plant in the mid-1960s. The plants were located in Portland, Oregon; Pomona, California; and Vancouver, British Columbia. (*Photo courtesy of Ray Halloran.*)

When outside suppliers were unable to provide aluminum castings, CF organized ConMetCo in 1964. ConMetCo supplied customers across the country and its product line expanded to include aluminum wheel hubs, radiators, heater cores, mufflers, and other components. It also acquired aluminum foundries in Washington, Ohio, and North Carolina as well as die-casting facilities in Oregon.

Manufacturing capacities at the Pomona and Vancouver plants doubled by 1965. That same year, Freightliner produced 10 experimental tractors called the Turboliner, which used Boeing gas turbine engines. These engines were 2,400 pounds lighter than comparable piston-driven rigs and were initially seen as an improvement when compared to other engines.[26] Lighter was not always better, however, and the project was cancelled after four years because the gas turbine engine used six times as much fuel as a comparable diesel-powered unit.[27]

SEEKING IMPROVEMENT

In spite of White's restructuring efforts, CF posted a loss of $604,000 in the first quarter of 1963. During the summer, White recruited Emerson W. Swan, who was vice president of operations at Roadway, to manage Consolidated's motor carrier division. After serving in the Navy during World War II, Swan worked at Bridgeways, a large Midwest trucking company, before joining Roadway in 1951. In December 1955, Roadway, which was based in Akron, Ohio, was nearly acquired by CF Inc. until the owner refused to sell at the last moment.

As CF's executive vice president, Swan redirected the managers and salesmen to hold costs down, cut waste, improve service, and obtain higher-valued freight. One of Swan's first efforts to cut costs was to eliminate snow chains on trucks. While snow chains were a CF tradition, they burned extra fuel by adding 300 pounds of weight to every set of doubles.

Salesmen were instructed to be selective about the types of freight that were accepted as Swan worked to improve CF's operating ratio. While 95 was considered a healthy operating ratio in 1963 for a motor carrier, CF maintained a tepid 100.5 ratio. As the company gained higher-value cargos and shunned unprofitable freight, costs fell nearly 8 percent. Although operating revenues dipped 3.5 percent, it posted almost $600,000 in profit in the first quarter of 1964.[28]

In 1964, the corporate headquarters was moved from Menlo Park when White and a newly trimmed staff opened an office in San Francisco. The move effectively emphasized the difference between the motor carrier subsidiary—which remained at Menlo Park—and the operations of the holding company to investors, clients, and the public.[29]

PRACTICAL TECHNOLOGY

The company significantly boosted its computing power in 1962 by purchasing an IBM 1401 computer for its Portland office. Although primitive by today's standards, this computer's magnetic tape–based system reduced the time required to generate outstanding accounts receivable reports from 39 hours to two hours.

Assistant Controller Schoen and his Portland accounting staff, which included Moffitt, wanted to use the computer to its full potential. They developed metrics to measure profitability and track business trends, which became known as terminal income and expense (I&E) reports. Moffitt studied how other companies used and generated these reports. Swan understood the value of I&E reports, as Roadway was one of the first trucking companies to track terminal profits and losses, and he supported Moffitt's effort.

Although the metrics were crude initially, the reports recorded trends, giving managers and salesmen a baseline tool to measure staff performance and provide guidance when improvement was needed. By the end of 1964, Consolidated's operating ratio hit 95.2, the company's best level since 1950. The average length of LTL hauls reached 897 miles, about three times its 1960 level. Overall, CF's national sales exceeded $200 million for the first time, and net profit topped $6 million, about twice the levels of 1963.[30] Moffitt also helped devise a year-end incentive compensation program (ICP) for CF's salaried employees, using his I&E reports as a yardstick for awarding bonuses.

In 1965, Consolidated Freightways Inc.'s stock was traded on the New York Stock Exchange under the ticker symbol CNF. Previously, the company's stock had been traded over-the-counter. By 1970, CF became one of the 20 stocks of the Dow Jones Transportation Average, and some nine out of its 10 largest shareholders were institutions.[31, 32]

With White's leadership and practical management style, the company was finally headed in a positive direction. The only dark news was the death of the company's founder, Leland James, on October 20, 1964, in California. He was 72.

STRATEGIC ACQUISITIONS

As the corporation's financial situation improved, White, who became chairman in 1966, looked to grow the business in the Northeast, Southeast, and Southwest. In 1965, the ICC gave CF temporary authority to operate Southern-Plaza Express Inc. of Dallas. The motor carrier had 13 terminals serving Texas, Arkansas, Illinois, Missouri, and Tennessee. Once the purchase was completed in 1968, Southern-Plaza became the cornerstone for CF's new Southwest division.

In 1967, CF expanded into eastern Canada with the purchase of Hanson Transport Company. Renamed Canadian Freightways Eastern Limited, it served Toronto, Hamilton, and other Ontario industrial centers and connected with CF's routes in the United States at Buffalo.

By the mid-1960s, new packaging techniques allowed shipments to be lighter but bulkier, as cardboard boxes of individually wrapped items replaced the heavier wooden crates.[33] Changing manufacturing techniques that emphasized smaller stock inventories and more frequent shipments were a boon to the trucking industry, which could deliver freight faster than the railroads. CF made a brief but unsuccessful foray into parcel shipping with the creation of the Package Division. Launched in 1969 and modeled after United Parcel Service (UPS), it was discontinued after the 1970 Teamsters' strike. The division never turned a profit.[34]

Arrowhead Division, which specialized in owner-operator truckload operations, began in 1967. It transported ammunition and explo-

More than 350 employees in Portland's accounting office in the mid-1960s handled the complicated paperwork required, including generating revenue and collection figures, interim reports, and payroll for nearly 10,000 staff. Microfilm and an IBM mainframe computer supplemented the paper record-keeping system. *(Photo courtesy of Ray Halloran.)*

sives for the military and eventually expanded into refrigerated products, iron, and the steel-hauling businesses. This marginal division was disbanded after two years.

Entering the Southeast market in the late 1960s, CF purchased Dance Freight Lines, which served Alabama, Georgia, Kentucky, and Tennessee, as well as the Carolinas. It also purchased Lewisburg Transfer Co.—the deal was finalized in 1972—which had routes in Alabama, Tennessee, Kentucky, and West Virginia. During the next 10 years, CF acquired additional carriers and terminals in Alabama, the Carolinas, Florida, Louisiana, Mississippi, and Virginia. By 1978, routes were added from Arizona to San Antonio, and from Houston to New Orleans to increase the southern route system.

In 1969, CF turned toward the Northeast and gained temporary operating authority over Swan Transportation Inc. This added many points in Massachusetts; the sale was finalized the following

year. With other purchases, CF added service to New Hampshire and Maine and expanded in New York and Connecticut. Other mergers enhanced the company's coverage of California and the central states.

Consolidated purchased 51 percent of Pacific Far East Line Inc. (PFEL), for $25 million as it reentered the fishyback business in 1969. PFEL had 13 general cargo freighters and was constructing six more ships to transport 61-foot-long floating cargo containers called lighters. The company also invested in a 45-acre terminal near San Francisco. The lighters were supposed to launch from ocean vessels and travel through shallow waterways to service Asia's inland ports. The vessels, however, were plagued with technological glitches, and the response from shippers was small.

A decrease in trade from the Far East and port strikes added to the difficulties surrounding PFEL, which was shut down half of the time from mid-1970 through the end of 1972.[35] After five years, CF finally sold PFEL for a $20 million loss in 1974. The line went bankrupt a few years later.[36]

"We've really taken a bath in the ocean," said White, of the PFEL venture.[37]

YEARS OF STRIFE

Swan became president of the motor carrier and a member of CF Inc.'s board of directors in 1968. A year later, however, he resigned after a disagreement with White, who became president and CEO. The company's bottom line slipped toward the red due to a 5.3 percent Teamster wage hike, freight rates that remained the same, and an increase in unprofitable truckload traffic. To compound the situation, the national economy slowed while inflation rose.

Yet the interstate highway system was growing. In 1969, the ICC allowed motor freight carriers to operate on new freeways parallel to their established routes without seeking agency approval. This change in regulations permitted the construction of larger and more powerful trucks.[38]

Even with Swan's departure from the motor carrier and the tepid economy, by the end of 1969, CF's revenues hit a record $450 million. Freightliner contributed to its parent corporation's robust earnings as it sold 8,614 vehicles through White Motor Corporation; sales totaled $153 million.

A shipment is ready to clear customs at the Canada–United States border at Coutts, Alberta, which was added to the network by Canadian Freightways, a CF subsidiary. (Photo courtesy of Ray Halloran.)

This 27-door Des Moines, Iowa, terminal, which opened in January 1972, was constructed in a completely new design. Its features included offices at the ground level, while the mezzanine level housed dispatch, dock operations, and terminal manager offices. This improved access from the offices to the dock and also lowered construction costs. Previous CF terminals dispersed the offices over three levels.

The truck manufacturer added a new plant at Swan Island, while the old factory began producing parts. By 1972, Freightliner built a new factory in Chino, California, replacing its Pomona plant. CF's spring manufacturing plant in Fremont, California, which opened in 1966, became a division of Freightliner in 1972. Freightliner moved its corporate headquarters to Swan Island in 1976.

Not all of CF's manufacturing units did as well as Freightliner, however. Transicold Corporation, the refrigeration trailer manufacturer that Snead started in the 1950s, was sold in 1970 after years of marginal profitability.[39] The Teamsters were also having difficulties.

During the 1960s, the Teamsters became more influential under the leadership of James Riddle Hoffa. After years of pursuit by the U.S. Department of Justice, in 1967, Hoffa was sentenced to 13 years in prison (he was convicted of fraud and conspiracy in 1964 for diverting more than $1 million in union funds for personal use). President Richard Nixon commuted the remainder of Hoffa's sentence in 1971. But he never regained full power in the Teamsters and mysteriously disappeared from the parking lot of the Manchus Red Fox restaurant on July 30, 1975, in the Detroit suburb of Bloomfield Hills, Michigan.

Frank E. Fitzsimmons replaced Hoffa in 1967 as a "caretaker president." He faced a revolt from a number of strong Teamster locals who wanted to adopt a more militant approach to the trucking companies that were wringing concessions out of the 1970 National Master Freight Agreement (an agreement between major trucking companies that used a majority of Teamster labor and the Teamsters Union).[40]

A 12-week wildcat strike broke out in Chicago. The strike affected different parts of the country, turning violent in some places. In one incident, a sniper shot 30-year-old Gary Kistler, a CF driver, who was driving in a convoy near St. Louis. A father of four children, Kistler died two months later as a result of his injuries.

The "wildcatters" won a 13 percent wage increase for the next three years, which was higher than the 8 percent increase that the national union had negotiated. CF also faced a 13-week machinist strike at its Freightliner plant in Portland while rising inflation and interest rates continued hammering the national economy. Consolidated's earnings dropped 46 percent, from $2.59 to $1.39 per share.[41]

The Civil Rights struggle also came to the foreground of American politics during the 1960s and 1970s. CF drafted an equal employment opportunity policy in 1966 and created an office to implement it. In 1968, after the Justice Department's Civil Rights Office found Roadway in violation of the 1964 Civil Rights Act, CF reviewed its policies and hired a minority employment specialist. Despite conflicts with the union's seniority rules, the company began permitting minority pickup and delivery drivers to transfer to the higher-paying line-haul positions.

CF nearly doubled the percentage of minority employees to 7.2 percent of its workforce between 1965 and 1973. However, the Department of Justice sued the entire trucking industry—including CF, six major carriers, 342 smaller companies, the Teamsters, and the Machinist unions—for civil rights violations. In 1976, a consent decree set forth specific goals and timetables for the industry to boost minority employment levels.[42]

AIRFREIGHT FORWARDING

In 1970, CF established a new subsidiary, CF AirFreight Inc., which began with three terminals in Chicago, San Francisco, and Los Angeles, and agents in 150 locations in North America and overseas.

Airfreight-forwarding companies usually did not own their own aircraft. These sales-oriented

organizations maintained low overhead and expenses, and utilized their expertise assembling small shipments, creating larger cargo loads, and booking freight transportation on airliners instead of running their own "mini airlines." Customers and the airfreight forwarders benefited from this system as cargo rates were manageable.[43]

Airliner companies enjoyed the airfreight business. As aircraft grew in size to accommodate more passengers by the late 1960s and early 1970s, the amount of cargo that planes could carry increased threefold. Airliners began offering to move airfreight for 25 to 30 cents a pound to fill this space.

The genesis of CF Air occurred in the mid-1960s when CF attempted to buy an airfreight forwarding company called Star Forwarders Inc.[44] CF's efforts to purchase the company seemed in vain as the Civil Aviation Board (CAB) was reluctant to allow motor carriers in the airfreight business. Other airfreight forwarders objected to CF's plans, fearing it could suppress the development of the industry.[45]

After four years, the CAB gave its approval of CF AirFreight—and the airfreight forwarding subsidiaries of Navajo Freight Lines and Pacific Intermountain Express (PIE)—to begin operating a five-year, experimental trial.[46] CF AirFreight started slowly, but gradually carved itself a niche and became one of the 10 largest airfreight-forwarding companies. It was producing $400 million in annual sales by 1978 and had a network of 125 North American locations.[47]

GAINING SPEED WITH FERST

By 1971, CF began developing one of the trucking industry's most sophisticated computer systems. It signed an agreement with IBM, which provided the hardware and programming, to create the Fast Information Retrieval for Surface Transportation (FIRST) program. This management informa-

The certification of CF equipment required a staff of six people. About 100 state requirements had to be met, including plates, permits, decals, and emblems. These licenses were needed to satisfy state regulatory agencies, highway departments, use and fuel tax departments, and other taxing agencies in the United States and Canadian provinces. (Photo courtesy of Ray Halloran.)

Weather always proved to be a challenge when delivering by land. The cover of the March/April 1977 *Freighter* magazine shows a CF doubles combination making its way over a snow-slicked road during the winter of 1976–1977, which was one of the worst winters to date. *(Photo courtesy of Ray Halloran.)*

tion program kept track of the company's tractors and trailers and was used to track shipments, providing detailed freight and operations data used to improve efficiency. It was later renamed FERST—Freight and Equipment Reporting System for Surface Transportation.

The FIRST/FERST project began in 1969. In the late 1960s, CF was unable to keep track of the locations of about 25 percent of its 8,200 tractors and trailers. FERST not only provided the ability to locate equipment, it could identify the starting point of the delivery and then estimate delivery times.[48] This computer technology allowed CF to discontinue sleeper units and return to a relay system.

According to Jim Schlueter, who was vice president of administration at the time, the change from sleeper units to a relay system was long overdue. Schlueter explained:

It was the largest change of operations ever filed with the Teamsters at that particular time in 1971. I took 2,900 road drivers off the sleeper operation and was able to substitute, in order to provide a better level of service with the same amount of service, with 1,800 drivers, [in the relay system]. It shows you how terribly inefficient it was.[49]

Operating like the Pony Express, a driver took his semi-tractor trailer or set of doubles to a relay point where the equipment was handed off to a relay driver. Then, the first driver returned to his initial departure location with a different rig. Some shorter CF runs became one-day turnarounds. Although the relay system required precise timing, freight moved faster and more efficiently, and drivers never spent more than one night away from home.

The new computer equipment also had the luxury of being housed in a new building. An earthquake during the mid-1960s had shaken up Peake Block. A study commissioned by Moffitt, who was vice president of financial planning in the early 1970s, showed that the old Portland General Office building was "subject to sudden and catastrophic collapse in the event of even a moderate earthquake."[50]

Peake Block was replaced in 1973 with the three-story Leland James Center that housed the controller's office, the Portland collection office, revenue accounting, claims, licensing, traffic, area headquarters, and the computer center.

Computing power and more sophisticated programs allowed CF to automate more of its billing, equipment control, and rating systems. When D. Wayne Byerley Jr. joined Consolidated Freightways Corporation of Delaware (CFCD) as a systems analyst in May 1969, the company's billing clerks were typing out the nine-page freight bills.

"Then [the freight bill] went to the dock because the freight bill always had to move with the freight," Byerley said, adding that about seven hard copies of the bill were physically filed in different locations.[51]

By 1975, electronic freight billing was common. Instead of delaying the departure of loaded rigs until freight bills were prepared, drivers were dispatched as clerks used computers to complete the bills. The bill was then sent electronically to the destination while the trucks were en route.

The complicated and technical freight rating system, which remained based on the ICC's archaic tables, was computerized in mid-1977 at CF's Boise Rate Center.[52] By 1979, about 75 percent of LTL freight bills were rated by machine, although pricing specialists still oversaw the handling of complicated bills.

TRANSITIONS

White stepped down from leading the motor carrier, CFCD, in 1972. He tapped Curtis Crowe to become president of the motor carrier while White remained president and chairman of CF Inc. Although Crowe had become executive vice president of CFCD in 1968 and was named to the CF board of directors in 1969, White was slow to relinquish the reins, often stopping by the Menlo Park headquarters (corporate headquarters was in San Francisco). Crowe left the motor carrier a year later. This time, White turned to O'Brien, who was, at the time, vice president of finance.

"[White] comes into my office and says, 'I'd like you to go down and run the motor carrier,'" O'Brien recalled. "I said, 'Why would I do that?'"

"Because the board of directors wants you to," White replied.[53]

About the time O'Brien was settling into his duties as head of the motor carrier, Halloran was promoted to executive vice president of marketing and sales. Meanwhile, Lary Scott, who had been CF vice president for the Eastern Area since 1969 and a former Roadway vice president, was using a cost analysis of CF's traffic patterns to boost traffic on the company's most profitable lanes. Using a technique called "lane selling," the Eastern Area was more profitable than ever—even as its tonnage decreased.[54]

Lane selling used a tremendous amount of data to bring each trailer to maximum legal weight, while salesmen acquired more profitable freight. By 1977, the company began using a computerized rating system to provide price quotes instead of relying on hand calculation of shipping rates by studying dozens of rate books and schedules.

By the early 1970s, the heavily regulated trucking industry came under fire from consumer advocate Ralph Nader. After gaining national recognition for skewering General Motors for the deficiencies of the Chevrolet Corvair in his 1965 book, *Unsafe at Any Speed*, Nader and other activists founded Public Citizen, a nonprofit lobbying group. To investigate corporate power, Nader created the Corporate Accountability Research Group in 1971 to advocate greater competition in the market. Nader's group viewed the cartel-like trucking industry with distrust and felt the ICC supported large corporate profits and high union wages at consumers' expense. The group advocated complete deregulation.[55] The deregulation movement grew throughout the 1970s despite opposition from the Teamsters and the American Trucking Associations.[56] In November 1975, for example, President Gerald Ford began calling for reduced trucking regulations and appointed members who supported competition to the ICC.

"OIL SHOCK"

Even as Scott had found the key to boost profitability with lane selling, the struggling American economy, which faced high inflationary pressures, went into a tailspin due to an oil embargo. After Israel defeated the invading armies of Egypt and Syria in the Yom Kippur War in October 1973, Libya halted oil exports to the United States. Soon afterward, Saudi Arabia and the Shah of Iran led the Organization of the Petroleum Exporting Countries (OPEC) in an oil embargo against the United States, Western Europe, and Japan.

The embargo sparked an energy crisis in the West, which had grown dependent on Middle Eastern oil. The economy slid into a recession as gasoline prices doubled—and then tripled. The Nixon administration attempted to control the recession using heavy-handed

CF Inc. President William G. White, left, shook the hand of Eastern Area Vice President Lary Scott. The Eastern Area was awarded the President's Trophy for most improved safety in 1971.

Blizzards and ice delayed Chicago Driver Jerry Kluck during the winter of 1976-1977, when his normal nine-hour run from Cameron, Missouri, turned into a 46-hour ordeal. Safety Supervisor Burt Studt photographed the rig near Pittsfield, Illinois. *(Photo courtesy of Ray Halloran.)*

regulations such as gas rationing, closing gas stations on Sundays, and a 55 mph speed limit to conserve fuel. Congress passed laws mandating improved fuel economy for motor vehicles.

As the Detroit-based automakers suffered from declining sales while "fuel sipping" Japanese imports became more successful, CF and Freightliner both faced numerous new government regulations. The Clean Air Act of 1970 created the Environmental Protection Agency, which imposed new pollution standards, while truck manufacturers also had the burden of improving fuel economy. Traditionally, CF's costs for fuel and oil had averaged 2.6 percent of revenue. Although the company had been conscious of its fleet mileage, by 1976 its fuel costs spiked to 5.6 percent of its revenues.

Worldwide economic uncertainty continued into 1974 when President Nixon resigned due to the Watergate Scandal and even after the OPEC embargo was lifted. Dealing with "oil shock," CF worked to coax more fuel efficiency from its fleet. By 1980, the transmissions of CF's trucks had been calibrated to perform efficiently at 55 mph. To make its semi-tractor trailers more sleek and to cut wind resistance, air shields were installed on cabs; new radial tires improved gas mileage. CF was able to boost its average miles per gallon to 4.6 in 1979, up from 4.1 at the beginning of the decade. The company saved an estimated $8.6 million per year against 1979 prices.[57]

Freightliner also had to contend with federal laws that mandated new anti-lock braking systems in 1975. These changes caused a rush of orders in 1974—before new, expensive equipment came on the market—and led to a decrease in sales the following year.

TROUBLES WITH FREIGHTLINER

CF Inc. Chairman White commissioned a study in the early 1970s by McKinsey & Company to examine the trucking company's operations, including Freightliner.[58] The consultants recommended that Freightliner build a conventional cab—rather than COE—Class 8 tractor. The study found that other vehicle manufacturers had credit corporations to help customers finance their purchases, and Freightliner was encouraged to offer this service as well. Another recommendation was to establish a dealer network independent of White Motors, and CF took steps to separate Freightliner from the distribution deal it had established with White in 1951.[59]

In 1973, Freightliner introduced a Powerliner COE tractor that accommodated engines up to 625 horsepower. That same year, Freightliner unveiled its first prototype of a conventional Class 8 tractor. Able to pull more than 33,000 pounds, Class 8 commercial tractors were used by large manufacturers and interstate fleet operators in states where length limits were much less restrictive.

Freightliner's long-nose Class 8 tractor entered production in 1974 and accounted for 20 percent of its 14,344 sales for the year.[60] However, due to the 1974 to 1975 recession, Freightliner posted its first annual loss. Exacerbating the situation, Freightliner closed its assembly lines and furloughed workers in late 1974 when White Motors announced it could not accept any more trucks.[61]

"Back in the seventies, most of the U.S. truck manufacturers were getting into serious trouble," Moffitt explained. "White was approaching bankruptcy. International was approaching bankruptcy. Freightliner was having a hell of a time holding onto its market share."[62]

With Freightliner accounting for 50 percent of White Motors sales, CF executives—including Self, who had been made chairman of the truck manufacturer, and Freightliner President W. E. "Bill" Critzer—decided in December 1975 to terminate the sales agreement with the Ohio-based truck manufacturer effective December 8, 1977. It also terminated a similar agreement it had in Canada, effective January 1978. For two years, Freightliner established a network of 190 dealers across the

This gathering took place at the 1977 CF management meeting in San Diego, California.

continent. In 1978, Freightliner sold 13,577 units in the United States and Canada while its revenues hit $478 million.

By 1979, Freightliner began marketing Volvo Class 6, 7, and 8 diesel trucks in the United States under an exclusive agreement.[63] But the truck manufacturer was capturing only about 6 percent of the truck market, and with growing federal vehicle regulations, CF couldn't financially support the new machinery, tooling, and worker training needed to keep Freightliner viable.[64] Consolidated began looking for a buyer for the truck manufacturer.

CHANGE OF COMMAND

In 1975, White relinquished the title of Consolidated president to O'Brien, but he retained the chairman's office and accepted the title of CEO. Knowing that White often doubted the decisions made by his own executives as well as interfered in their daily operations, O'Brien had to be proactive if he were to take over effectively.

"I told [White] … 'You can't come to my office without an appointment if I take the job,'" O'Brien said. "I told him, 'I'll tell you anything you want to know, but I'm going to make the decisions.'"[65]

Once, White was invited to a meeting at Menlo Park. O'Brien excused himself just before the meeting began to take a phone call from a customer. When he returned to the boardroom about 10 minutes later, White had already started the meeting.

"I said, 'Let me tell you something. It's my meeting. So let's just start over,'" O'Brien said, adding that he, indeed, restarted the meeting. "[White] got the message. To his credit, he may have been critical, but he never interfered."

One of O'Brien's first executive decisions was to pick a president for CF Inc. He chose Ronald E. Burbank, CFCD's executive vice president of operations, who had also run ConMetCo in the 1960s. Scott later replaced Burbank. O'Brien also recruited Roger Curry to become president of the lackluster CF AirFreight. At the airfreight forwarder, Curry picked Richard F. Bryner, who had been with the subsidiary since 1970, to become his operating expert.[66]

O'Brien advanced to become CEO and president in 1977, and, when White retired in 1979, he also received the title of chairman.

ADDING CONSOLIDATION CENTERS

In 1975, Roadway surpassed CFCD to become the largest trucking company in America using a hub-and-spoke system where outlying terminals sent small loads to consolidation centers. Called the breakbulk system, Roadway made sure its trailers were at near-full capacity on its long-haul runs.

Under Burbank and Scott, CF launched the Freight Flow System during the late 1970s.[67] This network of consolidation centers was used to serve major traffic lanes. Satellite terminals, placed in large and small markets throughout the United States, sent freight to breakbulk centers where full truckloads of shipments destined for the same locales were assembled before shipping.

The Freight Flow System operated 24 hours a day, seven days a week. In 1978, its first consolidation center, the 110-door Pocono (Pennsylvania) facility, opened to serve spoke terminals in the New England and Mid-Atlantic states. By 1980, the company had 24 large consolidation centers throughout the country and greatly increased the number of its smaller terminals.

CF generated record-breaking revenue between 1976 and 1979, but there were a number of drawbacks to the Freight Flow System.[68] Additional smaller terminals serviced the consolidation centers, which increased costs, and freight traveled extra miles, which led to shipment delays. The average CF shipment moved more than 1,000 miles—the company's short-haul business became virtually nonexistent.[69]

As it built its consolidation centers and spoke terminals, CF also participated in a lawsuit that overturned Wisconsin's ban on double trailers on the interstates in 1978.[70] The company fought against state restrictions in Iowa, Pennsylvania, and other states, but the cases weren't decided until the early 1980s.[71] The formerly oppressive Oregon, on the other hand, had liberalized its truck length laws, and CF began experimenting with triple trailers in the late 1970s.[72]

MOVING AHEAD

As 1978 came to an end, and CF's 50th anniversary was approaching, its routes covered more than 100,000 miles. It had 267 terminals in 47 states and five Canadian provinces (the only states it did not serve were Hawaii, Vermont, and South Dakota). It had the most complete, single-line service on the largest route system in the United States and Canada. Its Freightliner subsidiary ranked among America's largest 500 industrial corporations, based on sales.[73]

Although there would be much to celebrate in the coming year, no one could predict the tumultuous times ahead. Another energy crisis was on the horizon, following the fall of the Shah of Iran and the Teamsters strike and national lockout. CF would also continue searching for a buyer for Freightliner and seek ways to expand CF AirFreight.

CHAPTER FOUR
LAUNCHING CON-WAY
1979–1983

I've always called it the Con-way mystique. Starting out small, they grew it over time ... very small, small steps, and their training, the pride and the esprit de corps that [Jerry Detter] built in that organization originally. It's still there today and has been the success of Con-way.

—Wayne Byerley, retired vice president of purchasing[1]

UPON REACHING ITS 50TH ANNIVERSARY in 1979, Consolidated Freightways (CF) reported on February 9 that its previous year's revenue reached a record $1.38 billion.[2] Net income had risen 18 percent to $62 million, and its earnings per share topped out at $4.82 compared to $4.24 in 1977. When Chairman William G. White retired in 1979, Raymond F. O'Brien, president and CEO, filled this role as well.

Relying on economic forecasts from CF's financial staff in Portland, Oregon, O'Brien struck an optimistic tone in his statement to shareholders regarding the deregulation efforts in the trucking industry. Although he warned that many economists were predicting a "mild recession" that could be coupled with a high inflation rate in the upcoming year, O'Brien predicted a positive future for CF:

Given reasonably stable economic conditions, we believe 1979 will be another excellent year for CF.[3]

His prediction, however, would be severely tested as the 1980s brought its share of economic difficulties. On January 13, 1979, the autocratic government of Mohammad Reza Pahlavi, the Shah of Iran, was overthrown. As a result, oil prices spiked, and the U.S. economy remained in jeopardy as the inflation rate jumped to 13 percent by the end of the

year. Unemployment hovered near 6 percent.[4] In addition, the trucking industry was about to face its biggest challenge yet.

LABOR AGITATION

The threat of federal deregulation of the trucking industry had been a possibility for years and was finally brought to fruition. Lawmakers were prompted into action by the 1979 "inflationary" labor contract.

CF's national, three-year agreement with the Teamsters was scheduled to expire on March 31, 1979. President Jimmy Carter's administration was well aware of the negotiations and attempted to influence the bargaining by providing "voluntary" wage-price guidelines to cap wage increases at 7 percent per year.[5]

Just before the Saturday midnight deadline, the union broke off talks—negotiations for the trucking

---

Above: President and CEO Raymond F. O'Brien also took on the role of chairman when William G. White retired in 1979.

Opposite: Con-Way Central President Jerry Detter, pictured on April 12, 1983, with Con-Way Central's first piece of equipment—tractor 414-3001—soon after it rolled off the Ford Louisville Truck Plant assembly line.

A CF semitruck traveled during the night in Atlanta, Georgia. With its acquisitions at the end of the 1970s, the trucking firm stated that it was accelerating the growth of its southern operations.

companies were handled by Trucking Management Inc. (TMI)—and the union announced selective strikes against 73 motor carriers, rather than a complete walkout, which would have crippled the economy.[6] Although the Carter administration lobbied behind the scenes to stave off the strike, Teamsters President Frank Fitzsimmons said that "interference by high-level government bureaucrats" was a key reason negotiations soured.[7] TMI also criticized the administration's interference even as trucking companies took measures against the union by locking out 300,000 Teamsters nationwide.[8] The union and TMI came to an agreement that hourly compensation would be increased by more than 30 percent

for the life of the three-year contract, well above President Carter's suggested 7 percent increase.[9]

By April 11, with both the union and TMI adhering to a 30 percent wage increase agreement, the Carter administration capitulated. Concerned that the strike would affect the economy, the government officially declared that the contract met wage-price guidelines. Soon afterward, the trucking companies asked for rate increases to cover the costs of the wage hike, and the ICC granted the requests.[10]

O'Brien described how important regulation had been to the industry:

Life was much simpler when we were regulated. Relationship [between trucking companies and customers] was more important than anything else because the rates were fixed. That was great. The union loved it. They'd get the wages up. We'd pass it on to the customers. Nobody ever took a strike. … If you've got a regulated industry, [the government] *ought to regulate the unions along with it, as they do with public utilities. Then you can't go along and get a $1.85 an hour increase because it won't get approved.*[11]

The acceptance of the 1979 Teamster contract was the spark that ignited the deregulation forces on Capitol Hill, especially with the annual inflation rate running at double digits. The politically charged atmosphere in Washington, D.C., was felt throughout the industry and acutely studied by those readying for the imminent effects of deregulation. At the time, Edward P. "Ned" Moritz had been working for the American Trucking Associations (ATA) conducting economic research.

"My primary job was to delay the action of deregulation. That's what I did for six years, just slow it down," said Moritz, who was then hired as director of economic research at CF in 1979.[12] During his first year and a half, he prepared a nationwide tariff

Right: A CF dockworker is pictured here in the late 1970s in what is probably one of the long-haul carrier's breakbulk terminals, where freight was consolidated from satellite terminals into truckloads before being shipped across the continent.

Below: A CF safety supervisor is shown here with a radar gun to monitor the speed of a passing CF semitruck. This was a staged photo used in the 1979 annual report to illustrate the company's commitment to both safety and strictly enforcing the 55 mph national speed limit set to conserve fuel.

and pricing system for CF in case the motor carrier rate bureaus were abolished.

THE MOTOR CARRIER ACT OF 1980

Despite opposition from the ATA and the Teamsters, the Senate passed a deregulation bill in April 1980. A less sweeping reform measure was passed in the U.S. House of Representatives by a vote of 367 to 13.[13] Facing impending deregulation, the ATA reluctantly accepted compromise legislation that lifted many restrictions that had prevented competitors from entering the market.[14] President Carter signed the Motor Carrier Act of 1980 into law on April 1. Other bills enacted that year boosted vehicle fuel economy, promoted energy conservation, and simplified federal regulations.

The ICC still reviewed trucking tariff rates and required trucking companies to purchase interstate operating authority from the agency, but the law greatly altered an industry that had been highly regulated since 1935. The act eliminated most restrictions on the types of commodities transported, the geographic routes trucking companies could travel, and also gave truckers a "zone of reasonableness" for pricing, which meant that rates could fluctuate within 15 percent of 1980 levels.[15]

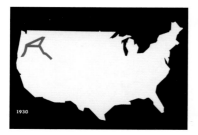
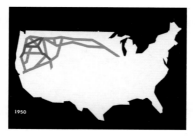

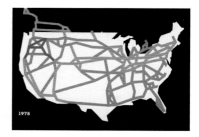

New trucking firms could enter the market easily, and companies could act as both common and contract carriers. Trucking companies no longer needed to purchase competitors to acquire new routes. Due to the new lack of restrictions, CF and other large trucking firms began rapid expansion programs. Although federal restrictions were lessened, individual states retained authority over intrastate traffic.

"The actual federal preemption of state-controlled intrastate traffic didn't end until 1992," noted John Hickerson, who joined the company in 1981 and eventually became president of Con-Way Southern. "For that twelve-year period after 1980, the states still tightly regulated intrastate traffic through various governing bodies and commissions. Texas was the worst and most notorious."[16]

These maps show the growth of Consolidated Freightways' route coverage in 1930, 1950, 1960, and 1978, including the expansion into Canada.

Many smaller companies trimmed their tariffs—the rate war had begun. CF's initial policy was to offer lower rates to customers on a case-by-case basis, not competing openly through pricing. Gregory Quesnel, CF's chief accountant at the time, said that discounts of even 1 percent would have "seemed like a mortal sin."[17] However, after competitors such as Yellow Freight—founded in 1924 in Oklahoma City, Oklahoma—began slashing rates across the board, Consolidated was forced to follow suit.

Donna Cottardi, who started at the company in 1969 and is current manager of Menlo

FORCES BEHIND DEREGULATION

THOSE IN FAVOR OF DEREGULATION—WHICH INCLUDED Ralph Nader, an outspoken consumer advocate; the National Association of Manufacturers; the American Conservative Union; Senator Ted Kennedy; and economist Alfred Kahn—had been gathering strength in the mid- to late-1970s. Kahn, whom President Jimmy Carter had appointed as chief of the Civil Aeronautics Board (CAB), had led the fight to deregulate the airline industry. Kahn then drafted the administration's trucking deregulation proposals. In Congress, Kennedy was chairman of the Senate Judiciary Committee and introduced a bill to strip away the regulations that prevented competition in the trucking industry.[1]

In April 1977, President Carter appointed Daniel O'Neal chairman of the Interstate Commerce Commission (ICC). O'Neal began dismantling the ICC's elaborate red tape, such as abolishing a rule that prevented retail companies such as Sears and Safeway from picking up backhaul cargo from other shippers after making deliveries to their stores.

Before the deregulation bills were able to make their way through Congress, however, the American economy was hit by the Iranian oil embargo.

Freight Payment, was a firsthand witness to the changes deregulation brought. Cottardi explained:

> *During those times after deregulation, it changed the whole makeup of how we did business. We went from a company that had all of our rates through the ICC, and now ... had to have everything submitted and approved. We suddenly were writing our own contracts and applying fuel surcharges. We were going through this tough time of not having fuel and having to pay high prices for fuel and customers being afraid that there wouldn't be fuel. That was a very volatile time in the industry because it was such a change. There were all these carriers going under, and that made it even worse. I mean, it was good for us because on one hand, we took the business, but it was a difficult time in the industry.[18]*

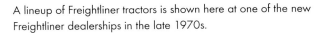
A lineup of Freightliner tractors is shown here at one of the new Freightliner dealerships in the late 1970s.

Following the fall of the Shah, the Muslim cleric Ayatollah Khomeini took over Iran. Khomeini was not an ally to the United States, which had supported the Shah for decades during the Cold War.

On November 4, 1979, some 500 Iranians stormed the American embassy in Tehran, taking 52 hostages. President Carter responded by halting imports of Iranian oil and freezing Iranian bank accounts in the United States. The Ayatollah persuaded the Organization of the Petroleum Exporting Countries (OPEC) to hike oil prices as punishment for the actions of the United States. The cost of oil skyrocketed virtually overnight from $12.46 per barrel to $35.24, marking the beginning of the second oil crisis and the onset of a deep recession. Despite a brief recovery near the 1980 presidential election, the economy didn't pick up until 1983—after the national unemployment rate had risen to 9.6 percent.[2]

Although unemployment in industrial cities, such as Detroit and Pittsburgh, reached Depression-era levels, CF was fortuitous in its planning. In 1979, for the first time in five years, the company borrowed money and boosted its debt level from 12 percent to 25 percent of its total capitalization to pay for improvements—it locked in its interest rates at 10 percent. Others had to contend with sharply rising interest rates as the federal prime rate reached 20 percent by April 1980. The Federal Reserve Board shrunk the money supply to fight inflation.[3]

The depressed economy was reflected in the plunge in overall North American motor freight tonnage. Tonnage peaked at 202.2 million tons in March 1979, and then fell to 133.9 million tons by September 1983. Retail sales of medium and heavy-duty trucks also plunged by 48 percent from about 213,000 units in 1979 to 144,128 units three years later.[4]

The Senate passed a deregulation bill in 1980, and President Carter signed the Motor Carrier Act of 1980 into law on April 1.

AIRFREIGHT OPPORTUNITY?

THE SAME 1981 BOSTON CONSULTING GROUP STUDY that identified the opportunity in the regional LTL trucking business also noted that airfreight forwarding, ocean freight forwarding, and customs brokerage services were prime targets for long-term growth.[1] Chief Financial Officer Donald Moffitt and CF AirFreight President Roger Curry began examining airfreight companies for possible acquisition, including Burlington Northern Air Freight, Airborne Express, Emery Air Freight, and Flying Tiger. They also reestablished contact with a business called Air Express International Corporation (AEI).

When William G. White first explored entering the airfreight forwarding business in the 1960s, he inquired about purchasing AEI, but its chairman and largest stockholder Joseph L. Mailman refused. By 1982, AEI posted a $4 million loss, and Mailman, who was 81 at the time, was finally ready to sell his company. Moffitt and Curry thought AEI's operations would complement the services that CF AirFreight offered.[2]

Remaining profitable during the recession, CF Air served 76 American cities, while AEI operated in 35 nations and provided service in the United States, Europe, and Asia. There was little overlap between the two companies, and the merger would make CF Inc. a global corporation. The asking price—between $40 million and $46 million—was tempting.[3] At the same September 1982 board meeting where Raymond O'Brien presented the launch of the regional Con-Way trucking firms, Moffitt and Curry also presented the option of negotiating with AEI to increase CF Inc.'s market share of the airfreight business.[4]

By January 1983, CF Inc. had formulated a plan to merge its CF AirFreight subsidiary, which had annual revenues of $91 million, with AEI,

An employee at a Freightliner dealer in 1978 used a computerized parts ordering system called S.O.S. Parts Express to identify the nearest parts center that has an out-of-stock part.

A number of long-established carriers went out of business within the decade, unable to adapt successfully to the changes. CF was also hampered by Freightliner, its truck manufacturing subsidiary, which needed major investments to stay competitive in the commercial vehicle industry.

With all of the deregulatory legislation, the former Cornell University economist Alfred Kahn joked, "Motherhood and apple pie are being taken care of in other legislation."[19]

"I debated [Kahn] once," O'Brien said, in a 2007 interview. "He said everything was going to be great after deregulation. Well, in a sense, he's right. You can ride airlines today and be treated like cattle. It's true you can get cheaper fares, but the fact is that the airlines are broke, and the employees are losing their pensions."[20]

As it turned out, CF didn't need the pricing system that Moritz had created. Moritz then went into "operational planning" for the next year and a half, learning about the shipping docks and interacting with the Teamsters.

which generated $125 million in annual revenues. The total cost estimates for the deal, however, had climbed to $63.3 million. Despite the added financial burden, O'Brien announced that he hoped the merger would be completed by midyear.[5]

AIRFREIGHT MERGER COLLAPSES

Anticipating the purchase of AEI, CF spent approximately $250,000 on marketing materials in preparation of the event, according to Moritz.[6] CF Inc. information technology employees also had begun "taking over" AEI's computer systems.

Although it had been discovered that AEI had some questionable business practices, the merger appeared on track with AEI shareholders scheduled to vote on June 29, 1983—a little more than a week after Con-Way Central Express began operating. Another issue surrounding the merger was that CF AirFreight was a nonunion entity, while the Teamsters represented a number of AEI workers.

The labor situation was partially responsible for the merger's collapse. Teamsters Local 851, which represented AEI's workers at New York's John F. Kennedy International Airport, filed a federal lawsuit to block the takeover. According to the agreement between Local 851 and AEI, the union had veto authority over a merger if the acquirer refused to accept the current collective bargaining agreement. There were also rumors that the local union was controlled by the Mafia.

Negotiations between CF and AEI broke off by early August. CF filed a lawsuit against the airfreight carrier, arguing that the company had not met its disclosure obligations—AEI launched a countersuit. Adding to the tumult, two Federal Bureau of Investigation agents appeared at Palo Alto and subpoenaed Moffitt as a witness for the government in a racketeering case that involved AEI. Moffitt and other CF Inc. executives had to testify to a federal grand jury about what they had learned about AEI's activities.[7]

CF Inc. settled its own dispute by paying AEI an undisclosed amount of money in 1984 for the merger's collapse. Mailman resigned as chairman, in an attempt to distance himself from the company, which lost $34 million in 1983.

FREIGHTLINER WOES

After a 32-year career, Kenneth Self retired as chairman of Freightliner on October 1, 1979. O'Brien named William E. Critzer as president and CEO.[21] CF's subsidiary had grown substantially and employed 7,130 people by adding new assembly plants—such as one in Charlotte, North Carolina, which was still under construction as 1979 began. Its own network included almost 200 dealers.[22] But Freightliner remained a cash drain on the corporation.

Consolidated's stock suffered on Wall Street due to the difficulty of classifying the holding corporation. According to Donald Moffitt, chief financial officer, some analysts did not know whether to identify it as a manufacturer or as a motor carrier. Moffitt explained:

Our stock was being hurt badly by Freightliner. Put that together with the fact that the business cycles in the motor freight and commercial vehicle manufacturing industries are different. Trucking does well as a recession ends, but it does very poorly before a recession begins. That's when people quit stocking, quit ordering from the warehouse. Truck manufacturing is exactly the opposite.[23]

Freightliner signed a deal with AB Volvo in August 1978 to become the exclusive marketer of the Swedish manufacturer's Class 6, 7, and 8 diesel trucks, but the agreement did little to rectify a difficult situation.[24]

Freightliner continued to falter during 1980 as production dropped from 57 trucks per day in February to 20 per day by August. It closed all seven of its American plants for periods of time; furloughed workers for a month at its Vancouver, British Columbia, plant; and permanently shuttered its Chino, California, factory. Critzer resigned before the year ended, and Freightliner posted a $16.6 million loss.[25] Ronald E. Burbank, who had just become CF Inc.'s president and COO, took over Freightliner as well.

Freightliner's Charlotte, North Carolina, factory was under construction in the late 1970s. Once completed, it increased the truck manufacturer's production by 50 percent.

"Moffitt and I talked about what we were going to do with Freightliner," O'Brien said.[26]

The manufacturer needed money for engineering as well as marketing. Its dealers were underfinanced and also in need of assistance, and it was clear that a hard decision had to be made. Volvo, realizing the vulnerability of the manufacturer, approached CF and offered to purchase Freightliner through a stock exchange.

"I was the chief financial officer by this time," Moffitt said. "I didn't want paper in a European company that I didn't understand."

As CF continued negotiations with Volvo as well as the bankrupt White Motor Corporation that had expressed interest—the company had entered bankruptcy in 1980 while other large truck manufacturers suffered severe sales and revenue declines, casting a pall over the industry—the German conglomerate Daimler-Benz AG learned of Freightliner's situation. Chairman Gerhard Prinz called O'Brien directly to discuss a possible sale.[27] Moffitt was assigned to handle all the negotiations surrounding Freightliner, meeting with both Volvo and Daimler-Benz. Cash strapped, Volvo eventually fell out of the running as a potential buyer. That left Daimler-Benz.

"This was the largest acquisition that Daimler-Benz had ever had to that point," Moffitt said. "It took a long time of negotiating in four or five European cities, in London, New York, and San Francisco. The deal fell apart once, and we put it back together."

O'Brien told Daimler-Benz that the asking price for the truck manufacturer was $300 million, although he didn't think the German company would be receptive to such a high figure.[28] The negotiations broke off. Then Prinz called

O'Brien while traveling in South America, and the talks resumed.

The two companies reached an agreement on March 5, 1981.[29] CF decided to sell Freightliner, its assets, and other manufacturing subsidiaries for $284 million—$204 million in cash and the rest in notes effective July 31, 1981.[30] Moffitt remembered:

When we did the closing in Germany, they had a special performance in the Stuttgart Opera House, and the prime minister made a speech. He says, "The people of Germany are in your debt." Can you imagine that?[31]

With a combination of the principal and interest, CF received about $300 million from the deal, O'Brien noted.[32] A few manufacturing subsidiaries not related to Freightliner, such as California-based CF Road Systems Inc., a trailer producer that was created in 1980, remained with the trucking company.

"The sale of Freightliner was good for everybody," said Wayne Byerley, CF vice president of purchasing. "It took away a cash drain on Consolidated Freightways, and it gave the Freightliner people an opportunity to go sell their product, which was—and still is—a superior tractor."[33]

In August, Freightliner ended its marketing agreement with Volvo, and Burbank resigned from his position at CF to remain with the truck manufacturer.

STUDY CHANGES COMPANY FOCUS

The recession continued in 1981 under President Ronald Reagan, who trounced former President Carter in a landslide election, and the motor carrier industry remained sluggish. More than 200 common carriers reported net losses in excess of $12 million by the end of the year.[34]

Undaunted by trying economic times, CF Inc. moved its headquarters from downtown San Francisco to a new 30,000-square-foot building next

WHEELS ON WALL STREET

NEW YORK STOCK EXCHANGE COMPOSITE

1981-80 High	Low		Tues. Close Mar. 10	Change For Week
$13^3/4$	$6^7/8$	Arkansas Best Corp. .60	$11^1/2$	$- ^3/4$
$16^3/8$	$7^3/8$	Banner Industries .16	$10^1/3$	$+ ^1/8$
$16^3/4$	10	Butler International .52	13	....
15	$6^1/4$	Carolina Freight Carriers .52	$14^1/2$	$+ ^1/8$
39	18	Consolidated Freightways 1.40	$37^3/4$	$+9$
$34^3/8$	$19^3/8$	Leaseway 1.40	32	$+ ^5/8$
13	$7^1/2$	McLean .32	$9^5/8$	$- ^1/8$
$19^7/8$	$11^5/8$	National City Lines 1.00a[1]	NA	
$38^3/8$	$17^3/8$	Overnite Transportation 1.40	$37^3/4$	$+ ^3/4$
18	8	RLC Corporation .64	$14^3/8$	....
$31^7/8$	16	Ryder System 1.08b	31	$+1^3/4$
$12^3/4$	$7^3/4$	Telecom Corp. .70	$11^3/8$	$+ ^7/8$
$7^1/8$	$4^3/4$	Transcon Lines .10	$5^1/8$	$- ^1/8$

AMERICAN STOCK EXCHANGE COMPOSITE

1981-80 High	Low		Tues. Close Mar. 10	Change For Week
$25^3/8$	$15^3/4$	Atlas Van Lines .10	$23^1/2$	$+1^1/4$
$4^3/8$	$2^3/8$	Branch Industries	$2^1/2$	$- ^1/8$
$4^7/8$	$1^5/8$	Cooper-Jarrett	$3^5/8$	$- ^3/8$
$3^3/8$	$1^5/8$	Eazor Express	2	....
$8^1/2$	4	Refrigerated Transport .36	$7^1/4$	....
10	7	Tri-State Motor Transit .80	$7^5/8$	$+ ^1/2$

to Hewlett-Packard's headquarters in July. Stanford University, which owned the property, feared that CF would open a truck terminal on the land. Located on Hillview Avenue, however, the corporate headquarters won a number of design awards and was ready to open in mid-1981.[35]

This move was also accompanied by a strict internal examination as far as the direction the company was taking. Prior to the sale of Freightliner, Moffitt commissioned the Boston Consulting Group to assemble a historical record of the U.S. transportation industry.[36] About the same time the new offices opened, the report was ready.

"In the end, [Boston Consulting Group] came up with a bunch of recommendations of where we should invest the Freightliner money," Moffitt remembered. "Number one on the list was regional trucking."[37]

Moffitt presented Boston Consulting Group's recommendations to CF's board of directors—many were surprised by the findings. With its growing Freight Flow System of large consolidation centers and satellite terminals throughout the United States, CF had become a specialized long-haul carrier, but the most profitable segment of the market identified by the study was freight that traveled less than 500 miles.[38]

"One of the things in the report that impressed me is that the average length of a freight haul in the United States is 500 and some miles," O'Brien said. "Our average length of haul was 1,300 miles. I thought we ought to be in that business. That's how the idea [for a short-haul LTL business] got started as far as I'm concerned."

Above: On the day the Freightliner sale was announced in March 1981, Consolidated Freightways' stock price rose by $9 a share to $37. (Photo courtesy of Ray Halloran.)

Below: This new ConMetCo custom-built machine automatically drilled, reamed, and tapped aluminum wheel hubs in a single operation. The machine increased ConMetCo's output of hubs by 50 percent.

CCX CON-WAY CENTRAL EXPRESS
SERVICE CHART
"Compare and see CCX's service quality"

From To	Chicago	Cincinnati	Cleveland	Columbus	Detroit	Grand Rapids	Indianapolis	Milwaukee	Minneapolis	Pittsburgh	Toledo
Chicago		1	1	1	1	1	1	1	1	2	1
Cincinnati	1				1	2	1	2		1	
Cleveland	1				1	1	1	2		1	
Columbus	1				1	1	1	1		1	
Detroit	1	1	1	1			1	1		2	1
Grand Rapids	1	2	1	1			1	1		2	1
Indianapolis	1	1	1	1	1	1		1	2	2	1
Milwaukee	1	2	2	1	1	1	1		1	2	1
Minneapolis	1						2	1			
Pittsburgh	2	1	1	1	2	2	2	2			1
Toledo	1				1	1	1	1		1	

1 - OVERNIGHT   2 - SECOND MORNING

This is the first service chart issued by Con-Way Central Express, showing its original 11 terminals. Initially, only three cities could serve the Minneapolis terminal, as other service centers were located beyond CF Inc.'s 500-mile restriction. The company also did not have intrastate operating authority in Michigan and Ohio.

Three decades before, Jack Snead Jr. had tried to reorganize Consolidated into a nationwide company that concentrated mostly on local cartage. Snead intuitively understood what the contemporary study had revealed, but was hampered when his divisionalization efforts failed.

"If you looked at what CF could do for you back in the early eighties, they'd go from [Detroit] to California, but they wouldn't go from [Detroit] to Chicago. They didn't want to," said Bryan Millican, who retired as executive vice president, sales and marketing, for Con-Way in 2005.[39] Because of the way the company was organized, it was uneconomical for the long-haul carrier to transport regionally.

Lary Scott and Robert H. Lawrence, executive vice president of operations for CFCD, examined not only how to improve long-haul operations, but also how to enter the regional short-haul LTL market effectively. Scott, at the time, was occupied with running the long-haul carrier and assigned Lawrence to tackle the daunting task.[40]

Lawrence, a former member of Philadelphia Teamsters Local 107, started his career in the industry as a dock foreman for the Ohio-based Norwalk Truck Lines. He then became the Philadelphia terminal manager for United Buckingham, a Seattle-based trucking firm. After Yellow Freight purchased United Buckingham in 1969, Lawrence became an assistant terminal manager at CFCD in Philadelphia. By 1973, Scott made Lawrence a staff assistant, and he proved his ability by resolving labor issues successfully.

Lawrence drafted a regional trucking business plan by late 1981, which was refined further by mid-1982. Moffitt noted that there were more than a dozen people who were involved in the development of the new business plans.

"You won't talk to any one of them who doesn't claim authorship for Con-Way," he added.[41]

Choosing a name for the enterprises was another obstacle. One source has credited Lawrence for creating the Con-Way name, reporting that he said: "We ought to do it the Consolidated way ... why don't we call it Con-Way?"[42]

Ray Halloran, though, recalls writing down a list of various names and expressing to other CF executives that the new regional businesses should tie into the Consolidated Freightways name by placing "Con" at the beginning.

"I've never been one to go out and say, 'Hey, I'm the guy that did it [created the Con-Way name],'" Halloran added, who at the time was the executive vice president of CF.[43]

The names would eventually reflect the geographic regions each division would cover—Con-Way Eastern Express (CEX), Con-Way Central Express (CCX), and Con-Way Western Express (CWX).

Once the decision to establish separate regional LTL carriers was finalized, Scott and Lawrence sought executives to head the divisions. However, CF's executives were uncertain whether to purchase existing companies as the foundation for the short-haul carrier business or to start their own companies.[44]

REFINING THE CON-WAY STRATEGY

CF considered an existing carrier, Motor Freight Express, as a possibility for the foundation of both the Midwest and Eastern Con-Way companies.[45] Located in the Detroit Division Manager Gerald Detter's hometown of York, Pennsylvania, Motor Freight was a unionized carrier, which also owned a subsidiary called Eagle Transfer. However, like scores of other trucking companies, Motor Freight had failed to adapt successfully to the deregulated environment and had more than $2 million in liabilities and obsolete equipment.

Even though the owners were willing to sell the company for only $1, Detter argued *against* the purchase as Motor Freight had lost much of its customer base to cut-rate competitors.[46] Detter convinced CF upper management to create a nonunion Midwest operation, rather than purchasing the company. Motor Freight eventually went out of business in late 1982.[47]

Although CF decided to form nonunion Midwest and Western regional LTL companies from the ground up, it continued to seek a trucking firm to purchase in the East. It was decided that entry into the challenging—and heavily Teamster influenced—Northeast market would be easier through an established presence.

O'Brien presented the launch of the regional Con-Way trucking firms at the September 1982 board meeting. After gaining approval for the short-haul carriers, Lawrence chose Gerald W. Dwiggins, division manager at Charlotte, North Carolina, to run the West Coast company. Detter would run the Midwest company, and George F. Craig would eventually lead the Con-Way presence on the East Coast. Dwiggins had 16 years of experience at CF. When chosen to head the Midwest regional carrier, Detter had been with CF for 18 years and was responsible for

In Rio Linda, California, Gloria Vanda, left, and Shannon Herkenham reviewed and filed customer requests. (*Photo courtesy of Ray Halloran.*)

23 terminals.[48] Craig had joined CF in 1964 as a sales representative in Rochester, New York, and later advanced to Rochester's terminal manager and then manager of CF's Buffalo, New York, division in 1970.[49]

Moritz' nationwide tariff and pricing system—the one he worked on when first hired by CF in case of deregulation—had never been utilized. It would eventually become the foundation for the Con-Way companies' initial rate structures.[50]

The situation in the trucking industry was about to improve even more. As CF Inc. prepared to launch the three Con-Way companies in 1983, it also won victories in the courts for the industry-wide use of double trailers.

USING "DUBS"

Consolidated led the battle in the courts and with state legislatures during the 1970s to legalize the use of tandem—or double—trailers. Nicknamed "dubs" or "double bottoms," CF, as well as other trucking companies, found that a 65-foot tandem trailer combination allowed trucks to operate with greater efficiency than a 55-foot single tractor-trailer combination. Trucking firms saw fuel savings of up to 20 percent using dubs instead of semi-trailers. Federal studies showed that the use of tandem trailers reduced wear and tear on bridges and expressways because weight loads were distributed more evenly across their axles.

Many state legislatures expressed concerns that double trailer combinations were more dangerous than a single trailer and banned their use. Those safety concerns began to recede when the U.S. Supreme Court ruled in 1978 that Wisconsin's prohibition on tandem trailers placed an undue burden on interstate commerce.[51] With that court victory, CF challenged similar bans on doubles in Iowa and Pennsylvania.

In 1982, Congress passed the Surface Transportation Assistance Act (STAA) that increased the federal fuel tax by five cents a gallon, up from the four cents a gallon set in 1959. The provisions of the act also set a maximum overall length of

combination vehicles at 65 feet, while trailer widths were widened to a maximum of 102 inches.

Even with the STAA, there were still skirmishes between the states and the trucking industry. Connecticut, for example, outlawed tandem trailers in 1983 only to have the law overturned by a federal district judge.[52] Although some differences remained among state truck regulations, CF won important victories when standardizing truck length and width limits.

COMPLETE REORGANIZATION

O'Brien, now 60, had been chairman of CF Inc. since 1979, and also CEO and president of the holding corporation for most of that time (Burbank was president between 1980–1981). His choice for a successor was narrowed to two candidates: Scott, who was president of CFCD, the motor carrier, and had created its rapidly expanding Freight Flow System; and Moffitt, who had negotiated the difficult Freightliner sale and was CF Inc.'s executive vice president of finance and administration.

While Scott knew the trucking industry from an operational standpoint, Moffitt was a superb financial executive although he lacked the experience of managing the practical day-to-day tasks. To further complicate matters, in April 1983, O'Brien restructured the corporation, creating CF Land Transportation Inc. and CF International & Air Inc.

Scott became an executive vice president of CF Inc., the holding company, and oversaw the CF Land Transportation unit, which included CFCD and all intercity motor carrier operations, including the three Con-Way companies.[53] At CF International & Air, Moffitt was charged with growing CF AirFreight, including handling the negotia-

tions of the purchase of Air Express International Corporation. He also oversaw CF Export-Import Services, a new subsidiary launched to provide customs brokerage and ocean freight forwarding services.

With the corporate restructuring, O'Brien had essentially placed Scott and Moffitt in competing positions with little incentive to work together.

"Lary Scott was running the trucking company at that time, and Lary was my competitor for CEO," Moffitt later recounted.[54]

CF Land Services Inc. also was created in 1983 and placed under Scott's control. This subsidiary oversaw the three Con-Way companies plus CF Arrowhead Services, which was an owner-operator network of special commodity type, flatbed, and heavy freight hauling; and CF Forwarding that handled truckload and container-load freight.[55, 56] Some have called CF Land Services the "holding company within a holding company" because of the role it served.

Robert T. Robertson headed CF Land Services Inc., which was based at CF Inc.'s Palo Alto offices. A native of Newark, New Jersey, Robertson joined CF in 1970, and by 1973, he had become the eastern area sales manager, reporting to Scott.[57] During the mid-1970s, he turned the Dallas terminal into one of CF's major consolidation centers and was promoted to division manager of Texas in 1978.

"[Robertson] was in charge of the Con-Ways' startup," O'Brien said. "They moved his office right down the hall from mine, so I'd go in and see him every day during the planning stage. I kept insisting that one thing we're going to do is we're going to give good service. That's the only way we're going to survive."[58]

DEVIL IN THE DETAILS

In creating the three Con-Way companies, CF Inc. officials were concerned it would be accused of double breasting—a labor term when a company employs nonunion workers in a separate division that does the same work as its unionized workforce—and the Teamsters would launch a strike. Yet the tide was turning as the Reagan administration was creating a pro-business climate, and the courts were deflating the labor unions in antitrust cases.

Legally, CF Inc. was the holding company that owned a number of subsidiaries, including the motor carrier CFCD. The motor carrier had spawned the parent corporation back in the 1950s to avoid ICC oversight of its non-motor freight activities.

"The money used to create Con-Way didn't come, at least directly, from the motor carrier. It came from the holding company," noted Eberhard (Eb) Schmoller, an attorney for CF MotorFreight who eventually became senior vice president and corporate general counsel for CF Inc.[59]

Yet the Teamsters did raise concerns about CF's plans. This directly affected how the Con-Ways functioned and the type of support the parent company provided to each division. Millican explained:

The company was formulated to fill the voids that CFCD couldn't handle. Our game plan was: How do you create a company that can't be related to CFCD? [CFCD] was Teamster. Con-Way was nonunion, or as we preferred to call ourselves, union-free, and had to be separate from it. No shared resources. No shared sales force. No shared marketing. We literally had to build a game plan to attack a [new] market from scratch. There was not going to be any transfer of customers, no sharing of business opportunities.[60]

The three Con-Ways were designed to fill the gaps in CFCD's route system. With its breakbulk and relay system, CFCD could not economically accommodate freight traveling less than 600 miles because of the extra mileage required to move cargo to a consolidation center and then make a delivery.

"They were very efficient at that, but it left market holes, and those market holes became where Con-Way was allowed 'to play,'" Moritz said.[61]

The unions did not strike because of double breasting; however, they threatened to strike against companies that bought products and services from nonunion companies. The courts eventually ruled in several cases that labor had violated antitrust and anti-competition laws by using strong-arm tactics, noted Schmoller.

"The unions were pretty wary about overextending and using their representation power in existing businesses against new business [such as the Con-Way companies]," Schmoller said.[62]

The three Con-Way companies began as independent entities, without any connection to each other. Additionally, Con-Way could only sell freight that traveled within a 500-mile radius of a terminal—freight could not be shipped to another destination outside the limit, even if it was within the company's territory. In the Midwest, for instance, Con-Way

Central's Cincinnati terminal was prohibited from sending shipments to its Minneapolis terminal because they were more than 500 miles apart, even though CFCD wouldn't accept the same shipment for economic reasons.[63]

CF Inc. supported the Con-Way companies, keeping their costs to a minimum by adopting key operating computer systems from the parent company's systems, as well as implementing operating procedures from CF administration manuals. The regional carriers, however, could not reference CFCD or Consolidated Freightways in their advertisements.[64] That prohibition also was reflected in the recruitment strategy of employees for the Con-Way companies.

For example, in early 1983, David McClimon, a future Con-Way president, answered a blind newspaper advertisement for a "new company" that was looking for sales personnel in Cincinnati.

"I didn't know the name of the company in my first interview—they never told me," McClimon said. "I had no sales experience. This brand new company hired me without any sales experience."[65]

Bob Bull, who was working for Associated Truck Lines at its Toledo, Ohio, terminal in 1983, was uncertain about the future of that company. Then he heard rumors that Consolidated Freightways was going to open a short-haul carrier.

"I knew the local CF manager," Bull said. "I called him up and I said, 'Hey, Mike. I heard that they're going to open up a regional carrier.' 'No, no, no, I don't know anything about that,' he said."[66]

Bull's friend, however, gave him a telephone number to a location in Ann Arbor, Michigan, and told him to talk to Brian Tierney. Tierney was Con-Way Central Express manager of personnel and safety. Because Tierney wasn't in the office the day Bull called, he talked to Kay Beher, the new office manager, and then directly to Detter. After being interviewed by Detter and having a follow-up interview with Dick Palazzo, who was vice president of operations for the fledgling company, Bull was hired as one of Con-Way Central Express' first employees.

CON-WAY WESTERN EXPRESS

Launching the three Con-Way companies was an enormous gamble and CF officers were afraid that the ventures would fail, according to Byerley, who became involved with purchasing the equipment for the enterprises.

"In the back of everybody's mind was the thought that if [the Con-Way companies] didn't make it, then the equipment, the tractors, trailers, and dollies could be brought right back into CF. So the equipment speced out almost exactly to the Consolidated Freightways specifications," he said.[67]

For Con-Way Western Express, CF bought Freightliner trucks while Con-Way Central Express received Ford tractors.

The regional carriers that became known as the "Con-Ways" were created to fill the short-haul gaps that CFCD was not able to fill. Each Con-Way was designated with a three letter name. This tractor shows CWX, reflecting its western market Con-Way Western.

OUR FIRST TRACTOR

Consolidated Freightways' executive Ray Halloran, left, is pictured with PGA golfer John Cook in 1983 when the trucking company became Cook's sponsor. (Photos courtesy of Ray Halloran.)

"The main reason we bought Freightliner tractors was that they were very well recognized in the West," Byerley said. "There was a longer length of haul and weight reduction was important out there from a serviceability standpoint."

Conscious of the weight of the equipment—lighter trucks allowed for more cargo—all early Con-Way tractors and trailers used wedge brakes, which were lighter than the industry-standard S-cam brakes. The drawback of the wedge brakes was that they were almost exclusive to CFCD vehicles. It limited the ability to hire outside vendors for maintenance, as they would be unfamiliar with the equipment. Early Con-Way trailers were also fitted with aluminum floors, rather than wooden ones.

According to Byerley, this was soon changed due to practical reasons:

Over time, we went to wooden floors for durability reasons, because there was so much more freight moved in and out [of the trailers] because of overnight deliveries. You were loading and unloading that trailer twice a day, every day, where in the Consolidated Freightways fleet, with the long-haul stuff, you loaded it in Portland, Oregon, and it may not get unloaded until five days later after it moved across the country.[68]

The first of CF's regional LTL companies to launch was Con-Way Western Express. It was headquartered in Orange, California, where Dwiggins also established a training center. The ICC granted Con-Way Western Express its interstate operating authority in March 1983, and California signed off on intrastate authority in early April. Con-Way Western Express had a sluggish start on May 16, with 11 service centers in California, Arizona, and Nevada.[69]

"I will never forget that first night," O'Brien said. "My wife and I had both quit smoking, but I went into Robertson's office, and I got so nervous that I had to have a cigarette. ... That first night, they only had eight shipments. I said, 'Gee, this idea may not be all that great.' We'd been promised all kinds of freight."[70]

Using aggressive discounting, Con-Way Western Express built up its tonnage and revenue, but not enough to offset costs.[71] By December, Dwiggins' company was forced to lease trucks because it needed about 100 tractors a day to support its operations, but owned only 43 units.[72]

CON-WAY CENTRAL EXPRESS

In Ann Arbor, Michigan, Detter took a more deliberate approach to building Con-Way Central Express. Signing his documents as "GLD," Detter became known to many CF Inc. executives by his initials—much like Lary Scott was called "One R" Lary. In November 1982, Detter moved his operation into a 118-year-old farmhouse—affectionately nicknamed "Tara" after the fictional plantation in *Gone With the Wind*—on Packard Road in a residential neighborhood.[73] The first clerical employee—and the first woman—to be hired was Beher.

Beher had responded to a three-line newspaper advertisement that described a job as "secretary to the president" and listed a phone number. She was attending school full time, almost ready to graduate, and in need of employment.[74]

About three months later, Beher received a call about her application; Detter hired her in early 1983. Beher recalled that Con-Way Central Express' "General Office" was in a farmhouse that didn't have equipment, although the living room had a fireplace and mantle.

"The first day I got there, I didn't even know the real name of the company," Beher said. "I went to answer the phone for the first time and it was, 'Uh... .' Fortunately, it was the boss' wife calling, so it wasn't too embarrassing."

Detter also wanted a finance person on-site who could provide forecasting, planning, and analysis instead of relying solely on CF Inc.'s main financial office in Portland. Kevin Schick, another applicant, was unimpressed with the farmhouse location initially and thought that the company was a simple "mom and pop" operation. He almost decided to skip his interview with Detter. After reconsidering, he went in and was hired as Con-Way Central Express' controller in March 1983.[75]

Detter, Palazzo, Millican, and Tierney already had offices throughout the house.

"Jerry said, 'There are two rooms left,'" Schick remembered. "'Whoever shows up first Monday—because a maintenance guy got hired—you'll have your pick.' Well, I got there before the maintenance guy did. I got this bigger room overlooking the street, and he got this narrow, cubbyhole-type room."[76]

Con-Way Central's first general office building was this more than 100-year-old farmhouse in Ann Arbor, Michigan. It was dubbed "Tara" after the plantation in *Gone with the Wind*.

On April 12, just 67 days before Con-Way Central Express began rolling, Detter arrived at Ford's Louisville Assembly Plant in Kentucky to drive the company's first power unit off the line. A 1983 Ford CL-9000 tractor, its numbers were 414-3001 ("414" represented the CL-9000 series, the "3" signified the year it was built, and "001" was the number in the manufacturing sequence of the series).[77]

Detter had wanted Con-Way Central Express to be operational by April 1, 1983, but the letter from the ICC that would grant the company operating authority didn't arrive until June 6.[78]

"I remember Jerry pacing the floor every day waiting for this document to come in the mail," Beher said. "We were getting closer and closer to opening day, and we still didn't have it. The day it came, it looked so insignificant. I stamped it and put it in his mail. Then he opens it up, and he was all excited … champagne started flowing."[79]

Con-Way Central Express officially opened for business on June 20, 1983, with service to 1,004 points from only 11 service centers: Chicago, Cincinnati, Columbus, Detroit, Grand Rapids, Indianapolis, Milwaukee, Minneapolis, Pittsburgh, Cleveland, and Toledo.[80] It did not have intrastate authority in most states. Additionally, because of the 500-mile radius operating restriction on the Con-Way companies, Con-Way Central Express' Minneapolis center could only be served from Chicago, Indianapolis, and Milwaukee.

With 56 employees, the company handled 89 shipments that totaled 179,160 pounds and earned $9,696.18 in revenue its first day.[81, 82] In Toledo, it was three days before the terminal had its first shipment for a customer named Temp Glass. The terminal had two drivers, two tractors, and six trailers, according to Bull, manager of the Toledo service center.

"The shipment was going to Pittsburgh, Pennsylvania," recounted Bull. "It was just a small shipment. We actually took it down and put it on a Greyhound bus to Pittsburgh. The manager in Pittsburgh went down and picked it up. They … put it on a truck and delivered it."[83]

Detter began calling service center managers and told them to get the drivers out on the road—whether the trucks had deliveries or not—to advertise the company.[84] Within 100 days, Con-Way

Central Express' on-time shipment performance reached 95 percent, and its workforce expanded to 105 people.[85] Service was emphasized, regardless of cost, to get the business growing.

"Once people started using us and found out that we actually did what we told them we were going to do, it was pretty easy to start gaining that additional business," said Bull.

While the initial success of Con-Way Central Express and Con-Way Western Express were welcomed, Craig was still working on establishing an East Coast regional trucking firm.

PENN YAN EXPRESS AND THE EAST COAST

If there was a successful formula for the creation of the Con-Way companies, it was because they adhered to on-time delivery service, and had uniformed, courteous driver-salesmen. The Central and West Coast organizations created by Detter and Dwiggins followed this plan. Craig, however, held to a more traditional and cautious strategy in starting a Con-Way presence in the Northeast.

"At Con-Way Eastern, somehow we conceived the notion when we opened it, it had to be unionized," O'Brien remembered.[86]

When Detter rejected the idea of purchasing Motor Freight Express, Craig proposed Penn Yan Express, a company located in Penn Yan, New York. The village was in an out-of-the way location to base a regional carrier, although three major interstates were nearby—I-90 to the north, I-390 to the west, and I-86 to the south. Seneca Lake bordered the town's eastern edge.

Owned by Robert L. Hinson and his family, Penn Yan was one of hundreds of traditional trucking firms that experienced severe difficulties as a result of deregulation. In 1982, it reported a net loss of $722,000 despite revenue of more than $31 million. To help save the company, the Teamsters had given back 15 percent of their wages, which was creating workforce unrest.[87]

Scott, Lawrence, and Robertson deliberated for about a year before giving the go-ahead to purchase Penn Yan Express. During this time, the company's situation had deteriorated. CF began proceedings to purchase the company despite the fact that Penn Yan Express had tractors and trailers

When Con-Way's regional carrier in the Northeast, Penn Yan Express, proved successful, its name was changed to reflect its roots in CF Inc. The abbreviation was now designated as CEX for Con-Way Eastern Express. (*Photo courtesy of David Faust.*)

that were not compatible with CF-owned equipment and also had a contract with the Teamsters.

In the third quarter 1983 edition of CF's employee magazine, *The Freighter*, it was announced that "Con-Way Eastern Express" was purchasing "Penn Yan Express" for $3.2 million.[88]

"Upon consummation of the merger, Penn Yan will retain its name and be operated as a regional carrier," said CF Inc. Chairman and CEO O'Brien. "The Penn Yan purchase will expedite CF's entry into regional trucking in the east."[89]

During the summer of 1983, CF purchased 58 percent of the company's stock and completed the deal that November for $3.2 million (about $7.50 a share). This included its 19 terminals in Delaware, Maryland, New Jersey, New York, and Pennsylvania. The terms of the sale dictated that the Penn Yan Express name remain in use, but the trucks were painted in a similar style as Con-Way Central Express and Con-Way Western Express, and its abbreviation also followed suit—PYX.

Wanting to offer overnight delivery service, Craig faced unfriendly Teamsters locals who were loath to change the work rules governing drivers and dockworkers. Union leaders felt that the workers had already made enough wage concessions to Penn Yan's former owners.[90] CF executives remained publicly supportive of the deal, considering the shaky start.

The carrier lost about $200,000 a month in 1983, despite revenues of about $30 million.[91] Under Craig, CF upgraded and modernized Penn Yan's fleet and its 19 terminals.

While the American economy gained momentum as 1983 drew to a close, many traditional trucking companies were failing as their cost structures hampered their progress in the era of deregulation. The Con-Ways would see success and failure, while struggling to remain solvent in a unionized market.

CWX PACESETTER

CON-WAY WESTERN EXPRESS

EMPLOYEE NEWSLETTER   OCTOBER/NOVEMBER/DECEMBER 1985

1985

Season's Greetings

Happy New Year

CHAPTER FIVE

EXPANDING CON-WAY

1980–1988

The transportation industry following deregulation presented opportunities for short-haul trucking, particularly a consistent, next-day product. ... We had to "raise the bar," set a service standard that was so much better than anything else that customers would become hooked.

—Robert T. Robertson,
president and CEO of Con-Way
Transportation Services[1]

CHANGE WAS INEVITABLE THROUGHOUT THE trucking industry during the 1980s, when more than 350 motor carriers as well as an untold number of owner-operators shuttered their doors. An estimated 125,000 workers were displaced, and long-established firms struggled to survive.[2] The Motor Carrier Act of 1980 placed an enormous strain on companies accustomed to the protections of a highly controlled business environment. Deregulation also created enormous opportunities for newcomers to thrive and for the largest motor carriers, including Consolidated Freightways, Roadway, and Yellow, to grow by entering new markets.

In 1984, CF Inc.'s long-haul motor freight carrier, which had been known as CFCD (Consolidated Freightways Corporation of Delaware), was renamed CF MotorFreight. Under the direction of Executive Vice President Lary Scott, it expanded its Freight Flow System by opening many new breakbulk and outlying terminals. Although initially successful, CF faced many difficulties in the years ahead competing with its nonunion rivals.

CF Inc. was in good financial standing after the sale of Freightliner in 1981. The corporation's nearly $300 million "war chest" allowed it to develop three regional less-than-truckload (LTL) carriers—Con-Way Western Express (CWX), Con-Way Central Express (CCX), and Penn Yan Express (PYX). Of the three, Con-Way Central Express grew the most

rapidly and was most promising as a sustainable, profitable business.

THE FALLOUT OF DEREGULATION

Many of deregulation's early casualties were motor carriers that were poorly managed or over-leveraged. Other firms struggled, such as ANR of Grand Rapids, Michigan, where David Miller worked before joining Con-Way in 1983.

"ANR is a now-defunct conglomerate that was comprised of three regional carriers, including Associated Truck Lines, Garrett, and Graves," Miller said. "All three were run by an ex-CF executive. He was trying to create three carriers to provide coast-to-coast services in regional short haul similar to Con-Way."[3]

Clashing corporate cultures and weak operating systems caused ANR to fail. Miller left the carrier before its collapse, after being recruited by a Con-Way sales manager, beginning a career

---

Above: To commemorate Con-Way Central's fifth anniversary, brass key chains with the CCX Service Excellence wreath were presented to all employees in 1988.

Opposite: The cover of the October/November/December 1985 issue of the Con-Way Western Express employee newsletter.

at Con-Way Central Express as a freight operations supervisor.

Despite the obvious difficulties that established carriers experienced, an Interstate Commerce Commission (ICC) study revealed that partial deregulation of the transportation industry had been a boon to most shippers and communities. Service had improved or remained the same while truckers were more willing to "go off route" to make pickups and deliveries.[4] Competition was intense, and traditional, unionized firms were at a pricing disadvantage as labor costs were much higher due to antiquated labor restrictions.

Between 1980 and 1984, about 15,000 new trucking companies entered the industry, concentrating on the truckload market. During the same period, the ICC also approved about 65,000 applications for new routes from existing carriers.[5] Competition was fierce in the contract carrier segment of the market—firms that could select their customers. In 1979, there were only about 4,000 ICC-licensed contract carriers, but four years later some 10,000 companies were registered.[6]

The law required common carriers, such as CF MotorFreight, to serve the public at large and provide a uniform bill of lading for each shipment. CF MotorFreight emphasized its most profitable selling lanes and initially reaped the benefits of the new rules governing the industry. Instead of joining the rate-cutting war among its competitors, CF MotorFreight created a number of value-added programs and promoted its service through 1984 and 1985.[7]

In November 1985, graduates of a Con-Way Central Express driver–sales representative training seminar show their certificates.

COMBINING FORCES

Although the adjustment to deregulation was challenging, large trucking companies were successful between 1980 and 1984, according to *Dun's Business Month* reporter Pat Wechsler in May 1984:

During the past four years, amid what were at best chaotic times for the industry, most of the largest companies shifted into high gear, spending millions for massive expansion of terminal networks and the upgrading of truck fleets. No longer fettered by a welter of Interstate Commerce Commission regulations, the Big 10 and other Class I carriers diversified, extended service to new regions and created subsidiaries in freight management, contract carriage, freight forwarding, and intermodal truck-rail transportation.[8]

CF MotorFreight, the nation's second-largest carrier at the time, had expanded dramatically, constructing more than 100 freight terminals between 1979 and 1984.[9] According to Scott, the company opened a terminal about every five days, using an expansion strategy to become "a very comprehensive transportation company that can service any marketplace in the free world."

CF's breakbulk centers serviced its large network of outlying terminals that combined numerous under-10,000-pound, less-than-truckload (LTL) shipments and sorted them according to destination. The long-haul carrier's LTL business rose from about 55 percent of its tonnage in 1980 to 68 percent by 1984, but its truckload business—like those of other big trucking companies—had fallen due to competition from upstart, nonunion firms.[10]

To boost productivity and on-time delivery performance, the long-haul carrier simplified its shipping, dock, and warehouse procedures. Using sophisticated computer data processing programs, CF partnered with manufacturers such as Snap-on Tools and General Motors (GM) Corporation's Buick Division to assist them in improving distribution and inventory control. CF developed a program for Snap-on in 1984 to ready shipments, load, and schedule outbound freight. At GM, the automaker had adopted the "just-in-time" inventory system in which suppliers shipped components to assembly plants as they were needed. Instead of storing and paying for several weeks' worth of parts in its factories, the burden of storing parts until needed fell to the

automotive suppliers.[11] CF MotorFreight was Buick's major transportation supplier. This type of shipping meant more deliveries to the manufacturers as parts could be ordered at any time.

In concert with CF AirFreight, the motor carrier started a coast-to-coast express delivery service called Super Daysaver via air in 1982. This program offered third-day delivery service for LTL freight between states that bordered the Pacific and the Atlantic oceans. Cargo was placed in widebody airline containers, and CF MotorFreight performed the pickup and delivery from airports to customers. Normal delivery times were reduced 50 percent with this coordinated airfreight and truck-shipping program.[12]

When the Con-Ways were created, establishing a professional, customer-oriented image was part of the main foundation. To ensure this dedication to the customer, even cultivating a professional appearance for drivers became part of the service the Con-Ways offered. Here, a uniformed driver from Con-Way Central approached his vehicle.

CF MotorFreight and CF AirFreight delivered electronic hardware and other cable components for Telecommunications Inc. Con-Way Central Express also partnered with CF AirFreight and created a similar program for Sherwin-Williams in 1984, delivering to its Midwest stores with a day's notice.

CF AirFreight offered warehouse and distribution programs, including refrigerated storage for Abbott Laboratories, a drug manufacturer, at its Chicago terminal. It also simplified its rate book, reducing it from 150 pages to 15 pages of customized tariffs on a computer diskette.

Although CF executives were reluctant to offer discounted services across the board like some competitors, Mattel Toys negotiated a new contract with the long-haul carrier in the mid-1980s. Mattel received lower shipping rates and expedited service in exchange for providing CF MotorFreight with increased volume.

GUARDIAN OF THE CON-WAYS

CF Land Services acted as the protector of the Con-Way regional LTL companies. Robert Lawrence, president, and Robert T. Robertson, vice president and general manager, insulated the fledgling regional carriers so they could become profitable in a reasonable timeframe, while cajoling CF for additional investment.[13]

CF Land Services kept CF MotorFreight "from trying to strangle the Con-Ways as they got out of the cradle—to keep them from 'killing the child' that was overtaking them," noted Miller, looking back at the mid- to late-1980s.[14] The Con-Way mission was to seek short-haul freight traveling less than 500 miles. This restriction frustrated Con-Way personnel and stifled some sales as CF MotorFreight, with its high overhead and hub-and-spoke delivery system, could not economically accept most freight that traveled less than 800 miles.

"Bob Lawrence was constantly telling Con-Way, 'No, you can't go there,'" said Edward "Ned" Moritz, who worked as director of marketing during the 1980s. "It was smart from his point of view because he wanted that business in CFCD."[15]

Early on, Robertson worried that the regional carriers' lack of intrastate operating authority would hurt the start-ups as in-state deliveries were a big portion of the short-haul business. Con-Way Central,

in particular, was hampered at the beginning because it did not have intrastate operating authority in most of its territory. For example, the Detroit terminal could sell freight to eight of the terminals outside Michigan—except to Minneapolis, which was outside the 500-mile limit—but it could not sell to Grand Rapids, located about 150 miles to the west-northwest down Interstate 96.

Because the three Con-Ways operated in different regions, the fact that they were organized differently wasn't an issue "as long as they kind of followed the major policies and procedures set down by the corporation," noted Rock Magnan, who was vice president of operations at CF Land Services and later became director of operations for Menlo Worldwide, another subsidiary. "There was no concept at that time of linking all the units together."[16]

Magnan started working for CF Land Services in 1984, serving as the operational assistant for Robertson in a four-person office that included Robertson's administrative assistant and a controller based in Portland, Oregon. At the time, he had seven years of experience working for other regional motor carriers in the LTL transportation field.

"I was kind of the jack-of-all-trades," Magnan said. "I helped write plans. I worked with the regional group wherever they needed the help, be that working on capital expense requests, doing presentations for the board meetings, just anything in general that Mr. Robertson needed me to do."

The three start-up Con-Ways were very different from each other, noted David McClimon, who began in sales at Con-Way Central Express:

Each company took on the personality of the president at that time, and Central was, by far, the most successful. So Jerry [Detter], at that time, wanted to provide the best practices to the other two companies. The managers at Con-Way Western and Eastern, of course, were resistant because they wanted to develop their companies as they saw fit.[17]

Each Con-Way company also had its own colors, which earned the trio the nickname, the "rainbow line." Con-Way Central Express' trucks, trailers, and terminals were painted in white with burnt orange and brown stripes, the colors of Bowling Green University, where Lary Scott attended college. Con-Way Western Express had gold and blue stripes to copy the colors of UCLA and Berkeley. Penn Yan Express (Con-Way Central Express) was red. Two additional regional trucking divisions opened later: Con-Way Southern Express used blue and aqua-blue colors, and Con-Way Southwest Express was blue and green.

CON-WAY'S SHINING STAR

Con-Way Central's business was tepid for its first week of operation, mostly because shippers were unfamiliar with the company. Additionally, Con-Way Central sales were hampered as it began with limited intrastate operating authority throughout most of its territory. Freight was occasionally shipped via Greyhound buses and then retrieved and delivered by a terminal manager because it was less expensive than sending a truck.[18] Hugh "Wes" Cornett, who was one of Con-Way Central's first drivers, recalled that his first run out of Cincinnati was hauling a set of doubles to Indianapolis to deliver one box. Once there, he switched trailers and hauled "one or two boxes" on the return trip.

"We didn't hardly have any freight, but [Detter] wanted the exposure. He wanted to get the equipment out. Run it so people would see it," Cornett recalled.[19]

Within the company's first 100 days, the on-time delivery ratio to its first 5,000 customers hit "an incredible 95 percent!" Detter noted in Con-Way Central's first newsletter, issued November 8, 1983. "This figure is even more outstanding when one considers that more than 80 percent of our market lanes have overnight standard!"[20]

Con-Way Central's workforce also grew from 56 to 105 employees.[21] By June 1984, the division averaged 1,000 shipments a day during its first full year of operation versus 89 shipments for its first day of operation. The company had grown from 11 terminals to 17, and its driver and sales personnel were supplemented by a telemarketing center.[22]

During the next four years, Con-Way Central experienced rapid, disciplined growth as it aimed to keep its delivery service above 95 percent.[23] The company's plan called for direct loading of freight with minimal rehandling at intermediate points. Drivers also did dock work.[24] Because Con-Way Central and the other Con-Way companies could access and implement CF's computer systems for operations, management, sales, accounting, and

David McClimon was one of Con-Way Central's first account executives.

customer support operations, the divisions were able to save money.

The growth of Con-Way Central was also facilitated by its location in the "Rust Belt," the traditional heart of America's automotive, steel, and other manufacturing industries as well as a more densely packed population than in the West or South. There were few nonunion competitors, so Con-Way Central could offer discounts, as well as added efficiency, supported by its flexible work rules. It became the glowing enterprise of the Con-Way system.

In May 1985, Con-Way Central opened five new terminals. Its network had increased to 26 terminals with a total of 950 doors (versus 11 original terminals and 289 doors when the company first opened). It employed more than 500 people while revenue levels hit $1 million per week.[25]

Spin-off terminals were added in Akron/Canton and Dayton, Ohio, and Aurora and Elk Grove near Chicago. A new 20-door terminal opened in Pontiac, Michigan, to serve the Detroit metropolitan area, and maintenance shops were started in Columbus,

Ohio; Chicago; and Fort Wayne, Indiana.[26] Later in the year, Con-Way Central's 27th terminal opened in Green Bay/Appleton, Wisconsin. This 32-door facility had a four-bay shop and was distinctly white with Con-Way Central's trademark brown and orange stripes.[27]

Con-Way Central handled its 500,000th shipment on June 24, 1985, which was 511 workdays after the company opened for business. It delivered its 1 millionth shipment less than a year later on February 26, 1986.[28]

KEEPING THE UNION AT BAY

Aside from transportation companies dealing with the effects of deregulation, the International Brotherhood of Teamsters was also hit hard. By 1984, the union suffered a permanent loss of 40,000 members, while more than 100,000 Teamsters had been laid off.[29] They became increasingly persistent in efforts to recruit new members from CF, although the new regional carriers were constantly making strides to ensure that the employees were satisfied.

Con-Way Central established a number of groundbreaking practices, including the training of its driver and sales personnel with the "30-second

sales call" and a telemarketing office that conducted nearly 9,000 sales calls each month to improve business.

A key motivator was the company's employee incentive compensation program (ICP). Detter extended the program to include drivers and dockworkers.[30] As the fledgling company made its goals, even when it was just barely profitable, all employees received a profit-sharing check, despite pushing Con-Way Central Express into the red.[31]

"Profit sharing was highly unusual in 1983, especially in our industry," Detter explained during a 2000 interview for *Transportation CEO* magazine. "But I felt if everyone had a little skin in the game, we would create a very efficient company. We would have a competitive cost advantage and a highly motivated and productive workforce."[32]

In 1985, Con-Way Central Express paid out nearly $1 million in ICP checks.[33]

Yet, the Teamsters were persistent. In 1986, the Teamsters' drive to obtain a presence at Con-Way Central terminals in the Detroit area and later into Buffalo, New York, were becoming more and more aggressive. Union demonstrators harassed Con-Way workers by throwing nails onto the road and sticking screwdrivers through truck radiators, Miller

DETTER'S WAY

THE DRIVING FORCE OF CON-WAY Central Express, which became the fastest-growing and most successful of CF Inc.'s first three regional LTL carriers, was its president, Gerald L. Detter.

"Jerry has a great grasp of businesses and business models, particularly the energy and the entrepreneurial spirit to bring something new into existence, but he also has the executive leadership skills to be able to keep it on track and really nurture it," said Douglas W. Stotlar, current CEO of Con-way Inc. "Like all great coaches, he could

identify talented people and push them to work harder. He expected more from us because he believed we had more capability."[1]

Detter assembled a team that had the right kind of attitude, added Wayne Byerley, who became CF Inc.'s vice president of purchasing. He built a company that could deliver freight overnight, relatively claim-free, while paying competitive wages and benefits.[2]

"Detter was aggressive and self-confident, I would say, but very, very positive," Byerley said. "He knew how to motivate."

said.[34] In the July/August 1986 newsletter, Detter reiterated the company's policy that Con-Way would remain union-free:

The "we–they" philosophy that almost all of us have seen in unionized companies is something we do not want, do not need, and will not willingly accept at CCX.[35]

"I can remember hearing a lot of stories when the Teamsters were carrying signs outside and harassing the drivers coming in and out of service centers," Byerley said. "One of the drivers came out, pulled his ICP check out of his pocket, and said to a Teamster, 'Do you get this?' He stuck it back in his pocket and drove off."[36]

By 1986, more than $1.5 million had been paid through ICP.[37] In 1987, Detter noted in the employee newsletter, the *CCX Milemarker*, that the company was setting aside "one dollar out of five for ICP." At the same time, the Teamsters' organizers made false accusations that Con-Way Central Express was paying substandard wages and benefits.[38]

Along with the ICP, Con-Way's five-day-a-week schedule was another big recruiting tool, said Cornett. A carrier where people were able to be home every day was "unheard of within other trucking companies."[39]

In 1985, Con-Way Central published this flyer to promote the opening of its Green Bay, Wisconsin, service center.

RAPID GROWTH

By the end of September 1986, Con-Way Central had 37 terminals, with a total workforce of more than 1,400.[40] Further growth included relocating the Cleveland facility from its original 28-door terminal to a renovated 72-door facility, while the Milwaukee terminal was relocated to a newly leased building that was expanded to a total of 53 doors. Two additional maintenance shops opened in Detroit and Cleveland, and Con-Way Central's rolling stock of tractors, trailers, and dollies exceeded 2,600 pieces of equipment.[41]

By the company's fourth anniversary, it had 1,700 regular employees. During a 15-day stretch in May, 11 new terminals opened, increasing its network to 48 facilities.[42] Con-Way Central now provided both interstate and intrastate coverage, and on-time delivery service averaged a nearly unheard of 97.6 percent.[43]

More terminals were added in 1987, and, by fall, Con-Way Central had 62 service centers, 812 tractors/trucks, and 2,040 trailers, and was making deliveries to customers at more than 14,500 locations.[44] In September, it produced its first $2 million pretax profit (profit after money set aside for the bonus program but before corporate taxes were assessed), and its operating ratio (a company's operating expenses divided by its operating revenues) was 82.2, which was one of the lowest in the industry.

"Profitability is a tool of measuring success," Detter wrote in the company newsletter. "Operating ratio is a yardstick used by all companies in our industry to determine our efficiency. Few motor carriers in the history of our industry have ever performed as well as your company."[45]

At the end of 1987, with the addition of the Marion, Illinois (XMA) terminal, Con-Way Central had nearly 2,000 doors. The company also delivered its 2 millionth shipment on February 25, and its 3 millionth shipment on November 11.[46, 47]

For its fifth anniversary year, Con-Way Central had grown to 81 terminals, including 13 maintenance shops, and 2,005 doors divided among six regions— up from its original three regions in 1983.[48] It employed more than 2,000 people and had about 4,100 pieces of equipment. Expansions that year included adding 36 doors to Fort Wayne, increasing its capacity to a total of 95 doors.[49]

Tonnage averaged 10 million pounds a day. Its on-time delivery service remained at an incredible 97.3 percent level. During its five years of existence, its workers moved more than 5.4 billion pounds of freight, drove more than 119 million miles, and

consumed more than 20 million gallons of diesel fuel (the equivalent of filling 400 Olympic-size swimming pools).[50] To help with training, a 72-seat amphitheater and cafeteria were built for its general offices in Ann Arbor, Michigan.

BEST IN THE WEST

Under its president, Gerald Dwiggins, Con-Way Western began operations with 120 people who handled 29 bills, 50,116 pounds of freight, and made $2,683 in revenue system-wide for its first day. Its 11 terminals in Oakland, Stockton, San Jose, Los Angeles, Phoenix, Las Vegas, Reno, Orange, Fresno, San Diego, and Sacramento served 739 points with "next day" deliveries in Arizona, California, and Nevada. By the end of 1983, the Santa Maria terminal opened, and Con-Way Western had 183 doors, 137 employees, and owned 43 tractors and

This chart shows Con-Way Central's more than 90 percent on-time delivery performance throughout 1985 and 1986.

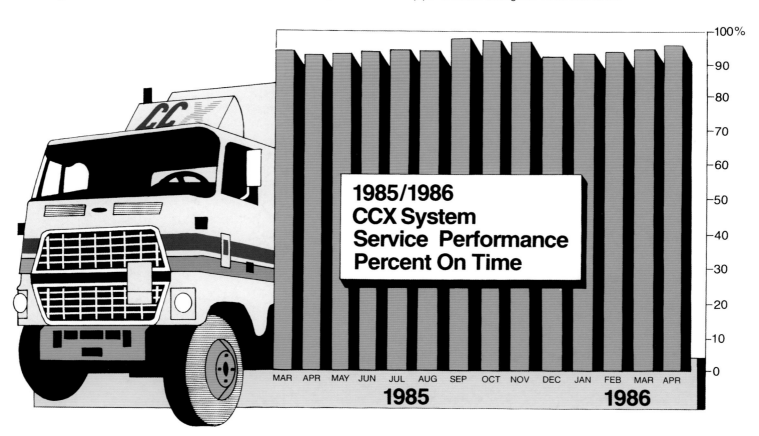

1985/1986
CCX System
Service Performance
Percent On Time

MAR APR MAY JUN JUL AUG SEP OCT NOV DEC JAN FEB MAR APR

1985　　　**1986**

147 trailers. Its on-time service performance to its 1,100 customers was 84.6 percent.[51, 52]

Costs exceeded revenues despite the company's rapid growth, and Dwiggins employed owner–operators to supplement the workforce while ordering 20 additional tractors.[53] Con-Way Western was in a tremendous battle for market share from the beginning, noted J. Edwin "Ed" Conaway, who joined CF in 1983 before moving over to Con-Way Western four years later.[54]

"In the west, there was Viking, which is now FedEx West, and they had grown tremendously as a union-free carrier," noted Conaway. "Viking was an excellent carrier, and they had a lot of market share. So we were measured against them all the time."

As costs exceeded revenues, CF Inc. executives replaced Dwiggins with George C. Reid, who had been with the company since 1972, to guide the company to firm financial ground.[55]

As Con-Way Western experienced double-digit growth and growing pains in its early years, its safety record began emerging as a problem, noted Sam Dunbar, Con-Way Western director of safety and zones.[56] Originally, the company only had a one-person safety office as part of the Personnel, Safety, and Training department. By 1985, an assistant

Brian Tierney (standing), Con-Way Central Express manager of personnel and safety, and Gerald Detter, president, reviewed the company's safety statistics in early 1987.

was added to the office, and, a year later, Bill Fyfe, who was previously a driver–salesman and freight operations supervisor, was promoted as its first safety supervisor.[57] Other safety officers were hired, but a separate safety department was not established at Con-Way Western until 1994 when staff training was implemented to maintain high standards of safety and to prevent incidents from occurring.

In 1984, the San Bernadino terminal was created as a spin-off from the Orange service center.[58] Con-Way Western also began to expand direct services to less populated markets and introduced DIRECT (Dial-In Retrieval of Electronic Customer Transactions), which allowed its customers to access Con-Way Western computer data files and trace freight, invoicing, and claims information.[59] The Las Vegas terminal was the first Con-Way Western location to become profitable in April 1984, and was soon followed by facilities in Reno, Los Angeles, and Orange.[60]

LEARNING CURVES

Con-Way Western employees faced a tremendous learning curve in 1985, noted Ted Regner, general sales manager, in the November/December issue of *Pacesetter*. Regner wrote:

We started slowly in sales growth in both revenue and tonnage. We changed our freight mix incrementally to improve operating efficiencies, profitability, and reduce costly empty miles where we were handling volume in headhaul lanes. 1985 marks our first profitable year ... October 1985 was CWX's first $3 million month.[61]

In 1985, Con-Way Western opened terminals in Tucson, Bakersfield, and San Fernando, followed by the Chico, Eureka, Flagstaff, Lake Havasu, Yuma, Ventura, and Santa Rosa facilities in 1986.[62] Con-Way Western was the first Western regional carrier to have fully uniformed driver–sales representatives. It also established a driver school at the Santa Fe Springs (ULA) facility.[63] From mid-year until the end of 1986, the company added 112 tractors, 200 trail-

Richard Palazzo, Con-Way Central's vice president of operations, left, and Gerald Detter, Con-Way Central's president, are pictured here at an annual sales award meeting in the 1980s.

ers, and 600 employees—increasing its workforce to 1,100 employees. Its upgraded terminals grew from 323 doors to 640 doors by the end of 1986, and it opened full-service maintenance facilities in Los Angeles and Oakland.

When Con-Way Western had been in business for four years, its management went to CF Motor-Freight searching for qualified staff available for promotion because the regional carrier had depleted its own ranks, according to Conaway.

"I got lucky and was able to jump from Consolidated Freightways to Con-Way Western," he added.[64]

Conaway came from a trucking family that had owned Gordon's Transports, once one of the top 50 trucking companies in the country. The family sold Gordon's in the late 1970s, and the combination of high interests rates and deregulation put the company out of business by 1983. Moving to California to pursue a music career—Conaway still plays the guitar—he landed a job at CF's Richmond terminal, becoming its manager two years later before transitioning to Con-Way Western.

"We were in a dogfight with a lot of really good union-free carriers," he noted.

In January 1987, Con-Way Western began running triple-trailer combinations between its Reno (URE) and Las Vegas (ULV) terminals in Nevada. To pull the greater weight, the company ordered four Ford tractors equipped with 350-horsepower CAT 3406B engines.[65] The company also began providing overnight service from Reno to Phoenix, Arizona, which was more than 750 miles one way.[66]

By 1988, Con-Way Western was still serving just three states—Arizona, California, and Nevada—but had more than 11,000 customers, 1,300 employees, and 33 service centers with 750 doors.[67, 68] Seventy percent of its business was concentrated in California.[69] It had 433 tractors and 1,087 trailers.[70] The California Public Utilities Commission finally gave Con-Way Western approval to use the zip code mileage–based tarrif system that Con-Way Central had been using for nearly five years.

On-time delivery service for Con-Way Western reached 96 percent in May 1988, while the company exceeded its goal of 95 percent on-time delivery service for most of the year.[71] The company also recorded its first 5 million pound day on July 27, and in August had its first 100 million pound month. For the fourth consecutive year, the company made ICP payments, which totaled $7.1 million since 1983.[72] It was also recognized by the California Trucking Association as one of the state's safest carriers.

TROUBLES OUT EAST

While the Central and Western carriers were growing, George Craig still faced numerous obstacles in his attempts to mold the struggling Penn Yan Express into Con-Way Eastern Express (CEX). After Craig fell seriously ill and stepped down in 1985, CF appointed Robert C. Sands, CF MotorFreight's eastern area vice president, to succeed him.[73] Sands had started at CF in 1969 as a dock foreman and held various positions, including being named manager of the Newark, New Jersey, division in 1975.[74]

Con-Way finally had a named presence in the east, as the Penn Yan Express name was retired and replaced with Con-Way Eastern Express. Sands also moved the company's headquarters to the metropolitan area of Rutherford, New Jersey.[75] In 1985, the company started providing service to the southern portions of the Canadian provinces of Ontario and Quebec. Con-Way Eastern also replaced its fleet of semi-trailers with double trailers, opened freight assembly centers, and began using the zip code mileage–based tariff system that Con-Way Central had proved was successful. Con-Way Eastern personnel were given new uniforms featuring red and blue jackets, light blue shirts, and dark blue work pants. These changes, while well-intentioned, were not exactly what was needed to bolster the struggling enterprise.

"[Sands] was a long-haul guy and he didn't think like a short-haul guy," Detter said. "Sands wanted to make Con-Way Eastern into a little CF, and it was a different business."[76]

Con-Way Eastern continued losing money, and Robertson reported to the CF Inc. board of directors that the carrier would rack up more losses as it tried to improve its market penetration. In 1987, Sands was replaced with Salvatore A. "Sal" Montforte, CF MotorFreight's Chicago division manager.

Con-Way Eastern opened or upgraded two terminals in 1987 and opened 13 new terminals in 1988, which CF Inc. financed.[77] Although Montforte negotiated a new contract with the Teamsters locals in 1988—which provided more flexible work rules and wage concessions than the national contract—the Teamsters International leaders temporarily suspended negotiations and took care of other business before approving the contract.

Even though Con-Way Eastern's performance disappointed CF Inc.'s executives, they turned their attention to realigning other business units and preparing a fourth regional carrier to target the Southern market.

CREATING CF TRUCKLOAD

Overall, CF Land Services was profitable for CF Inc. During the first half of 1986, it generated $152 million in revenue, $7.3 million in operating profits, and had a 95.2 operating ratio. During

A DIFFERENT KIND OF COMPANY

"**C**ONSOLIDATED FREIGHTWAYS COULD HAVE MADE Con-Way seem like just another trucking company, but they allowed us to differentiate ourselves through our people, products, and pricing," noted Bryan Millican, who was Con-Way Central Express general sales manager in the mid-1980s.[1]

One of the ways Con-Way distinguished itself from its rivals was by its user-friendly pricing system. It was one of the first companies to provide customers with shipping rates on diskettes. Decades later, the industry switched to providing rate information online via the Internet.

First impressions were also given priority. It was mandatory for driver–salespersons to wear a clean, white uniform shirt every day.[2] They were also taught the "30-second sales call" that included greeting customers positively and thanking them for the business. But this also included learning a different approach when speaking with customers.

"Instead of saying, 'I've got a shipment for you,' which [the customers] knew you must have or you wouldn't have backed in, say something like, 'Are you expecting a shipment from Baltimore? I've got it for you,'" Millican said. "Watch what they're probably going to say: 'I can't believe it. I just ordered that yesterday. It's here already?'"

The 30-second sales call helped reinforce Con-Way's image that it could deliver freight reliably in one to two days.

ANOTHER TYPE OF SALES CALL

Another early innovation at Con-Way Central Express was its business-to-business telemarketing office, which became known as the Account Management Center (AMC). Con-Way Central Express' account managers in the AMC

June 1986, each of the Con-Ways posted profits and had a composite operating ratio of 86.5.[78]

John T. Hickerson, who became the founding president of Con-Way Southwest, started working for Robertson in early 1986 when he became director of sales and marketing for CF Arrowhead Services in Fort Worth, Texas.

"Arrowhead was an owner–operator network of special commodity, flatbed, heavy haul-type business," Hickerson said. "I was offered the opportunity to make the assessment on whether or not that company was going to be a long-term CF company and if it fit strategically into our other offerings."[79]

Hickerson also looked at CF Forwarding, the intermodal rail subsidiary. In 1987, the decision was made to merge CF Arrowhead and CF Forwarding into one company that became known as CF Truckload.

"I became the vice president of sales for CF Truckload and, ultimately, the vice president and general manager of CF Truckload until fourth quarter of 1989 when I was asked to start up the southwest regional carrier for the LTL group," Hickerson added.

CON-WAY ROLLS INTO THE SOUTH

In early 1986, CF Land Services announced plans to open Con-Way Southern Express later that year and to launch Con-Way Southwest Express in 1987. That September, Robertson tapped CF executive Thomas C. Smith to organize Con-Way Southern. Headquartered in Charlotte, North Carolina, Con-Way Southern opened April 1, 1987. Initially, it had 130 employees, 15 terminals, 100 tractors, and 300 trailers. Serving North and South Carolina, Virginia, Georgia, and eastern

were responsible for developing and maintaining sales territories.

One of Con-Way Central Express' first telemarketers was Pat Jannausch, who later became Con-way vice president of Culture and Training. Formerly a music teacher from New England, she had moved to Michigan in 1982. After being interviewed by Millican, she was hired on November 14, 1983, as a telemarketing representative assigned to cover the Cincinnati, Ohio, area.

"When Jerry Detter established the telemarketing department, it was probably among the first, if not the first, telemarketing department in a trucking company," Jannausch said. "Jerry's vision was that the telemarketing office was going to bring in revenue, which it did, and it was going to give us the leaders of the future. It was going to be a management trainee program."[3]

Con-Way Central's telemarketers used CF MotorFreight's lead books. "We were offering regional trucking services whereas Consolidated Freightways was offering transcontinental services," Jannausch explained. "So it wasn't a conflict per se for us to call on the same customers in Cincinnati that Consolidated Freightways was calling. We were a sister company, and CF had an excellent reputation of service and quality and high standards."

In 1983, the immediate goal of the Account Management Center's five representatives was to spread an awareness of the company's existence to shippers. They generated 360 bills and $32,000 in revenue in August, the first full month of operation.[4] Telemarketing greatly multiplied the company's sales contacts. In 1985, the department started its direct-mail program to supplement its telemarketers. By 1986, the center had generated 11 percent of Con-Way Central Express' revenue. By October 1986, the center had 22 account managers, covering 30 terminal areas, and was responsible for generating 10,400 bills and $866,000 in revenue.

Business-to-business telemarketing is successful because it contacts people who are already at their desks, Jannausch observed.

"They probably prefer, in many cases, receiving a phone call instead of having someone drop in and take up time to drag them out to lunch or dinners or what have you," she said. "That department, at one time, had over 60 people in it. Eventually, I managed that department for nine years. It brought in millions of dollars in revenue and supplied the company with many of its future leaders."

Tennessee, it received intrastate operating authority from Georgia in October 1987.[80]

Although the Con-Way name was now becoming more recognized in the industry, there was always a need to maintain the service standard to customers. Smith, who died in 1997, described a customer interaction:

During our first week in business, a driver–sales representative and I are making a sales call on a local manufacturer. The customer takes us out on the dock and it's full of freight. I thought this could be our big breakthrough. He points to one 50-pound shipment and says, "I'm going to give this to Con-Way Southern Express, and I expect it to be delivered tomorrow."

I've never forgotten that because it reminds me that no matter who you are or where you come from, you still have to prove yourself every day with every shipment. Nothing sells like service.[81]

One of Con-Way Southern's first employees was James P. "Phil" Worthington, who joined the company in July as an operations assistant in the general offices in Charlotte, Con-Way Southern's largest facility. After two months, he was promoted to service manager in Macon, Georgia.

"I got involved in the industry right out of law school [at the University of Georgia] and went to work for Roadway Package System in Kernersville, North Carolina," Worthington said. A recruiter called him in early 1987 and asked if he would be interested in joining a new company.[82]

"I was real suspicious because I'd never heard about Con-Way before, but I had an interview ... and was intrigued by what [the recruiter] said," Worthing-

Con-Way Southern Express was added to the already successful roster of Con-Ways in 1987. By March 1988, its Richmond, Virginia, terminal was the first to reach profitability.

ton remembered, adding that he was convinced to join Con-Way Southern by mid-year.

The business model was far different than anything Worthington had ever experienced.

"It was interesting," he added. "One driver who did everything from dock work, line haul, keeping the unit clean, and everything else."

Con-Way Southern grew more slowly than Con-Way Central, but its general structure and operations copied Con-Way Central's proven best practices, including offering one-day delivery service. By March 1988, its Richmond, Virginia, terminal became the first Con-Way Southern facility to reach profitability. That August, *Distribution* magazine's annual reader poll named Con-Way Southern the quality southeast carrier of the year. At the end of 1988, its revenue had climbed 70 percent when compared to the nine months it had been in operation for 1987.[83]

CF AIRFREIGHT PARTNERS WITH EASTERN AIRLINES

Unlike its major competitors, CF AirFreight did not own or lease its own aircraft, and that was a strategic decision, according to Donald Moffitt, then chief financial officer. Owning or leasing aircraft would have added huge infrastructure costs to the airfreight forwarding company.

As commercial airliners added larger planes to their fleets, they had empty cargo holds underneath the passenger floors. According to Moffitt:

We began receiving offers from airlines to move our freight for 25 to 30 cents a pound because it was empty space. It was incremental profit to them. All of a sudden, hundreds of airfreight forwarders started going into business.[84]

In 1982, CF Air and the U.S. Post Office created an express shipment service, but the market remained challenging for the company. In 1984, CF AirFreight President W. Roger Curry trimmed personnel and raised rates to stabilize finances, but lost several major accounts in the process. Curry and Donald G. Berger, executive vice president of operations, cut nearly $200,000 in costs by signing an air-haul deal with the struggling Eastern Airlines.[85] By the end of the year, CF Air posted more than $3 million in operating profits.

CF Air expanded its partnership with Eastern Airlines in 1985, creating the "Moonlight Special" program, where it leased cargo space on Eastern Airlines' A-300 wide-body passenger planes. The aircraft flew at night when there was very little passenger traffic. They flew to a central hub in Houston where the freight was exchanged, and the aircraft returned to the spoke cities. This arrangement allowed CF Air to provide next-day, before-noon delivery service to major industrial markets in the United States, while Eastern Airlines utilized its idle aircraft and generated revenue.

As mid-1985 approached, however, shipping volumes fell on certain accounts and the rate of new customers requiring next-morning deliveries grew slowly. Competitors with their own aircraft reduced rates, forcing CF Air and similar airfreight forwarders to follow, depressing profits. The economy softened later that year, and CF Air was unable to fill Eastern Airlines' aircraft—costs exceeded revenues. By the year's end, CF Air had a $5.2 million operating loss that dragged CF International and CF Air's overall numbers down more than $1 million into the red.

Conditions worsened for CF Air in 1986 as competitors Emery Air Freight and Burlington Northern Air Freight slashed rates. CF Air suffered from a high customer turnover, while Eastern Airlines' financial situation worsened as it slid toward eventual bankruptcy. Although Curry was eager to rectify the situation, a management shift at CF Inc. rippled throughout the corporation.

SHIFT IN MANAGEMENT

Chairman, President, and CEO Raymond O'Brien named Lary Scott, then executive vice president of CF MotorFreight, as president and CEO of CF Inc. in 1986. In addition to becoming a board member, Scott was secretary of the American Trucking Associations (ATA), director of the ATA Foundation, and a member of the Western Highway Institute.[86]

At the same time, Moffitt was elected vice chairman and began serving on the board of directors. He was responsible for the corporation's financial and administrative activities and its subsidiaries. He was also a member of the ATA's National Accounting and Finance Council. Despite the move, Moffitt had been effectively removed from operational responsibility and became a less likely candidate in what would eventually become the race to succeed O'Brien.[87]

There was a chain reaction of other executive moves. Scott moved CF AirFreight President W. Roger Curry over to become senior vice president of marketing at CF Inc., while Executive Vice President of Operations Donald G. Berger took over as president of CF AirFreight. Robert Lawrence moved from president of CF Land Services to become president of CF MotorFreight, and Vice President and General Manager Robert T. Robertson took over the helm at CF Land Services.

CF International & Air started a new venture, CF Ocean Service, in 1986 at Long Beach, California, to coordinate the activities of the corporation's various international groups, including CF Export-Import Service, Container Management Corporation, and CF KAM Container Line. The new subsidiary worked with CF MotorFreight and the Con-Way companies.[88]

AIRFREIGHT EXPANSION

At CF Air, Berger tried to stem the airfreight forwarder's declining financial situation by promoting good service. He attempted to negotiate with Eastern

---

In 1985, CF AirFreight worked with Eastern Airlines to create a "Moonlight Special" program, where aircraft transported cargo at night to provide next-day, before-noon delivery. *(Photo courtesy of George Hamlin.)*

CF MotorFreight semi-tractor parked near a Tropical Shipping freighter in the early 1980s. CF and the West Palm Beach, Florida, ocean carrier teamed up to provide joint delivery service in the West Indies from the island of Grand Bahama south to Trinidad.

Airlines for price reductions, but the airline was already in a downward financial spiral. Frank Lorenzo, owner of low-fare passenger carriers Continental and New York Air, bought Eastern Airlines in February 1986. Lorenzo was known for slashing labor, and the airline's employee morale fell and service suffered, which caused delivery problems for CF Air.[89]

Despite the troubles, CF AirFreight opened a new $8 million facility in Los Angeles to handle its California business and operated 125 terminals worldwide. After losing $5.2 million in 1986, Berger argued that the company needed its own aircraft to improve its delivery reliability and stabilize its customer base and finances.

Leasing Boeing 727 and DC-8 aircraft in 1987, CF Air also leased a 300-acre facility in Indianapolis from Purolator, an air courier company, to have a major sorting hub located in the country's heartland.[90] Obtaining valuable contracts with Eaton Corporation, Intel, Nabisco, and Volvo White, the subsidiary's volumes increased, and CF Air purchased seven DC-8 aircraft to provide weekly service to Europe and Asia.

CF AirFreight posted $2.4 million in earnings in 1987 and $10.2 million in operating income in 1988. It owned 18 jet freighters and smaller feeder aircraft.[91]

PRESSURES ON CF MOTORFREIGHT

With more than 41,000 tractors, trucks, and trailers that supported more than 660 outlying terminals, CF MotorFreight was one of the largest transportation companies in the world by 1988.[92] As the 1980s progressed, falling diesel fuel prices reduced its operating costs.

Even with the moderation of energy costs, competitors offered discounts of 30 percent or more, cutting into the carrier's profits. As a result, CF MotorFreight began improving its efficiency. The largest user of double trailers, the carrier received a boost when President Ronald Reagan signed the Tandem Truck Safety Act of 1984 on October 30,

1984. Among its provisions, the act permitted 102-inch wide vehicles to operate on designated highways—most of the interstate system—but allowed states to opt out of the law if all adjacent states were in agreement.

The carrier used computer technologies, such as the customer computer access program DIRECT, which allowed customers to track shipments. A majority of the largest trucking firms in the nation had closed their doors during the 1980s, unable to compete in the deregulated industry. A rate war ensued during the fall of 1987 that decimated carriers' profits, but CF MotorFreight weathered the storm, adding new terminals to its Freight Flow System and modernizing its fleet.[93]

After serving 11 years as CEO, 65-year-old O'Brien retired to the role of administrative chairman. "The duties of the chairman are to run the board meetings. Period," O'Brien said. "I didn't believe [the chairman] should be second-guessing the guy running the company."[94]

In early 1988, as CF Inc.'s board of directors prepared to choose a new CEO to succeed O'Brien. Scott was an obvious choice. Scott was well-liked, according to O'Brien, while Moffitt added that his rival for CEO was "Hollywood's idea of a CEO …

good looking, tall, and smooth."[95] Moffitt decided to retire, effective April 25, 1988, after 32 years of service with the company.[96]

"I didn't get the job. When that happens, you don't stay on," Moffitt said.[97]

The future looked bright for the 52-year-old Scott who had started the Con-Way companies. As CF Inc.'s fifth CEO, he had management responsibility for all of the company's components, including CF MotorFreight, CF Land Services, CF AirFreight, and all financial and administrative functions.

Scott moved his office from Palo Alto to Menlo Park, where he and his staff began drawing up a five-year business plan. He wanted to take CF Inc. into the international transportation field to guard against foreign-owned competitors that might invade the North American trucking industry, much like they had done with the automotive, electronics, aircraft, and other sectors of the economy.[98]

Three out of the four Con-Way companies were growing, although the financial troubles of Con-Way Eastern still required attention. Corporate executives also were committed to growing CF AirFreight, and the most likely strategy appeared to be an acquisition. Two potential takeover targets were Flying Tigers and Emery Air Freight.

CON-WAY REGIONAL CARRIERS

THE OVERNIGHT SENSATIONS

CHAPTER SIX

WITH SUCCESS COMES DIFFICULTY

1989–1991

A board member was willing to put up $1 million of their own money to make sure that bank notes weren't called in. … Nobody ever knew how close to bankruptcy we were. The management of the company did a good job of insulating everybody from that. Another great lesson to be learned is while there are times of trouble … keep everyone focused on what they can do—and that was serving the customer.

—David McClimon, president, Con-way Freight[1]

THE SUCCESSFUL ESTABLISHMENT OF the four regional Con-Way companies—Con-Way Central Express (CCX), Con-Way Eastern Express (CEX), Con-Way Western Express (CWX), and Con-Way Southern Express (CSE)—showed a clear near-term path for success. The time was right for CF Inc. to expand in a new direction.

Lary R. Scott, president and CEO of CF Inc., set his sights on growing CF AirFreight. He was ready to take the airfreight forwarder global. As it would take years and millions of dollars in resources to grow an airfreight carrier organically, the simplest path to expansion was to enter the market through an acquisition. Emery Worldwide, an airfreight forwarding company that offered global possibilities, had been identified previously by Donald E. Moffitt, former vice chairman of CF Inc., as a possible acquisition. Scott resumed the inquiry.

ACQUIRING EMERY

In 1946, U.S. naval air transportation veteran John Colvin Emery Sr. founded Emery with three employees, two used trucks, and a $125,000 loan. The tiny carrier moved about 50 tons of freight and earned $30,000 during its first year. By the mid-1960s, Emery's net profits hit an average of $2.7 million annually, the company had 50 offices in the United States, and it also operated in Australia,

Canada, Europe, Japan, New Zealand, and the Philippines.[2] Despite rising fuel prices in the 1970s, Emery expanded its use of bicycle service in big cities, used chartered planes, and entered the overnight delivery service as its revenues grew.

In 1981, the company was renamed Emery Worldwide and purchased 24 Boeing 727 freighters and leased an additional 40 aircraft; its long-term debt grew to $130 million. By imitating Federal Express Corp.'s hub-and-spoke system, its profits rose to a record $25 million in 1983 on revenues of $683 million.[3]

"Emery, at one time, was the best in the business," said Moffitt.[4]

Emery opened a "super hub" in Dayton, Ohio, where packages were routed for reshipment regardless of size or destination. It opened a similar

---

Above: When Con-Way Intermodal was created in 1989, this advertisement provided information about its GlobalRate service, which was a simplified pricing system that included all points in the United States and most major markets around the world.

Opposite: For less than a year, after Con-Way Southwest Express opened in November 1989 until Con-Way Eastern was shuttered in September 1990, there were five Con-Way companies in existence.

In 1989, CF Inc. acquired Emery Worldwide for nearly $500 million in hopes of establishing a global airfreight business. *(Photo courtesy of George Hamlin.)*

European hub in the Netherlands by 1985. Despite the costs of transporting freight out of the way to its super hubs, Emery remained profitable.[5] Moffitt had approached Emery for a possible merger with CF AirFreight during the mid-1980s, but was rebuffed by John Emery Jr., its CEO at the time.[6]

In April 1987, Emery purchased the troubled Purolator Courier Corp., the fourth-largest U.S. ground-only small parcel carrier, for $350 million.[7] According to Moffitt, Purolator had intrastate authority that was "10 times better than FedEx."[8] Although Emery consolidated its operations, rising costs from the Purolator purchase placed it in a financial tailspin. CF Inc. made another unsuccessful overture to purchase Emery during the fall of 1988. In December 1988, with its fortunes sinking, the Emery board of directors removed Emery Jr. and named William F. Souders, retired Xerox Corp. executive vice president, as CEO and chairman.[9, 10]

In early 1989, as Emery approached financial insolvency, Souders called Scott to revive the merger talks.[11]

"On the asset side of the ledger, Emery gave CF AirFreight … a global doorway," said Eb Schmoller, then vice president and general counsel for CF AirFreight. "Emery offered at least the chance [to become a worldwide organization] in the guise of airfreight, but they also had some container shipping operations. That was the attraction. But the rose came with a lot of thorns. It turned out that the Emery acquisition was pretty costly."[12]

Theoretically, the Emery purchase would make CF Inc. a major force in the international airfreight business. Since CF had already compiled extensive research about Emery, Scott did not order a more thorough review of the air carrier's

financial state in 1989. This would prove a tremendous mistake.

"Emery's management was pretty desperate," Schmoller said. "The company was more unsettled than anybody [at CF] had figured out."

Although CF Inc.'s board of directors had misgivings about buying Emery, Scott had a successful track record. On February 14, 1989, CF announced it would acquire Emery in a cash deal for $230 million and assume its $258 million of debts.[13] The Emery board accepted CF's offer of $4.75 a share in cash for all outstanding common stock and $21.10 per share for all outstanding preferred stock.

In March, a 10-bank consortium, led by Security Pacific National Bank of Los Angeles, provided CF with a three-year, $300 million line of credit.[14] With the security of this line of credit, CF completed the Emery purchase on April 3.

THE FINANCIAL ALBATROSS

Scott and his executives should have recognized how serious the problems were with Emery—it was losing approximately $1 million a week by the time the acquisition was completed. Meanwhile, Standard & Poor's had lowered its rating of the airfreight carrier's debt to junk bond status.[15] Nevertheless, Scott insisted that Emery's fleet of 55 planes and operations in 45 countries would bring important benefits to CF.[16]

Scott also had another calculated reason for the purchase of Emery. He viewed it as a "poison pill" defense against a possible hostile takeover by Arthur M. Goldberg, a casino mogul. Goldberg, CEO of Park Place Entertainment, had purchased 4.9 percent of CF Inc.'s stock—there were also rumors that Goldberg's partners controlled about 13 percent of the trucking company's shares.[17, 18]

Before the acquisition, CF's $300 million surplus from the Freightliner sale made it a tempting takeover target for speculators. By putting the corporation heavily in debt, Scott hoped to thwart any potential suitors, including Goldberg. Unfortunately, CF had now inherited a financial albatross. In another move, CF AirFreight President Donald G. Berger dismissed almost every one of Emery's senior managers immediately, replacing them with his own people.

"[Berger] put in his own CF AirFreight people, and they just didn't know how to do it," explained Raymond O'Brien, chairman of CF Inc. at that time. "I think the merger was mismanaged, and maybe the timing of the acquisition was wrong."[19]

Employee morale at Emery was shattered.

Although the merger between Purolator and Emery had been completed two years prior, it was soon appallingly clear that the two accounting systems, as well as operations, had not been fully integrated. Gregory L. Quesnel, CF vice president of accounting, was sent to Purolator's offices in Scranton, Pennsylvania, to organize the hundreds of clients and contracts that each company—CF Air, Purolator, and Emery—shared.[20]

Other missteps by Berger and CF managers included raising the company's fuel surcharge by 4.7 percent even as an accounting program error overcharged hundreds of customers during the summer of 1989. Customers fled the airfreight carrier, and its tonnage dropped.

The financial difficulties at Emery were growing exponentially, threatening the entire corporation. The airfreight carrier's losses reached $18.7 million in the third quarter of 1989, and skyrocketed to $40 million by the fourth quarter—about half in write-off costs for Emery's flawed billing system.[21] Scott and Berger maintained their position that the company just needed more time to become profitable, although their mantra was beginning to fall on frustrated ears.

SUCCESS IN TRUCKING

Although the attempt to expand the airfreight business was progressing poorly, the trucking divisions were doing well. In mid-August 1989, CF Land Services was renamed Con-Way Transportation Services (CTS). Toward the end of 1989, CTS President Robert T. Robertson announced that CTS would spend more than $75 million in the coming

CF Inc. executive Ray Halloran, left, posed with Lary Scott after he was elected to become the corporation's president and CEO. *(Photo courtesy of Ray Halloran.)*

year on capital improvements, including $40 million for new tractors, trailers, and delivery trucks.[22] Out of the remainder, $6 million was spent for dock equipment, including forklifts, and $30 million was spent to build new service centers and upgrade existing facilities.[23]

At the time, the four Con-Way carriers collectively had 232 separate service centers, reaching about 50,000 communities with next-day service, and maintained an overall 97 percent on-time delivery. The carriers employed 5,700 and moved about 25 million pounds of freight every day.[24]

As the 1980s came to a close, Gerald Detter, president of Con-Way Central Express, reflected on the Con-Way companies' evolution from an idea, to a business plan, to successfully functioning operations. He discussed this in his column in the November/December issue of the *CCX Milemarker* employee newsletter:

In 1983, our goals seemed aggressive, our desire to establish and maintain a high quality, superior service product company that involved the input, cooperation, and dedication from all its employees seemed very possible with the rapidly

This "Thanks for Choosing CCX" button was created in September 1989, by Pat Light Jr., the 12-year-old son of Safety Supervisor Pat Light Sr. of Sandusky, Michigan. It was used by driver–sales representatives for Con-Way Central's "30-second sales call."

changing environment of our industry. The '80s saw CCX go from a nonexistent company to the No. 1 LTL revenue-producing carrier in its marketplace.[25]

Although the Con-Ways' parent company had inherited what was beginning to be seen as insurmountable problems with Emery, Con-Way Central, Con-Way Western, and Con-Way Southern all experienced growth and increasing profits. Only Con-Way Eastern faced continued difficulties. And a fifth company—Con-Way Southwest Express—launched in November 1989, targeting the large Southwestern market.

Con-Way Central remained the most profitable and largest of CF's regional carriers, and it experienced a major expansion in May 1989 with six new service centers in Aliquippa, Pennsylvania;

Hillsboro and Uhrichsville, Ohio; Keokuk, Iowa; Mason, Michigan; and Richmond, Indiana. There were now a total of 116 terminals, 1,218 tractors, 2,539 trailers, and 2,700 employees.[26] By June, Con-Way Central had opened a new 160-door, 30-acre Chicago terminal, which was the largest service center at the time.[27]

Although growing at a slower pace than Con-Way Central, Con-Way Western opened one of its largest facilities in early 1989, as the 44-door, 15,000-square-foot San Francisco terminal became operational. Employing 150 people, the new freight service center served customers in San Francisco's Financial District and industrial regions to the south of the city.[28] In March 1989, Con-Way Western's on-time delivery service also reached 97 percent for the first time.

Con-Way Southern also undertook a major expansion in 1989, increasing the number of its terminals from 27 to 40 and adding 132 employees. The company served 6,500 communities in the Carolinas, Georgia, Virginia, Tennessee, and Alabama. In May, it entered Florida when it opened its Jacksonville service center.[29]

Although it faced tough competition from other regional LTLs, including Carolina Freight Carriers Corp., Southeastern Freightlines Inc., Overnite Transportation Co., and Estes Express Lines Inc., Con-Way Southern's on-time delivery service hit 98 percent while employee turnover was a scant 2 percent.[30] By August, Con-Way Southern was making its first monthly profit.[31]

A SIX-WEEK DEADLINE

While in Philadelphia, CF Truckload Vice President John Hickerson received a call to return to Fort Worth, Texas, to meet with Robertson. CTS' intra-Louisiana operating certificate was about to expire. Robertson wanted to use that authority to launch Con-Way Southwest Express even though the

Con-Way Central's 48-door Grand Rapids, Michigan, service center opened in May 1989, and employed 45 people. It replaced the original terminal that was one of Con-Way Central's "Original 11" terminals from 1983.

company had not locked down intrastate authority in Texas, which was the largest market in the region.

"Robertson wanted to know if I was interested in becoming president of Con-Way Southwest. Of course, I was," Hickerson said. "We literally did this on the fly. From the time that the CF board approved the plan in September 1989, we had six weeks to get the company up and running to operate this authority before it expired."[32]

The frenzied effort to create a company in less than 45 days was daunting as there were no service

CWX
CON-WAY WESTERN EXPRESS
THE WEST'S FASTEST GROWING REGIONAL OVERNIGHT CARRIER, PROVIDING NEXT-DAY SERVICE TO ANY MAJOR MARKET AREA IN ARIZONA, CALIFORNIA AND NEVADA.

CSE
CON-WAY SOUTHERN EXPRESS
CSE PROVIDES THE HIGH STANDARDS OF CON-WAY SERVICE IN SEVEN STATES: ALABAMA, FLORIDA, GEORGIA, NORTH CAROLINA, SOUTH CAROLINA, TENNESSEE, VIRGINIA AND WASHINGTON D.C.

CSW
CON-WAY SOUTHWEST EXPRESS
CSW IS THE NEWEST MEMBER OF THE CON-WAY FAMILY, SERVING ARKANSAS, LOUISIANA, MISSISSIPPI, OKLAHOMA AND TEXAS WITH THE SAME SUPERIOR OVERNIGHT SERVICE YOU'VE COME TO EXPECT FROM THE CON-WAY FAMILY.

This map shows the geographic areas covered by Con-Way's five regional carriers. The regional carriers did not cover the Northwest, which was Consolidated Freightways' home territory.

centers, tractors, trailers, or employees. Obtaining equipment was the easiest issue to handle. With Con-Way Western, Central, Southern, and Eastern already in business, it was a matter of diverting vehicles already on order to Con-Way Southwest and repainting them.

Next, CF purchased the intrastate license of the defunct Brown Express Inc. of San Antonio, giving it the temporary right to operate in Texas.[33] Con-Way Southwest would not receive final approval until December 16, 1990.[34]

To secure the facilities that the start-up needed, Hickerson and Rock Magnan, vice president of operations for CF Land Services, took a three-day road trip through Austin, Corpus Christi, Dallas, Houston, Fort Worth, San Antonio, and Waco in October 1989, to scout properties to lease or purchase.[35] Similar leasing and purchasing blitz tours also occurred in Louisiana and Oklahoma. Next, Hickerson and his team conducted mass interviews in the Dallas–Fort Worth area to search for qualified employees.

On November 6, 1989, Con-Way Southwest opened for business.[36] Headquartered in Dallas, Con-Way Southwest started with a $25 million stake from CF Inc. and initially had 15 freight terminals—seven in Texas, six in Louisiana, and two in Oklahoma—and 100 tractors, 200 trailers, and 150 employees. It specialized in overnight and second-day delivery of LTL freight and operated in Texas, Oklahoma, Louisiana, and Arkansas (points in Arkansas were initially served through freight terminals in Louisiana). Con-Way Southwest used the same computer rating system and shipment tracking technology as the other Con-Way companies.

"In these smaller markets, it was just a matter of having our managers go out and knock on doors and saying, 'Hey, we're here. Give us a try.' It was literally that simple," Hickerson explained. "Everybody had a shipment on the opening day except Austin, Texas, and it took them about a week to get their first shipment."[37]

By June 1990, Con-Way Southwest had expanded its network by adding eight service centers in Arkansas, Mississippi, and Tennessee. It handled its 100,000th shipment by October, and by the end of the year had a 99.68 percent cumulative on-time delivery rate.[38]

Like most of the Con-Ways, Con-Way Southwest quickly built a successful track record and became a positive light for CF Inc. during the struggle with Emery's dismal financial situation. The carrier situation was not so promising in New England, however.

CON-WAY EASTERN SHUTTERED

Except for a scant few quarters of profitability, Con-Way Eastern (the former Penn Yan Express) lost money every year, including losing $7 million on revenues of $67 million in 1989.[39] Even so, CF supported the struggling regional carrier with a $6 million expansion between 1988 and 1989 that included purchasing 60 new line-haul tractors, 100 new trailers, and boosting its terminals to 37 service centers in the United States and eastern Canada.[40, 41]

In April 1989, Con-Way Eastern inaugurated an express service for freight shipments to Puerto Rico. The service combined next-day delivery capabilities in the Northeast with regularly scheduled sailings from its ocean shippers in Newark, New Jersey, and a special customs documentation program to expedite deliveries in San Juan, Puerto Rico.

Yet, intractable labor-management problems plagued the carrier. After Con-Way Eastern's union contract expired in 1989, Robertson took a two-pronged approach. Company negotiators stayed at the bargaining table, but he assigned Con-Way's outside legal counsel, James Smith, to study plant closure laws. Smith advised him that the union—not Con-Way—could be blamed for closing the eastern subsidiary if the Teamsters called a strike.[42] This was an important point because it meant that should the company close, Con-Way would not be at fault and could reenter the market with a non-union facility at a later time.

Starting in the winter of 1989–1990, the Teamsters again tried organizing the other Con-Ways and sent invitations to Con-Way Western and Con-Way Central employees to attend meetings and join the union.[43]

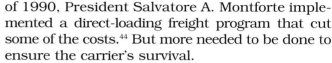

Sal Montforte, former president of Con-Way Eastern Express, joined Con-Way Western as its vice president of operations in December 1990.

When Con-Way Eastern lost $2.7 million during the first quarter of 1990, President Salvatore A. Montforte implemented a direct-loading freight program that cut some of the costs.[44] But more needed to be done to ensure the carrier's survival.

By June 1990, as the national economy was slipping into a recession, Con-Way Eastern and labor bargainers reached an agreement to permit more flexible work rules—such as allowing drivers to help out with dock work. At first, the Teamsters refused to allow the Con-Way Eastern union members to vote on the contract. CF filed a complaint with the National Labor Relations Board, which cited the Teamsters for unfair bargaining and ordered a vote. Con-Way Eastern workers rejected the contract by a 60–40 percent margin.[45]

On Friday, August 31, 1990, some 750 Con-Way Eastern Teamsters went on strike. CF executives acted a week later after they were convinced that obtaining an acceptable contract from the union was impossible.[46] Con-Way Eastern officially closed September 7, 1990.[47]

Employees from other Con-Way companies arrived at Con-Way Eastern's 14 largest terminals by 5 A.M. Within four hours, they had removed all pre-designated equipment and had driven the tractors to Emery's facility in Newburgh, New York, before the Teamsters had a chance to react.[48] According to Richard Palazzo, Con-Way Central vice president of operations:

CEX was not a profitable company. Their losing situation was directly attributable, among other things, to the unwillingness of the Teamsters to recognize and negotiate restrictive work rules out of their contract. In short, the Teamsters refused to cooperate in allowing CEX to become ... a successful carrier.[49]

CF Inc. incurred more than $11 million in losses for shuttering Con-Way Eastern—about

CON-WAY INTERMODAL

IN 1989, CF TRUCKLOAD WAS RENAMED AND revamped as Con-Way Intermodal (CWI), making Jim Hertwig president and CEO.[1] Based in Fort Worth, Texas, this subsidiary company was renamed again as Con-Way Truckload Services (CWT) in the mid-1990s, although its purpose remained the same—providing full-service, multi-modal transportation for truckload shippers.

Con-Way Intermodal/Truckload was comprised of rail, ocean, and trucking divisions. It offered door-to-door domestic intermodal movement of full-truckload shipments as well as international export shipping services to more than 200 major ports worldwide. Its trucks also provided contract container drayage throughout the United States.[2]

In 1988, the company implemented piggyback or container transfer services with major railroad companies, and also stationed its first pickup and delivery equipment and drivers in Dallas and Seattle that August. The following year, a central transportation control facility was established in Fort Worth, Texas, that included customer service operations. Premium 500, a service that guaran-teed on-time deliveries or offered customers a $500 refund was established in April 1990.[3]

In 1990, CWI introduced Con-Quest, an intermodal rail transportation program for full-truckload shippers that combined CWI's resources with major railroads for expedited door-to-door service. The following year, CF Inc. provided the company with a $4.9 million expansion, doubling its capabilities, by adding 300 containers and 200 chassis. In July 1993, CWI opened sales offices in seven cities—Charlotte, Jacksonville, Cleveland, Kansas City, Memphis, Oakland, and San Bernardino.[4]

It also improved its Ocean Services unit with a program called GlobalRate. Aimed at importers and exporters, GlobalRate provided customers with single-source pricing and routing for international shipments less than 10,000 pounds to points around the world. Traditionally, shippers had to use multiple service providers to ship freight internationally, which generated multiple bills of lading. GlobalRate significantly simplified the billing process.[5]

Since most cargos were distributed within 200 to 300 miles of their ports of entry, this was

---

$7 million for workers' compensation and $4.3 million in other closing costs.[50] For more than a year, Con-Way had no presence in the Northeast.

THREATS OF BANKRUPTCY

Although Consolidated Freightways had built a solid reputation since 1972, long before the Freightliner sale, the tide was turning. By the end of 1989, CF MotorFreight's profits dipped due to higher fuel costs and pressures from competition to cut rates, but the carrier transported a record 15.2 billion pounds of freight for a record $2 billion in revenue.[51] The Con-Way companies, despite the losses at Con-Way Eastern Express, earned a total operating profit of $40.4 million on revenues of $558.5 million.

Emery lost $66 million for the year, and there was an additional $31.4 million one-time charge related to closing redundant Emery–CF Air facilities and other merger issues.[52] The troubles at Emery negated any gains made by CF MotorFreight and four of the five Con-Ways, and CF Inc. reported a $35.5 million loss for 1989.

Emery's woes only worsened in 1990 when it lost $68.5 million during the first quarter of the year, including burning through $18.8 million in March. CF Inc.'s stock price took a hit, dropping from $18 a share to less than $12.[53] The company's debt had jumped from $47.7 million before the acquisition to $486.2 million in a little more than a year. The banks notified CF that they were displeased with its financial condition.

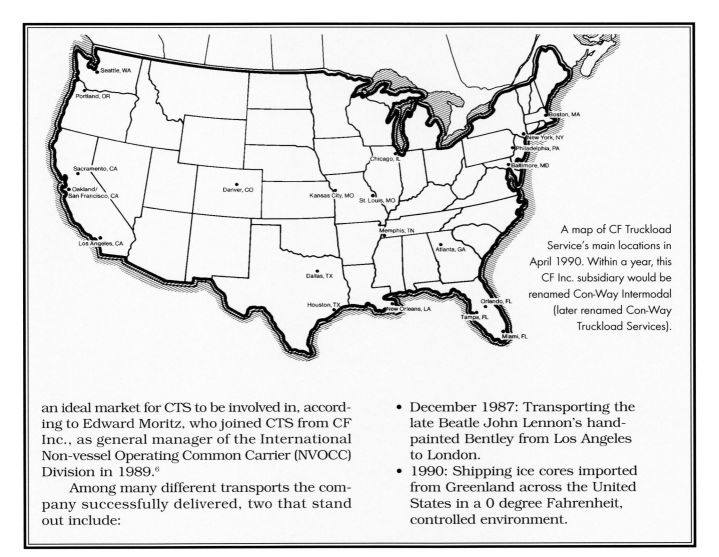

A map of CF Truckload Service's main locations in April 1990. Within a year, this CF Inc. subsidiary would be renamed Con-Way Intermodal (later renamed Con-Way Truckload Services).

an ideal market for CTS to be involved in, according to Edward Moritz, who joined CTS from CF Inc., as general manager of the International Non-vessel Operating Common Carrier (NVOCC) Division in 1989.[6]

Among many different transports the company successfully delivered, two that stand out include:

- December 1987: Transporting the late Beatle John Lennon's hand-painted Bentley from Los Angeles to London.
- 1990: Shipping ice cores imported from Greenland across the United States in a 0 degree Fahrenheit, controlled environment.

With its stock price plummeting, Scott authorized a dividend payment to reassure shareholders about the corporation's long-term future. Although Norman R. Benke, senior vice president of finance, and Frank Roberts, treasurer, assured him that the dividend payment would not violate the terms of the company's $300 million line of credit loan, Security Pacific Bank objected.

The bank's loan portfolio and balance sheet had been wrecked by the sluggish economy and the southern California real estate crash.[54] Also stung by the savings and loan crisis that had grown to scandalous proportions by 1990, Security Pacific declared that CF had defaulted on its loan agreements although the corporation had only used $18 million of its $300 million line of credit. Its assets were valued at

$2 billion, and it should have been able to secure additional financing.[55]

Emery's problems trickled down to the Con-Way companies, noted Kevin C. Schick, who had been named vice president and controller of CTS in 1989.

"We faced a liquidity crisis. Our vendors started calling, complaining about lack of payment," Schick said. "Con-Way was a well-run carrier, well-run organization, but we were caught up in this maelstrom."[56]

With its line of credit canceled, CF executives scrambled to satisfy its bankers. Adding to Scott's headaches, Benke unfortunately needed a leave of absence for open-heart surgery—CF was now without financial guidance at the most crucial point in the company's history. By June 1990, CF brought in bankruptcy consultants after warnings from Security Pacific.[57] According to Schick:

In the spring of 1990, things were very bizarre, very surreal. There were strange people in the corporate office. I was called by people I didn't know to run forecasts and provide them numbers and data. Bob Robertson just shrugged his shoulders and said, "Go over to corporate office, and provide the information they need to run their models."[58]

Chemical Bank of New York promised to pay the Security Pacific consortium by restructuring the trucking corporation's debt and selling off certain operations. Chemical Bank offered a $900 million loan, but demanded an up-front payment of $85 million.[59]

"I remember hearing stories that we were literally hours, maybe days, away from bankruptcy," said David McClimon, then Con-Way Central's regional manager in Chicago. "CF Inc.'s management did a good job of insulating [the Con-Ways] from that. It allowed us to focus on what we could do, which was serving our customers and growing our business."[60]

As had happened more than a quarter century before, the CF Inc. board of directors stepped in to resolve the crisis. The board appointed a special committee headed by Chairman O'Brien to review the situation. Along with O'Brien were two men who had been on CF Inc.'s board since the mid-1970s—Robert L. Chambers, president of Wilson & Chambers, a management and investment firm; and J. Frank Leach, who had more than 20 years of experience in the auto industry, and was former chairman, president, and CEO of Arcata Corp.[61]

MOFFITT'S RETURN

Cruising on a Sunday afternoon aboard the *White Bear*, his 44-foot sloop, Moffitt was relaxed, enjoying the beauty of British Columbia's Gulf Islands while sitting in the captain's chair.[62] During the two years since he had retired from CF, he established a consulting firm on the East Coast to save troubled companies, including Circle Express, an Indianapolis-based trucking company.[63] He received an unexpected phone call from his former boss, O'Brien, asking him to return to CF.

When Moffitt left CF in 1988, its stock price traded between $38 and $39 per share, and the company had $300 million in the bank. The transportation corporation was now faced with a potential bank-ordered breakup as its stock sunk to $9 a share.[64, 65]

After speaking with O'Brien, Moffitt immediately flew to California to examine the financial details. O'Brien, Chambers, and Leach briefed him on the situation and asked if he would offer assistance. Moffitt agreed to return to CF, under the condition that he report solely to the board and not be answerable to

Above: Con-Way Central Express provided pins and buttons for its driver–sales representatives.

Left: A motivational sign in Con-Way Central's Des Moines, Iowa, service center reminded employees that "The Day You Are Satisfied Growth Comes to a Halt!"

Robert P. Mallon, chairman of the Automotive Hall of Fame, left, is pictured with Raymond F. O'Brien, CF Inc. chairman and CEO, in 1991. O'Brien became one of only 323 individuals since the Hall of Fame's inception in 1940 to win its prestigious Distinguished Service Citation.

Scott.[66] For the next several weeks, he worked on a strategy to meet the corporation's financial obligations and to circumvent the demands of Chemical Bank.

"They [Chemical] were structuring a loan we couldn't possibly get out from under," Moffitt said.[67]

A flurry of management changes followed. On July 30, 1990, the board forced Scott to resign. O'Brien was named chairman and CEO, while Leach became president and chief operating officer. Moffitt was made CF's executive vice president of finance. Quesnel also replaced Roberts as vice president and treasurer.[68]

Ditching Chemical Bank, Moffitt suspended the corporation's common stock dividend payments. He also secured a $75 million line of credit from Bank of America, the financial institution with which CF previously had had a good history.[69]

Instead of selling Emery, Moffitt took the airfreight carrier out of the letter-mail and small package business and concentrated on overnight delivery of freight packages weighing more than 70 pounds. The airfreight company trimmed its payroll by 2,000 employees in 18 months, shrinking its workforce to about 8,000.[70] With Moffitt working to get the company back on its feet, there was a bit of optimism in the air.

"The company actually sought buyers at first [for Emery]," Moffitt explained at the time. "We've had an assortment of would-be buyers approach us and some bizarre proposals. The truth is there are no buyers for Emery, and we aren't looking for any. Emery is going to be fixed."[71]

To lead Emery, the CF board replaced Berger with Arthur C. Bass, who had been the former vice chairman and president of Federal Express.[72] Emery, however, continued to lose money—$13 million

Above: A Con-Way Central Express booth at a trade show, circa late 1989 to 1990.

Below: After Emery Worldwide was acquired in 1989, CF AirFreight President Donald G. Berger dismissed Emery senior managers and replaced them with CF employees while the two companies integrated operating procedures. *(Photo courtesy of George Hamlin.)*

in January 1991, which climbed to $16 million in February. Losing patience, O'Brien and Moffitt fired Bass and replaced him with CF veteran Roger Curry.

As Emery was undergoing severe restructuring, CF MotorFreight and the Con-Ways faced rising fuel costs in the wake of the 1990 recession, and the long-haul carrier faced increasing price pressures from competitors.

COPING WITH RECESSION, FUEL PRICES

For the first time in years, Detter noted in his end-of-the-year column to Con-Way Central employees, the company did not expand significantly in 1990. It did add spin-off terminals—facilities added in already established geographic locations where the sheer volume of traffic and freight needed more support—in Gary/Hammond and Columbus, Indiana; Iron Mountain and Cadillac, Michigan; Mason City, Iowa; and Mentor, Ohio. Its Milwaukee, Wisconsin; Columbus, Ohio; Bridgeview and Palatine, Illinois; Pontiac and Holland/Muskegon, Michigan, service centers moved to larger, newly built or renovated facilities.

All of the changes increased Con-Way Central's total door capacity from 2,357 to 2,796.[73] Con-Way

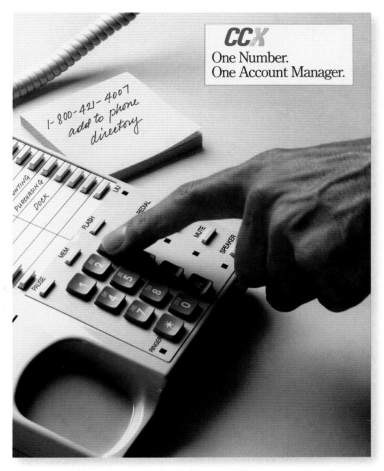

An advertisement from 1990 features Con-Way Central's telemarketing department. Con-Way was one of the first trucking companies to have such a department.

Central also exceeded $250 million in sales for the first time in 1990.

"This is significant in that no other LTL carrier in the history of U.S. transportation has ever grown at this pace before. This alone sets us apart from any other trucking company," Detter said.[74]

Con-Way Southwest struggled through the early 1990s servicing its rural markets and was unable to work with the neighboring Con-Way Southern and Con-Way Western companies, noted Hickerson.

"The Con-Ways never interchanged freight with each other. It was taboo because it would run afoul of the Consolidated Freightways organization," Hickerson said.[75]

Even with the difficulties that Con-Way Southwest faced, it provided 100 percent on-time service for three out of four weeks in February 1990.[76] In January 1991, it added three new service centers, and by the end of the year it had 42 service centers, 595 employees, and 1,551 pieces of equipment.

In 1990, Con-Way Southern purchased McMinnville and Hohenwald Truck Lines, and acquired intrastate operating authority in Tennessee.[77] The following year, there was a ferocious battle in the transportation industry for market share, and discounting reached an all-time high as competitors promoted price to attract customers. Although this battle hurt the Con-Ways—Con-Way Central, for instance, experienced a quarter where its revenues dropped below those of a comparable quarter from the year before—it also marked the beginning of the decline of CF MotorFreight.[78]

THE CHALLENGE OF CHANGE

The freight delivery business was undergoing a fundamental shift in demand. More customers requested just-in-time delivery service instead of longer service, such as a five-day transcontinental shipment. UPS, FedEx, airfreight carriers, and even regional carriers, such as the Con-Ways, were cutting into CF MotorFreight's share of the market.[79]

The long-haul carrier's Freight Flow System had been designed to take advantage of growth, and full capacity peaked at 689 terminals in 1991. With high overhead costs, it was now vulnerable to dropping tonnage.[80] CF MotorFreight's tonnage fell by 18 percent during the last quarter of 1990 and into the first quarter of 1991, forcing it to lay off more than 1,000 employees. To slash costs, the long-haul carrier returned much of its rented equipment and postponed buying new tractors and trailers.

By spring 1991, it barely earned a profit. It was saddled with a national Teamsters' contract that hiked wages as fuel prices rose, while competitors launched a new round of deep discounts. The carrier's operating profit declined from $108.5 million in 1990 to $52 million by the end of 1991.[81]

As 1992 dawned, the Con-Way companies faced a brighter future and the Emery acquisition was being more competently handled, but the original carrier began facing its hardest times yet.

CHAPTER SEVEN
A SPLIT DECISION
1992–1996

Many times business has been described as just a game. If transportation was a board game and CCX was part of that game, our objective would obviously be to finish first, gain the highest score, and eventually win.

—Gerald Detter, president of Con-Way Central Express[1]

CONSOLIDATED FREIGHTWAYS INC. (CF) was headed toward financial security in the mid-1990s after surviving the Emery crisis, thanks to the strength of the Con-Way regional less-than-truckload (LTL) carriers.

The company turned its attention to a developing industry, bolstered by a wealth of technology and customer initiative. With customers requesting that transportation of freight be as easy and seamless as possible, the time was right for the creation of a professional logistics operation to meet this need.

CREATION OF MENLO LOGISTICS

The idea for Menlo Logistics was developed in the late 1980s.[2] John H. Williford, CF Inc.'s then director of marketing, presented the venture—an organization that offered warehouse, inventory, and transportation management as well as full integration of supply chain links through customized systems and software—to upper management. He estimated that CF could capture a meaningful share of the $50 billion market but, at the time, the company was dedicated to solving the Emery financial crisis, and his idea never went any further. In the meantime, a chief competitor, Roadway of Akron, Ohio, started its own logistics firm.[3] After Donald Moffitt returned to CF Inc. and was named president and CEO in 1991, the idea for the new enterprise was given more attention.

On October 26, 1990, Menlo Logistics Inc. was formed. The name was a deliberate choice to prompt an association with California's Menlo Park, which was well known as the home of venture capitalists and high-tech industries. Logistics consultants and warehousing experts ran the dedicated, contract carriage operations. The start-up was "carrier neutral" and did not give special treatment to its companion organizations, such as the Con-Ways, CF MotorFreight, or to any particular outside carriers.[4]

The initial business plan was to create, implement, and manage logistics projects for its customers.

"These tended to be single custom solutions for each customer," noted Gary Kowalski, who eventually became the chief operating officer of Menlo.[5] Some companies were conducting business with

---

Above: Con-Way Central Express' first tractor was refurbished and placed on permanent display in the lobby of the company's new office at 4880 Venture Drive in Ann Arbor, Michigan, which opened in May 1993.

Opposite: The "Chicagoland" area is the largest freight-producing region in the 13 states served by Con-Way Central Express.

both the Con-Ways and CF MotorFreight and wanted to manage those carriers and others more efficiently.

Robert L. Bianco, who was working at CF Motor-Freight as its manager of operations research and was responsible for optimizing its freight network models, was one of Menlo's first employees.[6] He explained:

In the late eighties, customers were coming to corporations saying, "You do a great job moving my goods from point A to point B on trucks, but I really need somebody who can not only do that, but someone who can also run a warehouse for me." Or, "You're really good moving my goods from point A to B, but this other guy that I use is good from C to D. Now, I want to use both. I need someone to manage that for me." It was from those initial requests that John [Williford] crafted the business model for Menlo Worldwide.[7]

One of Menlo's early success stories was its successful bid on a $100 million distribution contract with Sears.[8] The department store wanted to close its internal distribution system, which cost Sears about twice as much as its competitors at 7 percent of its sales.[9]

"CF MotorFreight and the Con-Way Group had a lot to do with putting [the Sears] bid together," said Rock Magnan, then vice president of operations for Con-Way Transportation Services (CTS). "Once it was awarded, we needed a neutral third party within the company to arbitrate who was going to manage the respective parts of the business."[10]

After launching with Sears, Menlo signed contracts with Ford Motor Company and Hewlett-Packard. In 1993, Menlo was given a warehousing contract from Coca-Cola and a truckload management contract from Frito-Lay.[11]

This bottle of Dom Pérignon champagne was given to Con-Way Southwest on its first business day in November 1989. It was not to be opened until the company reached profitability, which occurred 27 months later in March 1992.

THE CON-WAYS MOVE FORWARD

By the beginning of 1992, the four Con-Way regional carriers operated a fleet of more than 11,000 trucks, tractors, and trailers.[12]

On April 1, 1992, a federal law was implemented requiring commercial driver's licenses (CDLs) for all commercial truck drivers. The law established competency and educational standards and was intended to prevent those with poor driving records from obtaining a license in another state. Robert T. Robertson announced the day before the law was to take effect that all Con-Way driver–sales representatives had already passed the examination successfully and received CDLs.[13]

Con-Way Southern Express (CSE) added Puerto Rico to its list of destinations in September 1992. Shipments bound for the U.S. protectorate were taken to a freight assembly center and combined with other cargo to create container loads for sea shipment. Con-Way Southern also handled return shipments from Puerto Rico.[14]

Con-Way Southwest Express (CSW) received a boost from the Texas Railroad Commission in October 1992 when it allowed direct service between its two existing operating authorities in Texas. Before this time, Con-Way Southwest was greatly restrained. It could haul freight from Dallas to Harlingen on the Mexican border, but it could not go from Harlingen to Amarillo in northwest Texas. The state even prohibited indirect service from Harlingen to Amarillo through Dallas.

The ruling allowed the carrier to decrease route times greatly and improve service, according to Con-Way Southwest President John Hickerson.[15]

In December 1992, Con-Way Western (CWX) had its first expansion beyond its original three western states, when it opened a new expedited freight shipping service to Hawaii. It provided regular service to Hawaii through container ships out of Long Beach and Oakland, California.[16]

Con-Way also established a presence in Mexico in 1992 with a sales office in Monterrey. This operation later became known as Con-Way Mexico Express.

MORE DIFFICULTIES WITH EMERY

At Emery Worldwide, President Roger Curry and his team faced a yearlong battle with the U.S. Postal Service when its bid for the Midwest Express Mail service became embroiled in Congressional politics. Part of the political—and what turned into a legal—battle included allegations that Emery had overcharged the government during the Persian Gulf War. CF Inc. filed countercharges that the Postal Service was showing political favoritism to other airlines, as well as improprieties of employment offers to postal employees by other carriers during the bidding process.[17]

Emery was in danger of losing postal contracts for 20 years, but in October 1992, CF Inc. won a legal victory. A federal judge ordered that Emery could transport overnight mail through the summer of 1993. Legal wrangling continued, however, until April 1993, when Emery received a 10-year contract to deliver the daylight Express Mail Fleet.

The fourth quarter of 1992 was an important one for Emery—the company posted a $1.5 million profit, its first in seven years. Also, the company signed a $200 million contract with General Motors and an express freight deal with Chrysler Corporation.

REENTERING THE EASTERN MARKET

After Con-Way Eastern was disbanded following the Teamsters' strike of 1990, CTS began planning how to reenter the important regional market. CTS took a two-pronged approach that was a ruse.

CTS knew that the Teamsters were waiting for another company to enter the Northeast market, and the company examined its options to recover the lost territory, according to Robert W. Coon, then CTS director of human resources. Creating a company called Con-Way Northeast, CTS announced that the new carrier would serve the region formerly covered by Con-Way Eastern.[18] Concurrently, it readied Con-Way Central for eastern expansion expecting the unions to be disruptive to a new carrier.

"Con-Way Northeast appeared as a real, viable company. It was organized. We actually had a president named," Magnan added.[19]

Con-Way Central then expanded into Con-Way Eastern's former territory. The union could not raise the same legal objections against

Caught, Mike Yuenger, Con-Way Central Express' controller, displayed his collegiate loyalties during the early 1990s. A real "Cheesehead," Yuenger graduated from the University of Wisconsin and joined Con-Way Central in 1991.

Con-Way Central's presence as it could against a new company.

With little fanfare, Con-Way Central opened a terminal on the outskirts of Buffalo, New York, on October 1, 1992, sparking protests from the Teamsters who began picketing.[20] Con-Way Central President Gerald Detter announced the company would expand into 10 cities in Western and Central New York and Pennsylvania.[21]

The union filed a complaint with the National Labor Relations Board (NLRB) against Con-Way Central after the company refused job applications from four former Con-Way Eastern drivers who were also union members. The Teamsters began picketing the company's locations and accused Con-Way Central of trying to avoid Con-Way Eastern's labor contract.[22]

"One day we were having real problems with the union in the terminal outside Buffalo. We went to the courts and got an injunction against the Teamsters, who were encroaching on our property with their informational pickets," Coon said. He continued:

We took it to the police department to have it delivered, and the desk sergeant laughed

at us. He said, "You've got to be kidding." We asked, "Why?" He said, "Do you realize what union represents my police officers?" It was the Teamsters.[23]

The Buffalo Regional Office of the NLRB, however, ruled that the Teamsters' picketing violated labor laws. In late November 1992, a federal district judge backed the board's ruling and ordered the Teamsters to end the protest.[24]

The Teamsters responded by planning a national campaign against CTS and filed an appeal of the NLRB's decision.[25, 26] The union, however, was facing additional pressure as the Yellow Freight System of Delaware, then the largest LTL carrier, announced that it was buying Preston Corp., which was the holding compay for the highly profitable Saia Motor Freight of Louisiana. Roadway Services also announced that it was buying Central Freight Lines, the largest nonunion carrier in Texas.[27]

A CHILLY BUSINESS

IN SEPTEMBER 1993, CON-WAY TRANSPORTATION Services (CTS) signed a five-year deal with the Pallet Reefer Co. of Houma, Louisiana, where the Con-Way companies would be among the first in the LTL industry to use refrigerated containers, called pallet reefers. Pallet Reefer Co. was a joint venture between the inventor, Louis Saia III, and Grumman Allied of Montgomery, Pennsylvania, a subsidiary of Grumman Corp.[1]

Robert T. Robertson, president and CEO of CTS, believed pallet reefers would open new markets to the Con-Way companies, allowing the transport of chemicals, pharmaceuticals, foods, and other freight that required cooling.[2, 3]

"The pallet reefer was a product line we started to get into the refrigerated and frozen transportation market," said John Labrie, who

headed the program in January 1994. "The invention, an interesting concept, created a self-contained, cryogenically cooled unit designed to allow dry van carriers to handle LTL quantities of refrigerated and frozen product."[4]

The lockable, one-ton pallet reefers stood 7 feet tall and had a storage volume of 72.3 cubic feet.[5] With microprocessor-controlled cooling systems and four liquid carbon dioxide tanks to provide cooling down to minus 40 degrees Fahrenheit for up to 48 hours, the pallets were used at Con-Way Southern and Southwest, and phased into Con-Way Central and Western.[6, 7]

Although the pallet reefer program looked promising, moving empty containers and positioning them properly throughout the Con-Way system became problematic. Con-Way exited this business after Saia and Grumman Corp. became involved in a legal dispute, and the trucking company's access to new units and spare parts diminished.[8]

CTS sold its pallet reefers to Dippin' Dots Ice Cream, which had been a user of the Pallet Reefer Service.

Driver–Sales Representative Alex Stroinski stood next to a self-contained, refrigerated shipping container. These containers were a value-added service used briefly before they were sold to Dippin' Dots, a customer.

By December 1992, the ICC granted Con-Way Central's application to operate under Con-Way Northeast's operating authority.[28] In the meantime, Con-Way Central extended its service to Ontario, Canada, and Pennsylvania.[29]

The task of opening Con-Way Central's operations in Canada fell to Gary Vianueva. He had started at Con-Way Central in February 1984, becoming a regional manager at the Detroit service center. At the time, Con-Way Central's territory was "hot," because Detroit's automotive industry was rebounding from the early 1980s recession.[30]

"There wasn't much discussion. In a staff meeting in March or April of the same year, they told me, 'Vianueva, you'll open Canada by October 1992,'" he said.[31]

The first Ontario cities to be served by Con-Way Central were Toronto and London, which were within a two-hour drive from Detroit. Aside from hiring a team, Vianueva had to find facilities that were close to Canadian Customs.

"We would be dealing with international shipments that have to be cleared," Vianueva said. "You want to be in a bonded warehouse or be close to Canadian Customs so you're not losing a lot of travel time. Finding a location in Toronto wasn't too difficult. London, on the other hand, was more difficult. We ended up with warehouse space and trailers for an office."

Con-Way Central was relatively unknown in Canada. This caused difficulty in finding both employees to staff the Canadian locations and potential customers. Another difficulty was retaining workers, as trucking firms in Canada typically experienced a high turnover rate.[32]

"We had an engaged sales force in the United States selling Canadian-bound freight, but we initially had more incoming than outgoing," Vianueva said. "It was slow starting. Once we started moving freight and dealing with customers, we succeeded in Canada."

THE TEAMSTERS' PROTEST

Under Teamsters' President Ron Carey, the union began lobbying CF Inc.'s major institutional investors before the company's 1993 stockholders' meeting at the Pan Pacific Hotel in San Francisco, claiming that the expansion of the Con-Ways was

Gary Vianueva, who joined Con-Way Central in 1984, was responsible for opening Con-Way Central's first terminals in Canada.

at the expense of CF MotorFreight.[33] The union also rallied CF MotorFreight workers, who controlled 13 percent of CF Inc. stock, to submit a number of proposals aimed at weakening the Con-Ways. All of the union's efforts failed.[34]

Although one trade magazine called the 90-minute shareholders' meeting "orderly," Moffitt recalled it as contentious.[35] About 400 to 500 Teamsters attended, along with Carey. Despite concerns of CF officials, Moffitt went to meet Carey, who didn't immediately recognize the CF president and CEO.

"It began to dawn on [Carey] that I'm the guy that they came to trash, but they didn't know what to do," Moffitt said. "At the meeting, they started yelling and screaming. The San Francisco Police

Donald E. Moffitt (right), CF Inc. president and CEO, presented a $115,000 check to the Boy Scouts in 1994. Teaming up with Moffitt are (left to right): Life Scout Paul Stooksberry (son of Con-Way Western Account Manager Paul Stooksberry), Life Scout Jake Riley, Boy Scouts of America Finance Director Walter T. Weaver, and Cub Scout Jack Allen (son of CF Inc. Vice President Jim Allen). Seated is Mike Riley, Jake's father and account manager for CF MotorFreight.

grabbed me and were trying to take me out through a side door, and somebody grabbed me from behind. I never knew who it was. The police pulled him off me and led me out."[36]

Because the Teamsters had no direct influence on the Con-Way companies, they protested CF MotorFreight whenever operational changes were proposed.

"They'd say, 'Okay, give us Con-Way, and we'll approve a change in operations,'" Moffitt added.

Although CF Inc.'s financial condition was improving, the corporation posted a net loss of $97.7 million in 1992.[37] The corporation's bottom line was hurt by a fourth-quarter loss of $11.8 million at CF MotorFreight and a full-year loss of $32.7 million at Emery.

On the bright side, Moffitt reported that CF Inc. had reduced its debt by $164 million, while its common stock price had rebounded from $9.50 in December to the $17.25 range by the time of the shareholders' meeting.[38] Emery signed a 10-year, $880 million contract with the U.S. Postal Service in early 1994. Also, CTS had an operating income of $53.7 million in 1992, making it "the third-most profitable company in the trucking industry," Moffitt noted.[39]

But the future for traditional long-haul companies was uncertain, according to a freight analyst with Merrill Lynch in New York, who claimed that the market would continue to lose business to United Parcel Service, Roadway

Package Service, railroads, airfreight, and truck-load carriers.[40]

CON-WAY'S 10TH ANNIVERSARY

In 1993, the Con-Way companies celebrated their 10th anniversary. Robertson reflected:

We have earned the respect of the market because Con-Way people have demonstrated their commitment to common goals of integrity, quality, and reliable error-free service that provides a competitive advantage to our customers. ... Our history of growth and accomplishment is a testament to the personal pride and dedication of Con-Way employees.[41]

Its regional trucking companies had exceeded its original goal of 95 percent on-time, next-day service, achieving a 98 percent rate.[42]

One of the shining examples of the four regional carriers was Con-Way Central. With approximately $300 million in sales, it was one of the most successful companies in the regional LTL business,

according to an industry analyst.[43] Since its inception, Con-Way Central had an average annual growth in revenues of 34 percent, although it slowed to about a 20 percent growth rate during the early 1990s recession. By 1993, Con-Way Central operated 5,000 trucks, tractors, and trailers in 153 terminals, serving 42,000 communities in 13 states and Ontario, Canada, and also employed 4,026 people. CTS' revenues exceeded $750 million in 1993, and it was the most profitable trucking company in the United States.

"We took a position that failure is not acceptable," Robertson said. "We have changed the way business is done in a regional environment."[44]

According to Don Gold, a distribution manager at the Wixom, Michigan, office of Stanley Bostitch Inc., a manufacturer of fastening systems, his company was more than satisfied with Con-Way's performance.

"I'll be honest—we haven't had one damage claim in the last two years," explained Gold. "And the products are delivered 100 percent on time."[45]

JOINING FORCES

As the smallest of the Con-Ways, Con-Way Southwest was locked in fierce competition with Arkansas Freightways (later called American Freightways before it was absorbed into FedEx Freight), noted Hickerson, Con-Way Southwest president. By 1992, Con-Way Southwest had saturated its five-state market, but needed to expand into other states to meet customer requests.

In 1993, Con-Way Southwest launched a $3.4 million terminal expansion to double its freight capacity. This project included constructing a 160-door freight processing facility on a 20-acre site in Dallas to replace its 80-door terminal. The new terminal included a 65,000-square-foot freight dock, 37,000 square feet of office space, and would employ 250 people with an equipment pool of 85 tractors and 250 trailers.[46] The company moved its Fort Worth, Texas, operations from a 30-door to an 80-door facility. By this time, the company had 47 service centers in eight states.

TEN YEARS

AND ROLLING...

THE CON-WAY

COMPANIES

In 1993, the Con-Way companies celebrated their 10th anniversary.

Above: Tom Smith (left), president and CEO of Con-Way Southern Express, and John Hickerson (right), president and CEO of Con-Way Southwest, worked together to merge the two companies seamlessly.

Left: Robert T. Robertson, president and CEO of Con-Way Transportation Services, in 1993.

Although Con-Way Southern and Con-Way Western already were operating in the states adjacent to Southwest's territory, the companies were not able to interchange freight with one another. This restriction was embedded in the founding mission of the regional LTL carriers—they were not to compete with CF MotorFreight.

Con-Way Southern Express and Con-Way Southwest were sharing a terminal in Memphis, Tennessee, but a physical wall separated the employees. The cultures of the Con-Way companies were noticeably different, with the employees taking pride in their own company rather than in the whole organization.[47]

"Our companies were defined by location codes," recalled Ed Conaway, who had become Con-Way Southwest's vice president of operations in 1993:

CCX service center codes start with an X. Southern started with an N, and if you were in Charlotte, your service center was NCH. Southwest was an L. People defined themselves as N people or L people. People would try to define me as an L because I was with Southwest. I said, "Oh, no, I'm a 'U' guy because I started at Western."[48]

In late 1992, Hickerson approached Robertson and asked if it would be possible to open five terminals in Alabama to meet customer requests for additional service. Alabama, however, was Con-Way Southern's territory. Instead, Robertson asked Hickerson and Con-Way Southern

President Tom Smith to develop a plan to interchange freight.

"It was sort of blasphemy at that point, but I said, 'We can do it,' " Hickerson said.[49]

Hickerson and his team met with Smith's people in Charlotte, and within 24 hours they created a plan to allow these two Con-Ways to interchange freight without spending any expansion capital. The move would catapult the Con-Ways into the long-haul business—and into competition with CF MotorFreight, which would upset the Teamsters.[50]

Although concerned that the Teamsters would accuse the company of illegal "double breasting" and rally its workers to shut down CF MotorFreight, Con-Way Southwest and Con-Way Southern began interchanging freight in early 1993. The union complained, but there weren't any wildcat strikes.[51]

"At that point, we literally began to compete with Consolidated Freightways for longer haul freight," Hickerson added. "All of a sudden, we exponentially expanded our market punch with no infrastructure or employee investment."[52]

With the interchange of freight, in the latter half of 1994, Con-Way Transportation Services introduced its own generic 28-foot trailers and dolly converters. The white trailers were painted with two gray stripes down the sides and the words "Con-Way Transportation Services." Additionally, the doorframe, rear, subframe, landing gear, hubs, and wheels were painted gray.

"We always called them the 'gray ghost' trailers," said Wayne Byerley, who was in charge of purchasing equipment for CTS in the mid-1990s. "They were designed to fit with the different company colors at the time. We had called the Con-Ways our rainbow truck line, which had blue and gold, brown and orange, and green and turquoise."[53]

Soon afterward, Con-Way Southwest began interchanging freight with Con-Way Western. However, it was not until April 20, 1998, that Con-Way Central began interchanging freight with Western.

THE 1994 TEAMSTERS' STRIKE

In 1993, CF Inc. climbed solidly into the black with a strong performance by CTS that generated an operating income of $71.9 million while its gross revenues increased by 34 percent to $818.3 million.[54] Emery's operating income increased to $16.6 million on revenues of $1.26 billion. CF MotorFreight had $2.5 million in net income in the fourth quarter of 1993, even though its gross revenues for the quarter fell 1 percent to $532.1 million. Its stock price had climbed to $26.63 in March 1994, although it was still below its pre-Emery acquisition mark of $37.75.[55]

However, the corporation's labor relations deteriorated. About 80 Teamsters attempted to enter CF Inc.'s Palo Alto headquarters on January 21, 1994, but were locked out. The labor members threw toilet paper around the exterior of the building before police escorted them away.[56] Moffitt immediately penned a letter to Carey asking for payment for the cost of cleanup, adding that his teenagers thought the prank was funny.

Trucking Management Inc. (TMI), the industry's bargaining organization, and the union were now locked in a bitter disagreement. Among its demands, TMI wanted to trim starting wages from $14.45 per hour to $11.40 to reduce costs, use part-time help during peak periods, and gain the right to use more intermodal transit. The Teamsters opposed the job cuts and fought against part-time workers performing union jobs. Carey was also struggling with opposition from within his own union.[57]

Negotiations dragged on until the end of the contract on March 31, 1994, when TMI offered a revised proposal to increase wages by 13 percent during the next four years. It also limited intermodal operations and restricted the use of part-time employees. The proposal was rejected. About 80,000 drivers, dockworkers, mechanics, and other union members set up picket lines at 12:01 A.M. on April 6. The 24-day strike was damaging to both sides, as the union spent $28 million from its strike fund, and the unionized carriers faced losses.[58]

Analysts projected that the "Big Three"— Roadway, Yellow, and Consolidated Freightways—

A Con-Way Central semi-tractor trailer is parked near a generic "gray ghost" trailer. Although these trailers are interchangeable among the Con-Way companies, they were a color uncharacteristic of the Con-Way's "rainbow line" of vehicles.

each lost about $10 million in daily revenues. During the strike, one of TMI's members, Churchill Truck Lines, closed its doors permanently.[59]

The Teamsters won guarantees to protect workers who might have lost their jobs to intermodal operations, plus a $3.20 per hour wage and benefit increase over the life of the contract. In turn, the carriers could reduce costs by using "piggyback" rail operations and gained the option to supplement the regular workforce with casual workers.[60]

The strike, although detrimental to CF Motor-Freight, was a financial boon to the nonunion Con-Way companies. These companies struggled to transport the enormous influx of freight to meet the needs of customers affected by the long-haul strike.

ALL HANDS ON DECK

At Con-Way Central's Toledo service center, manager Bob Bull remembered calling Bryan Millican, vice president of sales, to tell him that trailers were arriving with freight, but he had no way to transport it.

"I said, 'Bryan, if they keep bringing this stuff in here, I'm going to start stacking it out in the yard because I don't have the equipment to put it on to move it,'" Bull said.[61]

"I was vice president of national sales, and I was in Chicago at that time," said David S. McClimon, who was with Con-Way Central. He recalled:

We called customers to try to schedule freight deliveries. People were working 20-hour days and doing extraordinary things to address the influx of freight. We had to look for ways that we could limit the amount of freight we were bringing in. We'd only pick up a certain number of shipments from customers, certain size shipments. It couldn't be over 5,000 pounds ... trying to limit the amount of freight because there was just so much there. So much of the industry was unionized, and they had

Con-Way Central employees and their children participated in the annual spring spruce up in May 1996. Throughout the month, employees, friends, and family painted and cleaned the terminals.

shut down. It all went to predominantly smaller companies like ourselves who were union-free.[62]

After a short while, Con-Way Central focused on delivering freight for its core customers first, while limiting the number of new customer shipments to avoid further gridlock on the dock.[63] Other nonunion LTL carriers took advantage of the opportunity, accepting all the freight that they could—and over-saturating their systems, unable to handle the unusually high volumes.[64] Con-Way Central resorted to hiring people they wouldn't have otherwise had circumstances been normal.

"We got sloppy in some of our disciplined processes," McClimon explained. "It took a considerable amount of time to get back the discipline and the processes to the service levels that we saw just prior to that strike. It was a learning experience."[65]

The Con-Ways had built a reputation on superior service, with an on-time delivery rate of more than 98 percent, according to Ned Moritz, then CTS director of marketing.

"When that strike hit, it was impossible to keep up," Moritz explained.[66]

According David Miller, Con-Way Central's southwest regional manager during the time of the strike, service levels fell to 93.7 percent.[67] To move the freight, Con-Way Central President Gerald Detter made an "all hands on deck" call.

"Everybody stopped what they were doing in their day-to-day activities, went out, and, literally, moved freight," remembered Kay Beher, then Con-Way Central's office manager. "The system was so clogged. Customers were clamoring at the door, and phones were ringing off the hook."[68]

Even inside sales people were sent out into the "ordered chaos," said Pat Jannausch, who was Con-Way Central's manager of training in 1994.

"I remember sending some of them out," Jannausch said. "Jerry [Detter] came in, had them all line up one day during the strike, and asked, 'OK, who's ready to go out and hump freight? Who can go home and pack their toothbrush and a couple of pair of underwear and meet me back here this afternoon? We'll have plane tickets ready.' Off they went into the fray, and some of them got the best training of their lives."[69]

Freight also logjammed at Con-Way Southwest as its freight tonnages increased by 40 to 50

Pat Jannausch, manager of training, Con-Way Central Express, circa 1996. In July 1993, Jannausch was named manager of training for Con-Way Central and also worked with Con-Way Transportation Services to develop training programs for all CTS subsidiaries.

percent overnight as shipments poured in from Con-Way Western and Con-Way Southern, recalled Daryl Lafitte, who was a supervisor. Lafitte had started at Con-Way Southwest in 1989 as a driver–sales representative.

"At Southwest, we set up what we called 'the cavalry,'" Lafitte said. "Groups out of various service centers, say, close to Dallas or Houston or Shreveport, would team up and go work at the freight assembly centers every weekend to help push freight through. ... It was all hands on deck."[70]

Con-Way Central's business grew by approximately 30 percent during the strike. Afterward, many shippers returned to their original motor carriers, but many others had realized the quality of service that the Con-Ways offered, Miller said. Con-Way Central held onto about 80 percent of its strike growth.[71] The Con-Way workers were also rewarded when their incentive compensation checks were increased to the maximum for the year.[72]

STRIKE AFTERMATH

Regional carriers had become successful because small, rapid deliveries allowed customers to keep inventories low. About 90 percent of CTS shipments were next-day deliveries. Warehousing was also on a downward trend, with many goods being shipped directly to end-use customers.[73]

One result of the strike was another round of federal deregulation. President Bill Clinton's administration announced that the U.S. Department of Transportation (DOT) would be cut while in August the Republican-controlled Congress passed a bill to eliminate the Interstate Commerce Commission (ICC) by January 1, 1995. The legislation, which Clinton signed, also lifted most intrastate commerce restrictions, including regulating carrier entry, operations, areas of service, and pricing for intrastate shipping. However, states still had oversight of safety, truck size and weight,

financial responsibility, and rules for transporting hazardous materials.[74, 75]

"The act that ended the ICC allowed the carriers to use any pricing they wanted, any place they wanted, or to adopt the old rate bureau system," Moritz said later. "Between August 1994 and January 1, 1995, we—consultants and a lot of people in our IT department—created a whole new system. That's when what we called Con-Way Express rate came out. Since then, it has been our pricing system covering the whole United States and Canada."[76]

When the accountants examined the costs of the 1994 strike, CF MotorFreight had lost more than $46 million by April 1994. CF Inc. cancelled a $50 million planned expansion of its fleet to trim costs. The long-haul carrier also consolidated operations at 65 terminals and closed 22 facilities.[77]

Moffitt replaced longtime CF executive Robert Lawrence, then president of CF MotorFreight, because the carrier slipped behind Roadway and

CON-WAY INTERMODAL

PART OF CON-WAY INTERMODAL'S (CWI) STRATegy was to grow its European operations. In 1992, 15 percent of Con-Way's customers were shipping to Europe, and the business was expected to grow rapidly.[1] CF had a presence in Europe since acquiring Kam Container Lines a decade before—Kam was one of the units that formed CWI.

Using regularly scheduled ocean services, CWI used its hub in Rotterdam to tie into trucking networks in Belgium, France, Germany, Spain, Italy, Switzerland, Malta, and Scandinavia.[2] CWI also linked to the four regional Con-Way carriers to expedite cargo movements to ports in Atlanta, Chicago, Houston, New York, and Long Beach, California. From the ports, CWI operated like a non-vessel common carrier.

It began its Con-Quest expedited stack train service and door-to-door delivery for truckload shipments in 1992. CWI signed operating agreements with the Atchison, Topeka & Santa Fe, Union Pacific, Conrail, Norfolk Southern, and Burlington Northern railroads, creating a nationwide intermodal transportation network.[3]

In 1993, CWI planned to invest $4.9 million to purchase 350 new 48-foot-long, 9-foot-high rail containers and 300 chassis to add to its Con-Quest fleet. The company also opened a new Dallas–Atlanta service route; a link to Columbus, Ohio; a route from Charlotte, North Carolina, to Jacksonville, Florida; and a next-day link between Chicago and Memphis, Tennessee, via the Illinois Central Railroad.[4] The following year, CWI spent another $4.46 million to purchase an additional 300 intermodal containers and 300 chassis, bringing its Con-Quest fleet to a total of 900 containers and 650 chassis, anticipating that the federal government's Intermodal Surface Transportation Efficiency Act (ISTEA, pronounced Ice-Tea) would open additional business along the East

Yellow in profitability. First, he turned to Bob Robertson, but the head of the Con-Ways declined the offer. Next, Moffitt called Curry, who was in Hawaii on his first vacation since his appointment with Emery. Curry accepted the job.[78]

CONTEMPLATING A SPLIT

The idea for cleaving CF Inc. into separate pieces was based on Chemical Bank's "rescue plan" to bail the company out of its financial crisis in 1990. It had included selling off Emery and spinning off CTS from CF MotorFreight.[79] After the 1994 Teamsters' strike and the continued problems at the long-haul carrier, Moffitt knew that change was in order.

"We had to do something. We had to get out of it," Moffitt said.[80]

Approaching the board of directors in 1994, Moffitt first raised the idea of decoupling CF Motor-Freight from the rest of the corporation. He explained:

This was one of the real critical decision points in my entire life. I'm sitting here with the most profitable nonunion company in the world, and I'm sitting on a really large market share in with a union carrier. What am I going to do?

From a shareholder standpoint, the best thing is to split it up, give the shareholders from one company union and shareholders from another company nonunion, and let it go. This is where I made my good decisions and my bad decisions.[81]

The board and the management decided not to pursue the split at the time, as the carrier instead underwent a major restructuring effort.

CF MOTORFREIGHT CHANGES STRATEGY

CF MotorFreight's Freight Flow System, which was created as a long-haul business, was not efficient or cost effective in transporting

A Con-Way Intermodal truck with a Con-Quest container is parked on a viaduct above a Santa Fe locomotive.

Coast.[5] Taking effect in December 1991, ISTEA provided highway and transit funding and collaborative planning requirements for intermodal projects.

Con-Quest used double-stack rail cars, which allow containers to be stacked two high, and offered improved economies of scale to shippers, akin to how tandem trailers improved the efficiency of motor freight transportation.[6] CWI also expanded its coverage to Argentina and Chile with weekly ocean sailings for less-than–container load and full-container shipments.[7]

CWI, renamed on April 25, 1995, as Con-Way Truckload Services, began providing dedicated regional, inter-regional, and expedited transcontinental highway truckload freight service along with its rail intermodal capabilities. Con-Way Transportation Services invested another $25 million in the subsidiary, adding 175 tractors and 150 53-foot highway trailers to its fleet, plus new tracking and system management technology.[8]

In addition to Con-Quest, Con-Way Truckload launched its Express Service, providing expedited next-day and second-day deliveries to customers in 1995.

regional freight. Competitors also realized the problems of their own hub-and-spoke systems. Many former long-haul companies began competing in the short-haul market because price erosion and overcapacity (the number of carriers in the market had grown from 12,000 in 1980 to about 35,000 by 1994) were shrinking the transcontinental LTL segment.[82]

As manufacturers and retailers focused on just-in-time deliveries to reduce inventory costs, long-haul carriers lost business to regional carriers, according to Phillip Seeley, CF MotorFreight's vice president of sales and marketing. Running freight through a consolidation terminal could add 20 hours to transit time.[83]

CF MotorFreight closed about 250 freight terminals in 1995.[84] Drastic changes were needed to sustain the carrier. Curry advocated Network 2000, a freight-moving system designed by new Executive Vice President of Operations Patrick H. Blake. Under Blake's plan, freight would be rehandled no more than once as it moved in a more direct manner to its final destination.

Cargoes would only remain on the docks for six hours or less, instead of 24 hours, and would be moved according to priority rather than first-in, first-out.[85] The carrier also began moving trailers out at midnight regardless of the amount of freight instead of holding them only to fill the space completely. Quick, efficient service became the focus.

The Teamsters resisted the changes at CF MotorFreight, as a layoff of about 1,000 workers was also planned. The implementation of Network 2000 was ultimately delayed because of union negotiations, and instead of beginning during July, a slow month, the rollout was pushed into the fall. Curry could have waited another year, but instead went ahead with the plan, wary that another delay could affect implementation completely. The company was now moving toward efficiency and effectively attempting to compete with the Con-Ways in the short-haul market.

In 1995, CF Inc. officials revisited a potential spin-off of CF MotorFreight. However, because the long-haul carrier suffered heavy losses and was $100 million in debt due to the delay in initiating Network 2000, it could not be effectively marketed.[86]

MERGING CON-WAYS AND CULTURE

Toward the end of 1994, Tom Smith—Con-Way Southern's founding president—decided to retire. Instead of appointing a new president to the company, CTS merged the Con-Way Southern and Southwest operations. John Hickerson was chosen to run the combined organization.[87]

In November 1994, CTS announced that Con-Way Southern and Southwest would merge at the beginning of 1995, and would keep the name Con-Way Southern Express.

"When we faced the circumstances of the strike ... our companies' reaction to that and our employees' reaction to that were so phenomenal, it really opened our eyes as to what we could become," explained Phil Worthington, who was appointed president of Con-Way Southern Express in 2005. "It made the case for us that it made a lot more sense for us to act as one synergistic unit versus two entities."[88]

Operating in 13 states, the merged company had 101 terminals covering a roughly triangular area bounded by Baltimore, Miami, and El Paso, Texas, with 3,800 employees and 6,270 pieces of equipment.[89]

"The hardest part of putting those two companies together was closing the general office in Charlotte because most people did not move to Dallas. More than 100 people lost their jobs," Ed Conaway recalled.[90]

It took several years to blend the two company cultures together, Conaway admitted, but management took care to promote people in such a way as to minimize rivalries and grow a sense of teamwork.[91]

About the same time the two southern Con-Ways merged, the wall at the Memphis terminal was torn down as Con-Way Southern and Con-Way Southwest began interchanging freight.[92]

ADDITIONAL EXPANSION

When federal deregulation stripped the states of their powers to regulate intrastate trucking rates and routes, the Con-Way companies embarked on a series of expansions. Con-Way Western entered the Pacific Northwest, the traditional territory of CF MotorFreight.[93]

At the Hagerstown Service Center on March 16, 1995, Con-Way Central driver Paul Smith (left) and Con-Way Southern driver Phil Carter demonstrated the integration of the two companies after they began exchanging freight.

In early 1995, as part of a $9 million expansion, Con-Way Western opened 22 terminals in Oregon, Washington, Idaho, and British Columbia, Canada. Con-Way Western's network stretched from Canada to Mexico, and from the Pacific Ocean to New Mexico, Colorado, and Utah. At that time, it employed 2,500 and operated a fleet of 3,600 trucks, tractors, and trailers, while providing either overnight or second-day delivery service.[94, 95]

Using Lynden Transport as an extension of its network, Con-Way Western expanded its reach to Alaska, via containership from the port of Fife, Washington.[96]

In November 1995, Con-Way Western President George C. Reid left the company and was replaced by Charles E. "Chip" Boone, a 13-year veteran of Con-Way. He was vice president of operations for Con-Way Southwest and assisted in its launch in November 1989, and its subsequent merger with Con-Way Southern.[97]

Bolstered by the increase in business from the 1994 Teamsters strike, Con-Way Central constructed a $12 million, 85,000-square-foot terminal on 26 acres in Plainfield, Indiana. The 165-door facility, one of Con-Way Central's largest service cen-

ters, employed 150 people and doubled its freight handling capacity in the region. It was nearly four times the size of Con-Way Central's original Indianapolis terminal and could handle nearly 3 million pounds of freight a day.[98, 99]

Also in 1995, Con-Way Central opened two new service centers in Vermont; a new terminal in Campbellsville, Kentucky; two in Maine; a 15-door terminal in Sioux City and a four-door service center in Fort Dodge, Iowa; a 22-door facility in Chillicothe, Missouri; a 12-door facility in Alma, Michigan; a 14-door facility in Rock Falls, Illinois; six new service centers in North Dakota; and 21 facilities in Kansas, Nebraska, and South Dakota as part of a $5 million expansion. Before year's end, Con-Way Central had 222 service centers in the central and eastern United States that covered more than 70,000 points of service.[100]

In the early part of 1996, Con-Way Central launched a $5 million expansion to open service facilities in six locations in the Canadian province of Quebec, including Montreal, Quebec City, and Hull.[101] By mid-1996, Con-Way Central introduced its "Superior Service Lanes" for next-day deliveries up to 625 miles—two-day service had been considered the standard for shipments traveling beyond 500 miles.[102]

"It's a fundamental line-haul change to get freight further in an overnight environment," said Dick Palazzo, vice president of operations for Con-Way Central. "We have a real leg up in these markets. Nobody is pushing overnight service in these lengths of haul. Nobody is pushing the envelope further."

That July, Con-Way Central also inaugurated a new service link to Puerto Rico with scheduled steamship service from Elizabeth, New Jersey, while Con-Way Southern also expanded its service to the island departing from Florida.[103]

In October 1996, Con-Way Western was selected by Home Depot as its primary carrier for freight shipments between the retailer's 1,000 vendors and its 130 stores in the west. Con-Way Central also became Home Depot's backup carrier in its Midwest region, encompassing Minnesota, Wisconsin, Iowa, Missouri, Kansas, Illinois, Indiana, and Michigan.[104]

TECHNOLOGICAL EVOLUTION

In the early 1990s, the freight business was still a paper-intensive industry. The ICC required that trucking companies keep shipping documents on file for three years. CF MotorFreight and the Con-Way companies needed to store nearly 150 million pieces of paper, which required associated tasks that consumed about 500,000 man-hours annually. To ease the record-keeping nightmare, the long-haul and regional companies began using an improved image-processing system to file, store, and retrieve shipping records in 1991, well ahead of most.[105]

Con-Way Intermodal followed suit in 1992 and began using image-processing technology, shaving up to 10 days from the time it took to provide customers with copies of the bills of lading or receipts for proof of delivery, noted James R. Hertwig, president of Con-Way Intermodal. This system also sped up payments to the company.

Files older than six months were stored off-line and could be retrieved within one day.[106]

Con-Way Intermodal's computers in Fort Worth, Texas, were linked to the railroads' mainframe computers, allowing Con-Quest customers up-to-the-minute tracking with periodic updates 24 hours a day. This was important for customers operating with "just-in-time" manufacturing or "quick response" retail restocking systems.

The other Con-Way companies relied on Consolidated Freightways IT department. In August 1994, CTS became one of the first freight trucking companies to launch a home page on the Internet. The site was an information resource for customers, noted Carlos G. Fallas, executive vice president of sales and marketing. The Web site had e-mail capability, allowing visitors to ask about service standards, transit times, rates, specialized services and locations of business, as well as bid proposal information.[107]

In 1996, CTS launched its own IT group, based in Portland, Oregon, starting with about 40 people, noted Jackie Barretta, who joined CTS in 1996 as a systems analyst.[108] Barretta became the seventh employee of the Con-Way IT group, which grew to 190 employees within a few years.[109]

The previous information systems were not designed for Con-Way operations. Con-Way's IT group was charged with laying the foundation for a better system, according to Barretta, who became Con-Way Inc.'s chief information officer nine years later.[110]

"The old systems didn't talk to each other," Barretta said, explaining that information about the status of equipment or shipments had to be entered under separate programs, which required numerous manually keyed transactions. "We integrated all of those systems. We replaced all of the CF-based systems and made them much easier to work with."[111]

EXPEDITED SERVICE

Although the Con-Way companies consistently exceeded their on-time, next-day delivery goals of 95 percent, some shippers depended on expedited—also called emergency—services to maintain facilities that practiced just-in-time inventories and production. This type of expedited, LTL delivery had risen to about 26 percent of the LTL market, which totaled $16 billion in 1996, and CTS predicted it would expand to more than $19 billion by 1998. With an obvious market niche to fill, Con-Way NOW debuted in the Midwest in August 1996.[112]

With a $7 million investment from CTS, Con-Way NOW was based in Ann Arbor, Michigan, and started with a fleet of 125 vehicles that included Ford Taurus station wagons, Ford Econoline vans, and cargo trailers.[113] The division employed 250 on-call drivers and independent contractors who deployed from 30 staging areas in nine Midwestern states, noted Doug Stotlar, then vice president and general manager of Con-Way NOW[114]:

That company was a great lesson for me because we deviated from what the market norms were in that business. Instead of just trying to make a better mousetrap under the market norms, we tried to reinvent the whole wheel, and over time, we had to pull the spokes out of the wheel and re-spoke it. But we did start by putting some contractors in, and ultimately converted that whole company over to an owner/operator model, which was what was standard in the industry.[115]

The plan was to grow the business throughout the United States and Canada. Con-Way NOW offered a 50 percent discount for shipments that were more than two hours late. Shipments more than four hours late were free.[116] There were some missteps, such as the company's sales model, which was not much different from the LTL market, according to Stotlar.

"The value proposition was so much different that the market didn't catch on," he added. "It was Ed Conaway that really got the sales model fixed when he took over."[117]

Stotlar's Con-Way NOW, however, was not the first time that a Con-Way company had used the "NOW" expedited service idea. In 1994, Con-Way Western had launched its NOW Service that pro-

In 1993, Driver–Sales Representative Tim Bausch of Con-Way Central's Quad Cities terminal surveyed the damage of the Mississippi flood from his John Deere tractor. The "Noah's Flood Relief" campaign (inset) was sponsored by Con-Way Central and the University of Michigan to assist those affected by the flood. Donations of diapers, bottled water, and canned goods were transported by Con-Way Central's Jackson/Ann Arbor service center to the American Red Cross in St. Louis.

When I say **NOW,** I mean **NOW.**

At CWX we know when it has to be there.

Con-Way NOW Service, introduced in 1995, offered expedited service. The original employees of Con-Way NOW, in 1996, from left to right: Jim Fishpaw, Rob Schwalm, "Clay" the mannequin with the Con-Way NOW uniform, Matt Kloss, Michelle Potter, and Doug Stotlar.

vided shippers with a guaranteed delivery within two hours of the quoted arrival time or the delivery would be free. Con-Way Western used its own drivers and equipment, however.[118]

THE SPLIT DECISION

After a few years of indecisiveness, CF Inc. announced in August 1996 that the company would split from CF MotorFreight on December 2. The unionized CF MotorFreight long-haul unit, with 1995 revenues of $2.4 billion, would become the new Consolidated Freightways Corp.[119]

Much of the old CF Inc., including Con-Way Transportation Services, Menlo Logistics, and

Emery Worldwide, would remain under its old parent company, which was renamed CNF Transportation Inc. ("CNF" was the corporation's ticker symbol on the New York Stock Exchange. The word "Transportation" was later dropped from the company name as well.) As a separate entity, CNF's 1995 revenues were $2.9 billion, with an operating income of $178.3 million.

As the spin-off date approached, CF MotorFreight saw its stock price rise 16 percent. The "new" Consolidated Freightways would be the third largest of the long-haul carriers with 373 locations in 50 states, a fleet of 40,800 trucks, tractors, and trailers and approximately 21,000 employees. With Curry at the helm, Consolidated Freight established itself in the old Menlo Park headquarters building, and its board of directors included Raymond O'Brien, whose presence was thought to reassure investors and employees.

Staffing the new operations was a challenge. In one case, the technical staff in Portland, Oregon, was divided between CNF and Consolidated Freightways in a manner similar to a sports league draft, remembered Dave Anderson, who retired as human resources director of CNF Inc. in 2004.

"On Labor Day weekend in 1996, we sat around the table with the management of Consolidated Freightways, Emery, and Con-Way, and we went through every employee in Portland—all 2,000—and did an NFL-style draft name by name," Anderson said. "We flipped a coin, and CNF Inc. got to pick an employee and then Consolidated Freightways picked an employee until we had drafted out all management and hourly employees working in Portland."[120]

Curry said that he was "excited and optimistic" about the new CF in spite of it remaining a unionized company.[121] The Teamsters also applauded the spin-off, saying that its members "will now be working for management whose own fate is tied to the success of the unionized company."[122]

WEEK OF JUNE 2, 1997 $5.00

traffic

W🌐RLD

THE LOGISTICS NEWS WEEKLY

A coalition of shippers and truckload carriers wants to increase the maximum federal weight limit for trucks to 97,000 pounds. **Page 14**

Brazil is booming. So is the capacity being poured into the market by scheduled and charter carriers alike. **Page 26**

TRUCKING'S 'ROLLS ROYCE'

Shippers agree the total Con-Way package is often not the cheapest, but its combination of value and service is tough to beat.

See Page 10

CHAPTER EIGHT

BALANCING EARTH AND SKY

1997–2001

Without Leland James, CNF would never have been founded. Without Raymond O'Brien, this company would never have entered the modern era so successfully and with so much integrity. But without Donald Moffitt, there would be no CNF today. This company would not even exist.

—Gregory L. Quesnel
CNF Transportation Inc., president and CEO[1]

IN JANUARY 1997, SHORTLY AFTER Consolidated Freightways was spun-off as an independent long-haul carrier, CNF Chairman, President, and CEO Donald E. Moffitt, the Con-Way presidents, and other CNF Transportation executives traveled to meet with investors in four cities to highlight the "new" company's accomplishments. For the first time in nearly a decade, the parent corporation was on sound financial footing. Con-Way Transportation Services operated the leading and most profitable regional carriers in the industry.[2]

Menlo Logistics was growing at a rate of 30 percent a year, and Emery Worldwide was the No. 1 domestic air cargo carrier and the largest U.S.-based international airfreight carrier.[3]

Since 1994, the Con-Way companies had a presence in all 50 states, several Canadian provinces, Mexico, and Puerto Rico. Con-Way spent $322 million on capital expenditures between 1994 and 1997, dwarfing that of the four biggest unionized carriers.[4]

CHANGE OF COMMAND

Two of the newest members of CNF's board of directors were Keith Kennedy Jr. and William J. Schroeder. Kennedy, who was president and CEO of Watkins–Johnson Company, a manufacturer of equipment and electronic products for the telecom-

munications and defense industries, had been invited to join the board by Raymond O'Brien. Recruited by Moffitt, Schroeder was president and CEO of Diamond Multimedia Systems, with experience in the software and telecommunications industries.

"[Schroeder and I] both came from the electronics industries of Silicon Valley," Kennedy said. "There was a thought at the time that one of CNF's biggest growth areas was going to be Menlo Logistics, which included software and logistics. Bill and I had experience in that type of business."[5]

During the winter of 1996–1997, the nearly 65-year-old Moffitt told the CNF board of directors that he wanted to retire as CEO by the April 1998 board meeting, but remain on as chairman. The board interviewed a number of candidates to succeed him, including Robert T. Robertson, president and CEO of Con-Way Transportation Services; Gregory

---

Above: Gregory L. Quesnel was named president and CEO of CNF Transportation Inc. in 1998.

Opposite: *Traffic World* magazine identified CTS as one of the best trucking companies in the United States in terms of profitability and quality of customer service. *(Photo courtesy of Traffic World, Commonwealth Business Media.)*

L. Quesnel, CNF's chief financial officer; and David I. Beatson, who was hired to run Emery after Roger Curry was moved to CF MotorFreight.[6]

Although Robertson was well respected, there were concerns that he had little experience with the board, as a number of new members had joined in 1997.[7] The choice was narrowed to 49-year-old Quesnel, who had 23 years of experience with the corporation when he was promoted to president and chief operating officer on July 1, 1997. Quesnel took over the CEO title in the spring of 1998.

Sanchayan "Chutta" Ratnathicam, a veteran of CF AirFreight and later Emery, was appointed chief financial officer.[8]

Above: Robert T. Robertson, president and CEO of Con-Way Transportation Services, posed with the driver of Unit 432-5155 that was the 2 millionth truck produced at Ford's Kentucky Truck Plant on May 16, 1995. A special ceremony was held at the factory as Con-Way personnel took possession of the tractor that was painted in Con-Way Central's colors.

Right: In the late 1990s, Norm Wallace, Con-Way Central's manager of freight flow, challenged the freight assembly centers to increase trailer load factors, which were averaging a little more than 15,000 pounds per load. Wallace, a 14-year veteran of Con-Way Central, stands by his namesake "King of the Hill" trophy.

Robertson resigned. Gerald L. Detter, who had led Con-Way Central to become the largest of the Con-Way carriers, was appointed president and CEO of Con-Way Transportation Services, which oversaw all of the regional carriers, in late July 1997.

Dick Palazzo succeeded Detter at the helm of Con-Way Central. At the time, Palazzo was a 35-year veteran of the transportation industry and had been vice president of operations for Con-Way Central Express. Detter had chosen Palazzo to help form the carrier in 1982, and Palazzo was involved in starting up every service center including site selection, leasing, purchasing, and even hiring construction contractors. He was one of five CNF employees honored with the Raymond F. O'Brien Award of Excellence in 1997.[9] Known as a stickler for detail who balanced risk with prudent foresight, Palazzo was instrumental in making Con-Way Central the industry's most efficient and reliable overnight line-haul carrier.

After Detter began leading CTS, all the Con-Way companies began to be referred to as CON-WAY in official company press releases. In August 1998, at Detter's behest, CTS relocated its 35-person headquarters from Palo Alto, California, to Ann Arbor, Michigan.[10, 11]

BALANCING AIRFREIGHT AND TRUCKING

After Jerry Detter was appointed president and CEO of CTS in July 1997, he moved CTS headquarters to Ann Arbor, Michigan.

The three Con-Way regional LTL carriers—Central, Southern, and Western—and Con-Way Truckload were projected to earn $130 million in operating profits on $1.5 billion in revenues, about half of CNF Transportation's operating income in 1997. CTS' operating ratio that year was 92.2—the industry average was 98.[12]

Although the nation's fifth-largest LTL carrier in terms of income, CTS was the most profitable, offering "Rolls-Royce service at a Chevrolet price," according to Greg Smith, vice president of Colography Group, an industry research firm in Georgia.

"They are never the low-price carrier. They are never the highest, either. But their combination of service and price is hard to beat," he said.[13]

Con-Way driver–sales representatives were more flexible than the workers of Teamster-covered firms and typically made as much or more than Teamster drivers along with receiving incentive checks often totaling thousands of dollars a year.[14]

About six months after its separation from CF MotorFreight, *Traffic World* called CTS "Trucking's Rolls-Royce," because it stood out in profitability and quality of customer service. It took the Con-Way companies about 10 years to reach the milestone of $1 billion revenue per year.[15]

Con-Way Southern celebrated its 10th anniversary in April 1997. The company had grown from its original 15 service centers to 100 locations with 4,200 employees, including 300 at its headquarters in Charlotte, North Carolina, and 8,000 trucks, tractors, and trailers.[16]

At the end of October 1997, Con-Way Southern Express' first president, Thomas C. Smith, passed away at his home in northern Michigan. He was 57. He had served as Con-Way Southern's president from its founding in April 1987 until his retirement in January 1995.

"Tom Smith was a leader, a mentor, and a friend who helped instill the basic values that CSE follows today," said John Hickerson, Smith's successor as president and CEO of Con-Way Southern Express. "His influence over a distinguished career is well recognized within our company and our industry."[17]

EMERY SIGNS WITH USPS

In April 1997, Emery Worldwide Airlines began its 58-month, $1.7 billion contract with the U.S. Postal Service, the largest postal contract in transportation history.[18] Emery spent $64 million on the postal contract, but costs exceeded revenues, and the airline lost $13 million by the year's end.[19]

"The Postal Service was outsourcing a portion of its priority mail, and this had never been done before for a lot of reasons, including opposition from the postal union," noted Gary Kowalski, who was working at Emery at the time and involved

in securing the post office contract. "Emery ran their network in ten U.S. cities as a pilot program. Ideally, we were going to improve their service and costs prospectus and ultimately compete with FedEx and UPS."[20]

In 1998, Emery opened 10 new Priority Mail processing centers and doubled its mail sorting operations per hour through improved practices and automation.[21, 22] Yet, the air carrier faced rising costs, and by March, it trimmed 650 full-time positions from its workforce.[23] Its operating income fell to $85.8 million by the third quarter of 1998, a 4 percent decline from the previous year, because the amount of mail processed dipped.[24]

"We are disappointed with the break-even performance of our Priority Mail contract operations, which is due to a pricing dispute with the U.S. Postal Service," said Quesnel. "Although our Priority Mail performance remains very good within the Emery Worldwide Airlines system, the contract pricing dispute led to a decline in CNF group operating income for the first time in nearly two years."[25]

Beatson resigned from Emery in June 1998 to join a freight forwarding and brokerage company, Circle International Group, in San Francisco. Ratnathicam was placed in charge of Emery temporarily before Roger Piazza was named president and CEO in August 1998.[26]

Although the national side of the business was challenging, Emery's international freight forwarding operations recorded solid growth in Asia and were also strong in Europe and Latin America.[27]

CON-WAY "NOW" PICKS UP PACE

In late May 1997, Con-Way NOW planned to nearly double its network to 47 locations in 18 Midwestern and Southern states. The "emergency" delivery service operated 24 hours a day, seven days a week, and even used noncommercial vehicles, such as station wagons.[28]

Con-Way NOW's goal was to book shipments and assign a vehicle for pickup in less than three

This 2000 marketing piece cover featured a Con-Way Southern Express tractor-trailer on a New Orleans street, along with the Con-Way name written on a shrimp platter, hot sauce, and wine bottle.

Roger Piazza, president and CEO of Emery Worldwide, had 35 years of experience in the air freight business.

minutes.[29] Its services offered businesses a solution to tough situations.

"Maybe a manufacturing company has had to stop production as a result of a particular piece of machinery breaking down, or, upon unloading, it is found that some key convention materials have been forgotten. These are the types of situations we address," noted Doug Stotlar, the subsidiary's general manager and a CNF vice president.[30]

Con-Way NOW's first major geographic expansion was establishing operations in Minneapolis/ St. Paul, Minnesota; Huntington/Charleston, West Virginia; and Buffalo, New York, in 1997. Its state-of-the-art command center in Ann Arbor, Michigan, had centralized customer service, dispatching, and satellite global positioning systems. Twelve new service centers opened in Tennessee, Georgia, Virginia, North Carolina, and South Carolina.[31] It also added 70 company-owned vehicles, including cargo vans and tractor-trailers, bringing its fleet to 195 units.[32, 33]

In August 1997, Detter appointed Stotlar as vice president of operations for CTS. Ed Conaway replaced Stotlar as vice president and general manager of Con-Way NOW.[34]

By January 1998, Con-Way NOW served more than half of the United States when it expanded into the Northeast with centers in Maine, Vermont, New Hampshire, Massachusetts, Rhode Island, Connecticut, New Jersey, Delaware, and Maryland, plus additional locations in New York, Pennsylvania, and Ontario, Canada.[35] Texas and Arkansas were added in August 1999.[36]

THE DISNEY EFFECT

The Con-Way companies as a whole had grown significantly, and in so many directions, that it was time for a cohesive plan to incorporate one vision and direction for all. Detter was dedicated to creating a close, professional organization and was open to many different ideas to achieve this goal. During the summer of 1997, he approved Pat Jannausch and Dave Miller's request to attend the Disney Institute for Professional Development (later known as the Disney Institute).

The Disney Institute offered three-day workshops, including a service excellence program. Jannausch and Miller of Con-Way Central attended

THE "13 THINGS" LIST

AFTER ATTENDING A DISNEY INSTITUTE WORKSHOP in the fall of 1997, Pat Jannausch and Dave Miller of Con-Way Central discussed what they had learned and together created a list embodying that knowledge. This list would soon become the foundation of a cohesive "Con-Way Culture."[1]

1. That Con-Way does many good things now—we're ahead of many companies.
2. That Disney has applied basics and common sense in a brilliant and profitable way.
3. That attention to detail in all things is key to achieving excellence in any business.
4. That we don't take full advantage of our "natural resources," i.e., employees and customers, to improve our company and its profitability.
5. That we don't have a collaborative environment in all areas and we must.
6. That role modeling of correct principles must start at the top.
7. That all employees must understand and commit to standards of the organization—no exceptions, any time.
8. That many of our current processes only need small adjustments to be more effective.
9. That we are missing opportunities every day to gain a competitive edge with employees and customers.
10. That while what we are doing now will support us into the future as a good or even very good company, true excellence is not possible.
11. That additional study of and exposure to Disney practices would benefit our company.
12. That other key people need to be exposed to this experience and information.
13. That NOW is the time to begin to make the cultural changes that will position us for true excellence in the 21ˢᵗ century.

---

a workshop. It was the beginning of a cohesive "Con-Way Culture."

"Con-Way Central was not big on benchmarking for a number of reasons," Jannausch explained. "We were the leader [in the industry]. Who were we going to get ideas from?"[37]

In a class of nearly 70 people from a variety of industries and occupations, including healthcare, finance, and the military, Jannausch said that she and Miller were exposed to numerous business methods and strategies. On the flight home, they created a list of 13 lessons they had learned. Although they realized that Con-Way was ahead of other companies in many areas, they acknowledged there was room for improvement. Disney, as an example, had applied basic and common sense strategies in a brilliant and profitable way. They realized that Con-Way had not fully explored the potential of its employees and customers to improve the company and profitability, and that many of the Con-Way processes needed adjustments to be more effective.[38, 39]

In November 1997, Detter invited Jannausch to present the list of "13 Things" at an officer's meeting. The reaction to the information was so successful that ultimately 24 additional executives attended the Disney Institute. This effort led to the creation of a series of "Eagle Meetings" at Con-Way, which were dedicated to corporate strategy, leadership, and culture. The information gained from these resulted in the rollout of Con-Way's culture initiative, corporate constitution, and employee recognition programs.[40]

By the third Eagle Meeting in 1998, Con-Way executives had created a company mission statement—in a sense, a company constitution. In January 1999, Eagle Meeting Four was held at the Kennedy Space Center, and Don McMonagle, an astronaut and director of launch integration at the time, spoke to the company's managers.

"It was at that meeting that Jerry [Detter] said we needed to document the process and make a record of what we had done up to that point," said Jannausch, who became vice president of human resources for Con-Way in August 2000.[41] This led to the creation of the "Power of the Dream" video and the rollout of culture initiatives at all company locations that included banners, posters, flags, hats, and a recognition program based on the company's values.[42]

SUCCESS IN MENLO LOGISTICS

Menlo Logistics was expanding, carving out a sizable niche in the logistics industry. By 1997, it posted $17 million in profits on gross revenues of $456 million.[43] Menlo's major customers included many *FORTUNE*® 500 companies such as Dow Chemical, Hewlett-Packard, IBM, and Nike.[44]

During 1998, the Redwood City, California–based Menlo captured six major projects—for IBM, NCR, Haworth, H.B. Fuller, Ingersoll-Rand, and a major computer chip manufacturer—that totaled

more than $1 billion in gross revenues, for five years. Several Wall Street analysts ranked Menlo as No. 1 in the logistics field.[45]

With 9 million square feet of warehouse space, Menlo's 2,500 employees managed about 2 million shipments worth billions of dollars annually by the beginning of 1999.[46] The success of Menlo drew many people to join the CNF-owned company, including Bob Bassett, who became its director of business development in 1999. He had left the financially troubled Caliber Logistics, which was one of Menlo's biggest competitors.

"Both Caliber and Menlo were non-asset based, neutral logistics providers [called 3PLs]," Bassett said. "We would go to the marketplace and say, look, we're not beholden to our assets. We're not going to stuff you into our assets if that's not the right solution."[47]

The mindset at Menlo, which still prevails today, was that the Con-Way companies were not going to be treated any differently than other car-

Recent promotional items have included logos that are the result of strategic culture initiatives throughout Con-Way and its subsidiaries. This hat and coffee mug reflect the core values of integrity, commitment, and excellence.

A composite image of four semi-tractor trailers show the colors of Con-Way Western Express, Central, Southern, and Canada.

riers. However, in the years that followed, Menlo and the other companies have grown increasingly collaborative.

ACROSS THE NATION IN THREE DAYS

About a year after the separation from Consolidated Freightways, in late December 1997, Detter announced that Con-Way Western and Con-Way Southern would now deliver freight across 1,600 miles in two days.[48]

Con-Way Western and Con-Way Southern also provided an unheard of three-day service for coast-to-coast shipments, which was one to two days faster than what was then considered the best LTL industry's delivery standard. By mid-July 1999, Con-Way Central offered its customers a similar three-day service from western New York and Pennsylvania to California.[49]

Shippers noted that the latest Con-Way service was significantly better than any provided by traditional long-haul carriers. At the time of the announcement, Detter downplayed that the Con-Way companies would now be in direct competition with the big long-haulers.

"Regional next-day is our flagship product," Detter said. "Our total product line is now one of the most comprehensive in the industry. That's highly attractive to the customer, who generally wants to use as few carriers as possible."[50]

Con-Way's service propelled it toward a $144 million operating income for 1997, the most in the LTL market.[51]

The competition tried imitating Con-Way's model with mixed results. For example, Caliber Logistics failed in its effort to merge its Viking subsidiary with Spartan, Coles, and Central Freight Inc. After losing $200 million in the effort, Caliber closed Spartan and Coles instead and sold Central Freight.[52] In October 1997, Federal Express announced a $2.4 billion stock swap to acquire Caliber. It was predicted that FedEx would soon try to imitate the successful Con-Way model.[53]

THE DEMISE OF CON-WAY TRUCKLOAD

Due to railroad mergers and consolidations, by mid-1998 only four major rail providers were left, casting a shadow over the future of intermodal transportation for Con-Way. At an intermodal conference, sponsored by Con-Way Truckload (CWT), industry experts pointed out that the four major railroads would probably dictate the terms and conditions under which intermodal companies could operate.[54] And, indeed, the railroad companies eventually raised their rates by more than 30 percent in the mid-2000s.[55]

In the late 1990s, Con-Way Truckload had entered into an alliance with GST Corporation, a telecommunications company headquartered in

Allentown, Pennsylvania, to develop computer operations and systems to reduce costs and improve services for its intermodal customers.[56] However, the subsidiary's long-term business model was unprofitable. When Con-Way Truckload needed to replace its aging fleet of Freightliner tractors and trailers, Emery's costs hampered CNF from undertaking a large recapitalization.[57] CNF decided to dissolve Con-Way Truckload, selling off most of its assets in August 2000.[58]

SERVICE CENTER GROWTH

Between 1997 and 2001, Con-Way opened a number of new service centers, replacing older facilities with larger service centers that more than doubled its freight distribution capacity and expanding into other geographic areas. Some new facilities were large freight assembly centers that turned dozens of former second-day delivery lanes into one-day lanes, or three-day lanes into two-day lanes.

AIDING A SILVER SLUGGER

WHEN CHICAGO CUB'S BALLPLAYER SAMMY SOSA won his second Silver Slugger Award in 1998 for National League outfielders, his supply of bats was transported by Emery and Con-Way.

During the eight-month-long baseball season, in which Sosa threatened to break Roger Maris' 61 home run record, Emery's Louisville Service Center shipped out an average of one box of five bats each weekday—for a total of about 640 bats. The bats were taken by Con-Way Truckload to Emery's hub in Dayton, Ohio, before they were flown out to destination airports and delivered by Emery trucks.[1]

Emery had been shipping out bats for many Major League Baseball teams for years, according to Rick Clevinger, who had been general manager of Emery's Louisville Service Center.

When Con-Way Central expanded its service centers in 1999, its driver–sales representatives and account executives distributed flyers depicting the company's business relationship with professional baseball organizations.

CCX CON-WAY CENTRAL EXPRESS
Con-Way Transportation Services, Inc.

Con-Way Western expansions occurred in California, Arizona, and Wyoming.

In 1999, CNF invested more than $43 million in Con-Way Western's region to build six new major service centers and upgrade existing service centers. Adding 244 doors, 42 acres, and 105,742 square feet of dock space, new facilities were built in Blythe, Chula Vista, Fontana, and Kettleman City, California; Denver, Colorado; and Salt Lake City, Utah. Seventy-four acres, 334 doors, and 127,330 square feet of dock space were added to the operations by the 1999 projects alone.[59]

Con-Way Central's expansions included new, enlarged, or replacement facilities in Ohio, Illinois, Kentucky, West Virginia, Michigan, Connecticut, and Rhode Island. Con-Way Central also opened four freight assembly centers, including the 100-door Louisville, Kentucky, service center on 24 acres near I-65, in July 2000; the 100-door Salem, Illinois, service center that could handle close to 2 million pounds of freight a day on August 7, 2000; the 144-door Fremont, Indiana, service center that could handle 3 million pounds of freight a day (replacing the Coldwater, Michigan, service center) in May 2001; and the 58-door Clearfield, Pennsylvania, facility in October 2001.[60-62]

Con-Way Southern's expansions included new, enlarged, or replacement facilities in Georgia, Alabama, Louisiana, and Texas. Con-Way Southern also built three freight assembly centers, includ-

ing the 101-door Chester, Virginia, facility near Richmond in November 2000; the 100-door freight assembly center in Birmingham, Alabama; and an 80-door freight assembly center in Glenpool, Oklahoma, that replaced a 37-door service center in Tulsa.[63-65]

A RISING TIDE

In 1997, the top eight LTL carriers posted their best profits after many were plagued with years of red ink.

CTS had a 90 percent operating ratio with operating income of $147 million on $1.47 billion of gross revenues. Yellow Freight doubled its operating income for the year. Roadway Express saw a 69 percent increase of its profits; Overnite Transportation had its first profit in two years.[66]

Rounding out the results, U.S. Freightways had record revenue and earnings. Even Consolidated Freightways (now separate from the Con-Way Group) went from a $73 million loss in 1996 to net profits of $60 million, and ABF Freight System posted its best operating ratio in a decade.[67]

The Con-Way companies were the most profitable of the LTL carriers in February 1998.

CANADA AND MEXICO OPERATIONS

Con-Way Canada Express was officially formed in 2000 as Con-Way's Canadian subsidiary.[68] The new company received its 1,500th Sterling truck on May 1, 2000; opened a new headquarters building in Mississauga, Ontario; and expanded its operations into five more provinces with 27 service locations in Ontario, Quebec, New Brunswick, Nova Scotia, Prince Edward Island, Manitoba, Saskatchewan, and Alberta.[69, 70]

"Canada's trade with the United States and Mexico, as well as within Canada, is growing at a strong pace," Palazzo said at the time. "That is why we have announced this five-province expansion. We saw the opportunity for Con-Way Canada

Employees and family members of the Quad Cities terminal repainted carts in the 1990s.

John H. Williford was president and CEO of Menlo Logistics until 2005.

Express to provide superior on-time LTL service to Canadian companies who need faster, more reliable transit times, between more direct points of delivery to markets throughout North America."[71]

Richard "Rick" Smith, a Con-Way employee since 1995 and former service center manager at Hamilton, Ontario, was named general manager of Con-Way Canada Express in February 2001. When Smith joined Con-Way, he was put in charge of opening the Hamilton service center. His first "office" was comprised of his two kitchen chairs and a cellular phone placed in the middle of the dock.[72]

Although Con-Way Canada was small in terms of workforce, it covered a huge territory, mostly handling transborder shipments.

"Most of our business is international bonded freight—north and south. A small percentage is domestic within Canada," Smith said. "We take a lot of pride that when the cold weather comes, we don't use that as an excuse. We keep the same service levels. A lot of customers are very surprised by that. We run through conditions where most carriers are not even open."[73]

Con-Way Canada also added British Columbia (where Con-Way Western already had a presence) to the eight other provinces it served. It aligned with West Arm Truck Lines to serve the southern half of the province and Northwest Truck Lines Ltd. to reach northern British Columbia.[74]

CTS noted that the growth of NAFTA-related (North American Free Trade Agreement) traffic as well as growth of intra-Canada business made it the proper time for Con-Way Canada's 2001 expansion.

Jose Antonio Gonzalez was promoted to managing director of Con-Way's Mexican operation, which was renamed Con-Way Mexico Express (CMX)—a subsidiary of Con-Way Southern—in December 2000. Gonzalez had worked for Con-Way since 1992, helping to open its office in Monterrey, Mexico, and then built a sales team operating out of Mexico City and Guadalajara.

A NEW KIND OF LOGISTICS SERVICE

Although Menlo Logistics and Emery were well-established, CNF-owned enterprises, in October 1998, CTS started its own logistics company, called Con-Way Integrated Services. Among its services, Con-Way Integrated Services offered multi-client warehousing; warehouse and inventory management; transportation optimization and management; and light assembly, pick and pack, and packaging.[75]

Based in Chicago, Con-Way Integrated Services targeted small and mid-tier companies that needed economical logistics services, large companies that needed to supplement existing networks, and foreign companies seeking to enter the U.S. market. Con-Way Integrated Services' first facilities were located in Chicago, Los Angeles, and northern New Jersey.[76]

Con-Way Integrated Services used a different approach than Menlo, which still offered fully customized logistics programs for its customers' large, complex projects; or Emery Global Logistics that provided assembly, warehousing, and distribution services for international and American-based customers. Con-Way Integrated Services served smaller clients and combined much of the backroom functions, such as warehousing, to cut costs.

Safelite Glass Corporation, an aftermarket manufacturer, distributor, and retailer of automotive glass, became a major customer, signing a multi-year contract in February 2000.[77]

"We as a group of companies are strongly focused on the regional business, and that's not going to change," Detter said. "First and foremost, we are regional companies. Sixty percent of our business is overnight. It's what we are."[78]

Con-Way Integrated Services was renamed Con-Way Logistics in July 2001. The company also moved its headquarters to Aurora, Illinois.[79]

"We started with three warehouses in February 1999, and now we have seven large, modern facilities located throughout the United States," said Michael Bare, vice president and general manager of the subsidiary. "These facilities are strategically located to provide next-day distribution services to 85 percent of the population, and two-day service to virtually the entire country."[80]

A new "stacked" logo format was also introduced about the same time that Con-Way Logistics was launched. The "Con-Way" name was placed over the operating unit name for Con-Way NOW, Con-Way Air, and Con-Way Mexico.[81]

CON-WAY CENTRAL LINKS UP WITH WESTERN

The Con-Way business model was constantly evolving, beginning when the former Con-Way Southwest interchanged freight with Con-Way Southern and Western in 1993. Customers sought out regional carriers for long-distance shipping to avoid transit delays and costs caused by the use of breakbulk facilities.

The final coast-to-coast link in the Con-Way system was completed in April 1998 when Con-Way Central and Con-Way Western expanded interregional service. The reason, according to

This Con-Way Central Express handout promoting the Con-Way Guaranteed! service was distributed in 2001.

A Con-Way Central semi-tractor trailer was showcased at an unidentified school in 1998 during the annual Red Ribbon anti-drug campaign.

Palazzo, was that Con-Way customers wanted "three- to four-day service between the eastern and western parts of the country."[82]

"With Con-Way, we get three- to four-day service for a price cheaper than expedited freight. They don't sell on price. They sell on service. And they give dynamite service," said Tony Deely, director of distribution for New Pig Corporation of Tipton, Pennsylvania, a manufacturer of industrial absorbents and spill-containment products.[83]

Palazzo noted that the Con-Way companies would still maintain regional service.[84]

By the end of 1998, CNF Transportation posted a record net income of $130 million, a 16 percent increase over 1997 earnings. It also had a record operating income of $290.5 million, about a 10 percent increase from $264.9 million in 1997. CNF revenue was $4.98 billion, a 16 percent increase over 1997's revenue of $4.26 billion.

GUARANTEED! LAUNCHED; WAL-MART SIGNS UP

On February 1, 1999, Con-Way Transportation Services offered a new service option called Con-Way Guaranteed! Although the Con-Way companies had a 97.6 percent on-time record for 1998,

Detter explained that the guaranteed service soothed customers' minds without the elevated cost of using an expedited service. A 20-percent charge was added to customers' existing discounted price. Competitors charged a premium on nondiscounted prices for their time-delivery programs.[85]

Shipments not eligible for the program included those that required protection from freezing, shipments that were affected by abnormal weather conditions, or those destined for points not directly served by a Con-Way carrier.[86]

The nation's largest retailer, Wal-Mart, signed a three-year logistics agreement with the Con-Way regional carriers in March 1999. Con-Way routed LTL shipments from vendors to replenish Wal-Mart and Sam's Club stores in the 11 Western states covered by Con-Way Western and the stores covered by Con-Way Central.[87]

"Con-Way's track record of growth and reliability make them a good fit for the aggressive growth plans at Wal-Mart," noted Larry Duff, vice president of transportation for Wal-Mart. "We consume a large amount of transportation capacity across the country, and we are always looking for alliances that provide capacity, speed, and reliability at competitive rates. We believe Con-Way fits that profile."[88]

CRASH OF EMERY FLIGHT 17

In early February 2000, Emery announced plans to replace its entire fleet of DC-8s during the next year, but ensuing events halted that effort, including the aftermath of the crash of Emery Flight 17.[89]

On February 16, 2000, the weather was calm with surface temperatures about 46 degrees Fahrenheit. At 7:49 P.M., Emery Flight 17 roared down the runway of Mather Airport just east of Sacramento, California.[90] Carrying a three-person flight crew and nearly 64,000 pounds of cargo—including transmission fluid, clothing, and a small packet of detonators for auto air bags—the four-engine DC-8-71F airfreighter had flown twice before that day and was en route to Dayton, Ohio.[91, 92]

Within seconds of the wheels leaving the runway, the flight crew knew something was wrong. The pilot reported to air traffic control that there was a problem with the positioning of the plane's load, and he would attempt to return to the airport.[93] Banking left, the pilot and first officer fought to keep the DC-8 in the air, but it crashed into an automobile salvage yard about one mile east of the runway less than two minutes into its flight.[94] The crew died on impact. The aircraft and cargo were destroyed while flames burned through the vehicles in the salvage yard. It was Emery's first fatal plane crash.[95]

Initially, National Transportation Safety Board (NTSB) investigators thought that the plane had been loaded improperly.[96] After the crash, the CNF board decided it was time to sell Emery.

"[Quesnel] came back to the board in June 2000 and said, 'I can't get enough for Emery,'" Kennedy said. "I was one of three board members who stayed after the meeting to tell him he didn't understand. It's not how much can you get for Emery—it's get rid of it."[97]

At the same time Emery's maintenance and safety procedures were coming under question by the NTSB, the U.S. Postal Service wanted to cut the costs of its express, priority, and first-class mail. It questioned whether dedicated air transportation networks, such as Emery, were efficient and cost-effective.[98]

By autumn 2000, it became clear that the Post Office was seriously considering awarding its next mail transportation services contract to Federal Express Corp.[99] Another round of woes began for CNF's historically troubled airfreight carrier, exacerbated when the Postal Service terminated Emery's contract in November 2000. CNF filed a lawsuit on January 5, 2001, receiving a temporary restraining order to halt the Post Office/FedEx seven-year contract worth $6.36 billion in an effort to recover some of its lost postal business.[100]

The repercussions of the Flight 17 crash continued into mid-2001 when the Federal Aviation Administration (FAA) prepared to pull Emery's operating certificate after discovering more than 100 purported safety regulation violations. In an April 2001 incident, maintenance workers installed the wrong equipment in one landing gear, which made it ineffective. The DC-8 was forced to use its two remaining landing gears and a wing upon touch-down; fortunately, no one was injured. On August 13, 2001, Emery voluntarily grounded its fleet of 37 freighters.[101]

Emery leased aircraft from other cargo carriers to operate a full schedule of flights while its fleet was grounded. The company laid off 800 pilots, crew members, and administrative personnel out of its workforce of 1,100. There were reports Emery would remain grounded for at least 30 days as it addressed the alleged violations, but the events of September 11, 2001, would influence CNF to cease ownership of aircraft.[102]

CON-WAY NOW BY AIR; FORMING VECTOR SCM

With about 10 percent of its customers seeking an even faster expedited shipping service, Con-Way NOW began offering air service for transport to 24 cities in April 2000.[103] Its air express coverage was expanded by an additional 176 destinations by July of that year.[104]

Con-Way NOW also began expedited service for truckload shipments after experimenting with one-way and round-trip services with different equipment configurations from 53-foot trailers to 24-foot straight trucks. Ed Conaway noted that GPS technology allowed the company to monitor dedicated shipments and provide customers time-definite deliveries.[105]

Conaway became president and CEO of Con-Way NOW in October 2000.

In 2000, Menlo Logistics partnered with General Motors (GM) to create Vector SCM, a joint venture company to handle automotive supply chain management. Based in Novi, Michigan, Vector SCM was created to oversee most of GM's approximately $6.2 billion annual global logistics.[106]

"We had to figure out solutions to improve GM's supply chain and from those solutions, we drove cost savings," said Rock Magnan, who was director of ground transportation for Emery at the time but became Menlo's director of operations in 2002. "Supply chain management and supply chain technological solutions were evolving when we took on that project [Vector]. It had a very rapid start-up, a wide deployment, and used new and innovative IT."[107]

Vector began approximately the same time that Emery's postal contract declined, according to Kowalski, who became the first president and CEO of the joint venture. Kowalski had worked for GM for about 16 years before joining Emery and was familiar with a number of GM's people.

The major challenge was that the "different regions within General Motors tended to operate a little independently versus in a centralized fashion," Kowalski said. "They were changing their culture. Outsourcing their logistics was a big change for them. We had to learn how to work together."[108]

E-COMMERCE OVERHAUL

Since the launch of the Web site in 1994, CTS was continually updating the site to offer more services. By August 2000, shippers could receive specific rate quotes and listings of their top 20 vendors and customers. The site also offered shippers a lane analysis report that ranks shipment volume by origin or destination. By December, the site provided real-time information on shipment costs and allowed customers to track orders online.

"The customer-specific rating program will provide our registered customers with highly accurate data that can be utilized in their logistics planning," noted Bryan M. Millican, then Con-Way executive vice president of sales and marketing. "The availability of this company-specific pricing information will allow our customers to present final delivery costs to their customers."[109]

CTS added an interface to its site by June 2001 to allow customers to transmit bills of lading and order pickup data. The number of electronic orders increased. The link greatly sped up transactions and offered greater flexibility to Con-Way customers, noted Jackie Barretta, who became vice president of information systems in 2000.[110] In November 2000, CTS launched Con-Way Business Solutions, which

provided a full range of supply chain management to small to medium-size companies.[111] By August 2001, customers could access invoice status, obtain rate and delivery details on shipments, and get copies of shipping documents and delivery receipt.

"Internet technology and e-commerce can help companies effectively achieve [the balance between being profitable and meeting their customers' needs]," said Luis R. Solano, Con-Way Business Solutions' general manager.[112]

In August 2001, Con-Way Business Solutions was closed as a separate unit and its operations were folded into Con-Way Logistics.[113]

OPENING AIR EXPRESS

In May 2001, CTS opened Con-Way Air Express, an airfreight forwarding business. This start-up com-

This brochure cover helped introduce the Con-Way Air freight forwarding service in 2001.

CHAMPIONSHIP DREAMS

CON-WAY'S EFFORTS TO BOLSTER THE TRUCK DRIving profession's reputation began to show as record numbers of Con-Way drivers won first-place awards in their vehicle classes at state championships and then had stellar performances at the National Truck Driving Championships.

In 1998, nine Con-Way drivers were among the top 10 finishers in the 1998 National Truck Driving Championships—two were named to the American Trucking Associations' (ATA) prestigious America's Road Team as role models and spokespersons for key industry issues.[1] Bruce Andrews of Con-Way Truckload and Mark Stamper of Con-Way Western were named as two of 12 captains for the ATA's 1998 America's Road Team. Speaking on highway safety, Andrews and Stamper represented the industry before media, students, transportation officials, and government leaders. Collectively, the 12 drivers logged more than 235 years of safe driving and 21 million accident-free miles, noted ATA President Walter B. McCormick Jr.[2]

Additionally, veteran Con-Way Central driver Al Gerber became a captain to the ATA's prestigious America's Road Team for 1999. Gerber, who was picked from a group of 25 finalists, had been a professional truck driver for more than 28 years with more than 900,000 accident-free miles.[3]

In August 1999, the Con-Way companies sent 46 drivers to the national championships held in the United States by the ATA.

Con-Way Central driver Michel Roy, a resident of Terrebonne, Quebec, became the first Con-Way Canadian driver to win a national title in the three-axle class at the 1999 Canadian National Professional Truck Driving Championship held in London, Ontario. Working out of the Con-Way Central terminal in Montreal, Roy scored a total of 425 points (out of a possible 500) to take the first-place trophy.[4]

"Michel's accomplishment is truly his own, but having 47 total championship drivers in North America in 1999 is a wonderful reflection on the Con-Way workforce," Gerald Detter added. "Safety is the number one value in the Con-Way culture, and the award-winning performance by Michel and his 46 fellow drivers in

Con-Way Transportation Services sent a total of 46 state champions to the 1999 American Trucking Associations' National Truck Driving Championships held in August in Tampa, Florida. Seated from right to left are: Con-Way Central driver Morris O'Keefe of Providence, Rhode Island, the rookie of the year in the straight truck category; Con-Way Central driver Bruce Early of Cleveland, the 1999 U.S. champion in the three-axle category; and Con-Way Southern Express driver Michael Galbraith of Knoxville who won third place in the twin-trailer category. Standing from left to right are: Con-Way Central Dale Knox of Erie, who was the Pennsylvania champion in tank trucks; Con-Way Central Director of Safety Gerald Krisa; Con-Way Central President Richard Palazzo; CTS President Gerald Detter; CTS Director of Safety and Environmental Compliance Bob Petrancosta; and Con-Way Central driver Gary Wilkinson, Pennsylvania state champion in the three-axle category.

In 2001, Con-Way Western Driver Ina Daly (pictured here in 2007) was the company's first female driver named to the 2001 America's Road Team. She had more than 1 million accident-free miles and won four first-place state driving and safety competitions.

the U.S. speaks volumes about their commitment to safe driving."[5]

MORE CHAMPIONS

Darren Beard, a Con-Way Central driver from Watertown, South Dakota, became one of only 13 captains on the ATA's 2000 Road Team. He became the fifth Con-Way employee in four years to receive that honor.[6]

In 2000, Con-Way sent a record 49 drivers, who won state-level first-place finishes, to the National Truck Driving Championship, held in New Orleans.[7]

In 2001, Con-Way Western Driver Ina Daly and Con-Way Central Driver Robert Kleinschmidt were named to the 2001 America's Road Team.[8] Daly, who worked out of the Phoenix, Arizona, service center, was Con-Way's first female to receive this honor. She drove more than 1 million accident-free miles in her career and won four first-place state driving and safety competitions. Kleinschmidt, from the Detroit terminal, also had more than 1 million accident-free miles and had won first place in his equipment division. He was also named "Rookie of the Year" in the Michigan state driving championship.[9]

Con-Way's number of participants in the 2001 ATA National Truck Driving Championship in Minneapolis swelled to 60 men and women—with 59 winning state-level first-place finishes for their class. With a combined total of 70 million accident-free miles, the Con-Way contingent was the largest number of drivers ever sent by any one trucking company in the history of the competition.

"These men and women are among America's best drivers," Detter said. "Their total dedication to safety, customer service, and on-time performance make not only Con-Way proud, but also the trucking industry."[10]

REACHING NO. 1

Con-Way was named North America's No. 1 trucking firm—and was the only transportation company listed—on *Fortune*® magazine's March 1999 "America's Most Admired Companies" list. *Fortune*® created the list using an independent survey and ranked companies on several measurements including quality of service, management, financial performance, innovations, and environmental sensitivity.[11]

The recognition is an example of the many accolades that the Con-Way companies received over the years from state trucking associations, trade journals, and business magazines for high-quality safety and performance. For example, in 2000, Con-Way Central Express was recognized by three of its major customers—Moen Inc., Ryder System Inc., and the Additives Division of Ciba Specialty Chemicals—while Con-Way Western was recognized by the logistics company C.H. Robinson of Minnesota for superior service.[12]

pany began with 13 service centers, each with a dedicated operations and sales staff, and had an agency network to provide full coverage for all 50 states as well as Puerto Rico. This operation differed from Emery in that it was a domestic organization that scheduled cargo space on third-party aircraft.

Headquartered in Forest Park, Georgia, near Atlanta's Hartsfield International Airport, Con-Way Air Express linked to an extensive network of facilities and assets within the U.S. operations of Con-Way's LTL operations.

Heading up Con-Way Air Express was Gary Baude, who became vice president, general manager. Baude had 22 years' experience in the airfreight industry.

IMPROVED SAFETY FOR THE ROAD

In 2001, as part of its commitment to improved safety, CTS received 605 new Sterling tractors equipped with high-tech collision avoidance systems. With an additional cost of $1 million for the new units, the collision avoidance system used radar antennas on the front and sides of the tractors.[114]

Connected to an onboard computer that monitored the tractor's speed, the sensors kept track of vehicles in front of and beside the truck. The system sounded a warning when vehicles were detected in the "blind spot" on the right side of the tractor.

"The driver is still in control of the tractor, but this system acts as a separate set of eyes and gives the driver notice of a potentially dangerous situation," said Stotlar, then executive vice president of operations for CTS, when the new system was unveiled.[115]

SEPTEMBER 11 AFTERMATH

Air travel and international ground traffic crossings were severely affected by the terrorist attacks on New York City and Arlington, Virginia, that destroyed the World Trade Center and damaged the Pentagon on September 11, 2001. All civilian air flights were suspended until Thursday, September 13, and automotive traffic at international entry points into Canada, such as Detroit's Ambassador Bridge, was clogged for months because of security concerns.

The terrorist attacks brought a quick and historic response from many people in New York, and contributions from communities around America. The Con-Way companies also were involved in assistance efforts during the immediate aftermath.

By noon, the Federal Emergency Management Agency (FEMA) had contacted Grainger, the leading provider of maintenance, repair, and operating supplies, to obtain a set of 30 generators from Grainger's branch in Albany, New York. Grainger, in turn, contacted Con-Way Central.[116]

A Con-Way Central tractor pulling two trailers was dispatched to pick up the 14,000-pound load. FEMA made arrangements for the truck and its cargo to proceed directly to Ground Zero, the site of the destroyed World Trade Center towers, and the cargo was delivered by 7:30 P.M.

In the following days, Con-Way was asked to deliver numerous shipments to the disaster site. On September 12, Airgas Safety of Bristol, Pennsylvania, had a shipment of 15,000 coveralls, boots, 600 boxes of respirators, lanterns and batteries, a 60,000-watt laser light, and four 100,000-watt spotlights. Con-Way Central driver Bob Schaffer transported the materials under police escort by

In the aftermath of September 11, 2001, Con-Way donated more than $300,000 to the American Red Cross Disaster Relief Fund. The ceremonial check traveled to locations between Ann Arbor and Washington, D.C., where it arrived at the Red Cross headquarters on October 9, 2001. In Michigan, Kay Beher (left), Con-Way Central's manager of administration, is aided by Darrel Stoker, driver, and Tara Keezer, technical support analyst.

1:00 A.M. on Wednesday. Con-Way also shipped medical supplies into New York, as well as hard hats for recovery workers donated from Bullard Company of Kentucky.

Con-Way, on behalf of its employees, presented a $305,821.46 check to the Red Cross Disaster Relief Fund during a ceremony at Red Cross national headquarters in Washington, D.C., on October 9, 2001. Funds were collected during a two-week period, and the company matched employees' donations dollar for dollar.[117]

EMERY'S DIFFICULTIES CONTINUE

Emery elected to return the USPS network back to the USPS, once it was determined that the dispute could not be favorably resolved. On September 26, 2001, Emery and the Post Office entered into an agreement where the USPS paid $235 million to the airfreight company (plus up to an additional $70 million in provisional payments to cover costs and other claims related to the end of the priority mail contract).[118, 119]

That December, CNF announced it was discontinuing its Emery unit and selling its aircraft. The corporation took a $200 million charge to shutter Emery permanently, dismissing 130 of the airfreight company's remaining 200 employees.

Emery was folded into a new unit called Menlo Worldwide that included Menlo Logistics and Vector SCM. As part of this move, Emery was renamed Menlo Worldwide Forwarding.

"By altering the basic business model of Emery in North America, we are taking a major step in CNF's strategy of reducing assets in a way that will benefit both customers and investors," said Quesnel.

In August 2005, the final report by the NTSB was released regarding the crash of Flight 17. It claimed that a missing bolt, which was needed for the control of the plane's right elevator to control the pitch attitude of the aircraft, was responsible. The NTSB blamed faulty maintenance for the lost part, but investigators were unable to pinpoint exactly when the bolt was lost.[120]

By the end of 2001, CNF Transportation Inc. had weathered some difficult times and change was on the horizon in many forms. The company again changed its name, this time to CNF Inc. Its international freight operations were affected by the aftermath of September 11, 2001, which was one of the catalysts for exiting the air freight forwarding business. In spite of the challenges, there were new opportunities for the trucking transportation industry, and CNF once again looked to enhance its ocean freight forwarding operations.[121]

CHAPTER NINE

NEW MANAGEMENT STRATEGIES

2002–2005

We built a great organization under Jerry (Detter's) leadership. ... Just because Jerry is leaving doesn't mean that this team isn't in a position to do what Jerry taught us to do. Now it's our responsibility to take this organization into the future. It's our responsibility to build on the legacy and take this company forward.

—Douglas W. Stotlar,
Con-way Inc., president and CEO[1]

AS THE CORPORATION FOUNDED BY Leland James entered the 21st century, and Con-Way Transportation Services approached its 20th anniversary, the remnants of Emery continued to affect operating income for Menlo Worldwide, and in turn, the entire company. A major management shake-up in 2004 would find a host of executives leaving the corporation. Yet, the company continued to focus on its strength—the trucking industry.

CON-WAY FULL LOAD

In January 2002, Con-Way Transportation Services (CTS) launched Con-Way Full Load, a new truckload brokerage operation, which offered service throughout the United States and Canada.

"We're on very familiar ground. We contract with truckload carriers regularly for a portion of our line-haul service in our LTL operations, and we also manage a large group of contract operators in our Con-Way NOW expedite service. This experience has given us the expertise and systems necessary to manage a very substantial truckload brokerage operation," said Gerald Detter, president and CEO of Con-Way.[2]

In order to run the new operation, Con-Way utilized and scaled up the systems used by its NOW unit. Full Load's central operations and customer service center were placed adjacent to Con-Way NOW in Ann Arbor, Michigan.

Con-Way Full Load provided complete truckload service with Con-Way's reliability and excellent service standard, enabling Con-Way to offer its customers competitive pricing, complete shipment tracking, and single-source accountability.

BREAKING FREE

With the effects of Emery still weighing down Menlo Worldwide and CNF, talk circulated of spinning off CTS as a separate company in mid-2002.[3]

Some analysts firmly believed a spin-off would occur. Yet, a trucking analyst for Bear Stearns said it was doubtful that the Con-Ways would be severed from the parent corporation because their success balanced losses from CNF's other business units.[4]

At CTS, Detter remained unaffected by the potential separation from CNF. He explained:

We have an obligation [to shareholders] to look at a possible spin. It's up to what the markets think. If

Above: In 2003, Con-Way celebrated 20 years of working in North America with superior service through its regional carriers.

Opposite: Con-Way Central Express remained dedicated to providing superior service to its customers.

they value us completely, it probably won't happen. If they don't, then a spin is not out of the question.[5]

Ultimately, the board of directors, under Vice Chairman Keith Kennedy, decided to sell what was left of Emery, instead of pursuing the trucking split. During the last quarter of 2003, UPS offered to purchase Menlo Worldwide, which included Emery, whose name had been changed to Menlo Worldwide Forwarding following the formation of Menlo Worldwide. At the time, many members of CNF's board of directors were uncomfortable with the deal. The company, however, continued to negotiate with UPS.[6]

In October 2004, Con-Way agreed to sell UPS just the Menlo Worldwide Forwarding portion, including Emery's old hub in Dayton, Ohio; Menlo Worldwide Expedite!; the international trade unit; and Menlo Worldwide Trade Services for $150 million in cash with UPS assuming $110 million in debt. CNF retained only the logistics operations of Menlo Worldwide, including Menlo Logistics and Vector SCM.[7] According to Kennedy:

CNF will be in its best financial condition in 15 years. ... We are strengthening our business and serving the best interest of our shareholders, while enabling Menlo Worldwide Forwarding to join with one of the premier brands in the transportation industry.[8]

After the sale of Menlo Worldwide Forwarding, Con-Way Logistics was folded into Menlo's remaining logistics operation and consolidated into the same warehouse operations, saving the corporation $3 million to $4 million a year.

EXPANDING SERVICE

Con-Way had always relied on market demand to dictate the expansion of facilities or movement into new areas. Each division saw great growth during the 2000s, with new and expanded facilities.

Con-Way Central Express (CCX) opened new facilities in Williston, Vermont; Chicago; Marshfield, Missouri; and Florence, Kentucky.[9] It replaced its Greencastle, Pennsylvania, facility, which allowed for second-day deliveries to Miami, Oklahoma City, and Fargo, North Dakota.[10]

Con-Way Southern Express (CSE) replaced its Memphis, Tennessee, facility, which allowed for next-day delivery as far away as Milwaukee, Wisconsin. The Memphis facility also housed the general offices of Con-Way Truckload.[11, 12] New facilities were constructed in Glenpool, Oklahoma, and in Newnan, Georgia.[13]

Con-Way Canada Express opened two new terminals in Montreal, Quebec, and Windsor, Ontario, in early 2002. The St. Luc, Quebec, facility served the metropolitan Montreal market while the Windsor facility replaced a smaller 10-door terminal.[14]

"Windsor is the busiest international gateway between the United States and Canada, and our new facility will be instrumental in improving international

Vice Chairman Keith Kennedy led the charge to sell Emery Forwarding, which was part of Menlo Worldwide, to UPS.

Con-Way expanded and built new facilities across the country to accommodate rising customer demand.

and local service," said Rick Smith, general manager of Con-Way Canada Express.[15]

After Con-Way increased its freight assembly center network to 75 terminals strategically located around the country, it then focused on redefining next-day and second-day service for more than 6,000 U.S. cities and towns. Con-Way focused on extending its reach to cover two-thirds of U.S. markets.[16]

As part of a project called Extended Service Lanes, CTS conducted feasibility tests using tractors with sleeper cabs and teams of drivers to reduce transit times in May 2002. The tests proved so successful that by June 1, all three Con-Way regional carriers implemented the special tractors and driver teams.

"These new operating procedures will replace two-day service with next-day service in a large number of markets," Stotlar said. "Even though we're already a service leader, we don't want to rest on past performance."[17]

Examples of the new next-day service included shipping freight between Indianapolis and Charlotte, North Carolina, a 558-mile distance; between Detroit and Newark, New Jersey, a 610-mile distance; between Milwaukee and Memphis, a 619-mile distance; between Chicago and Sioux Falls, South Dakota, a 550-mile distance; and between Palm Springs and Redding, both in California, a 649-mile distance.

The new second-day lanes traveled between Buffalo, New York, and Dallas, Texas, a 1,353-mile distance; between Jacksonville, Florida, and Minneapolis, a 1,389-mile distance; and between Eugene, Oregon, and Colorado Springs, Colorado, a 1,315-mile distance.

SECURITY MEASURES

As a reaction to the September 11, 2001, terrorist attacks on the United States, both U.S. and Canadian customs authorities imposed new security inspections and documentation requirements for those crossing the border. These changes—while necessary—increased the cost and the time it took truckers and other travelers to cross international borders. Stotlar explained:

September 11 brought many changes to our lives. The need and concern for security is a goal we can all support, but it is having an impact on our operating costs. As government agencies on both sides of the border have continued to formulate and modify security plans, the increased costs have become a constant within our operations. It's now time to begin to recover these costs.[18]

After the September 11, 2001, terrorist attacks, CTS joined the Customs-Trade Partnership Against Terrorism program and urged its customers to become certified members to speed their deliveries across the United States–Canada border.

Gain Important Benefits for Your Company and Your Country.

Join the Partnership Against Terrorism with U.S. and Canada Customs.

Become certified in:
• Customs-Trade Partnership Against Terrorism
• Customs Self Assessment
• Free and Secure Trade
• Partners in Protection

CON-WAY

On November 11, 2002, Con-Way began applying an $8 "Homeland Security Surcharge" on all shipments moving north or south across the United States–Canada national border.

A U.S. national program, the Customs-Trade Partnership Against Terrorism (C-TPAT), was established to set new security standards for the LTL motor carrier industry. Con-Way worked with the Partners in Protection (PIP) security initiative operated by the Canada Customs and Revenue Agency.[19]

The American and Canadian programs were part of the Free and Secure Trade (FAST) Highway Carrier Application Process. FAST was created to tighten security at the United States–Canada border while maintaining the free flow of low-risk trade by using dedicated traffic lanes for trucks. Carriers and drivers received preapproval to cross the border with their shipments.

In early 2003, Con-Way Central, Western, and Canada Express received approval to participate in Canada's Customs Self Assessment, which was launched in 1998.

In this program, truckers are given bar-coded identification cards that notify Canada Customs that the vehicle, driver, importer, and shipment have preapproval by the agency to cross the border. No additional documentation is required, resulting in significantly improved crossing times.[20]

Con-Way also sought to improve its internal security. It appointed 12-year veteran Curtis Shewchuk to the new position of director of corporate security services. Shewchuk, who served as manager of corporate security services at CNF's Portland, Oregon, location, was placed in charge of a team of security specialists who would protect Con-Way's employees, facilities, equipment, and freight. A graduate of the Organized Crime Institute at the University of Georgia and the National Intelligence Academy in Fort Lauderdale, Florida, Shewchuk worked in law enforcement for many years before coming to Con-Way.[21]

CONTINUING TO INNOVATE

Con-Way helped set industry standards when it added thousands of cities to its next-day and second-day lanes and implemented Con-Way NOW and Con-Way AIR for customers who needed expedited shipments. For those who did not require next-day

Con-Way's next-day and second-day service demonstrated consistent on-time performance and set the standard for the industry.

or two-day service and wanted an additional 20-percent discount on their transcontinental shipments, Con-Way created a deferred service program in October 2002.[22]

PORTLAND'S VOTE

The decertification vote of the Portland employees who belonged to Local 11 of the Office and Professional Employees International Union (OPEIU) proved a key event in 2002. When the Portland office employees first voted, decertification won by seven votes, but the OPEIU challenged the result. Instead of going to court over the issue, CNF held a second vote. This time, the margin of employ-

ees willing to exit the union increased by about 20 votes.[23] David Anderson, then director of human resources, explained:

We were able to decertify the union in the Portland office, which in my opinion probably saved all the jobs there. I don't think the employees understood it at the time, but subsequent events have proven correct that their jobs were more secure because they're union-free.

It was still pretty close, but to my knowledge, since that happened, none of the employees have regretted it, and they know now that they're much better off in terms of pay and bonuses and other benefits they're receiving.[24]

Con-Way's philosophy has always been to maintain a nonunion—but not antiunion—atmosphere, noted Robert Coon, who became vice president of human relations for Menlo Worldwide.

THE DEMISE OF CONSOLIDATED FREIGHTWAYS

CONSOLIDATED FREIGHTWAYS CORPORATION SPUN off from CNF Inc. on December 2, 1996. It emerged as a unionized long-haul carrier with little debt and an improved capital structure. CFC President and CEO Roger Curry wanted to make the company a profit-generating enterprise.[1]

With its headquarters in Menlo Park, California, the "new" CF ranked as the nation's third-largest long-haul carrier with 19,000 employees and 40,800 trucks, tractors, and trailers. By slashing the number of distribution terminals from 700 to 373 prior to the spin-off, Consolidated Freightways became more cost effective. In its first quarter of operation as an independent, Consolidated Freightways produced a $3.3 million profit, and Curry introduced a stock grant program designed to encourage eligible employees to become shareholders and to foster an ownership culture.[2]

With a net income of $20.4 million on sales of $2.3 billion for 1997, Consolidated Freightways showed promise for the future. Its profitable period continued into 1998, when the company posted a net income of $26.3 million.

In 1998, Consolidated Freightways signed a five-year contract with the Teamsters union that provided for a moderate wage increase in order to ward off a potential strike. Unfortunately, CFC experienced difficulties in 1999 when it took on marginal freight and outsourced its information technology system, requiring a large investment. Consolidated Freightways' net income dipped to $2.7 million on sales of $2.38 billion that year.

Curry retired from Consolidated Freightways in January 2000 and Patrick Blake, a 30-year Consolidated Freightways veteran who began his career there, replaced him.[3] After he became CFC's president, Blake commented:

"The original management team at Con-Way came out of a unionized environment. They'd all learned to live with it. They all understood why there are unions," Coon added.[25]

MAGICAL MOVES

The Con-Ways participated in the delivery of more than 500,000 copies of the book, *Harry Potter and the Order of the Phoenix*, for Levy Home Entertainment in 2003. The undertaking involved 2,000 individual LTL shipments to bookstores throughout the United States for the opening sale day of June 21. Levy was one of several distributors chosen by Scholastic Books to handle the book's initial press run of 4.5 million copies in the United States and Great Britain.[26, 27]

Bruce H. Moss, vice president of Con-Way Central, said:

It was an exciting and challenging project for us. It's what we do best. It was about planning, execution, and precision. It was also fun because of the huge interest these books have caused among children around the world.[28]

Con-Way did not make any special arrangement for employees to receive books or early deliveries and instead focused on getting the job done successfully.

"My two sons waited in line at the bookstore on the day of the book's release along with everyone else," Moss said.[29]

Two years later, Levy Home Entertainment again enlisted the Con-Ways to make the deliveries for J. K. Rowling's sixth Harry Potter book, *Harry Potter and the Half-Blood Prince*, which was released on July 16, 2005. Con-Way service centers in Illinois, Virginia, and Utah handled the more than 4,000 shipments of 10.8 million books into the company's

The exterior of the former headquarters of Consolidated Freightways in Menlo Park, California, in August 2000. After CFC's bankruptcy, the building was demolished to make way for a new development. (Photo courtesy of Ray Halloran.)

We were called a mature company in a mature industry. The reason we saved the company was every employee, not just management, pulled together. We beat the odds many times. We're going to beat them again. That's our goal.[4]

The carrier closed its Menlo Park headquarters in August 2000 and moved to new offices in Vancouver, Washington. The company also bought FirstAir Inc., a Minnesota-based airfreight forwarder, and renamed it CF AirFreight. Although Consolidated Freightways brought in outside consultants in an attempt to maximize efficiency, the company reported a net loss of $7.6 million for 2000.

Consolidated Freightways continued to lose money in 2001 as it recorded a net loss of $104.3 million for the year. In response, Consolidated Freightways reduced its administrative staff from 900 to 800, and hundreds of employees were laid off across North America. Despite these efforts Consolidated Freightways' losses deepened further—it posted a net loss of $36.5 million for the first quarter of 2002.

Even after securing a $45 million loan in early 2002 to stay solvent, the company filed for Chapter 11 bankruptcy protection that September. The company liquidated its assets, and the historic Consolidated Freightways ceased to exist.[5, 6]

nationwide service center network for delivery within a 24-hour window.[30]

TECHNOLOGY ADVANCEMENTS

To increase the speed and convenience for shippers, Con-Way updated its Web site in 2002, creating a user-friendly interface for customers to easily create templates for electronic bills of lading (eBOLs) that are used for recurring shipments. The improved system also allowed customers to submit pickup notices electronically to a nearby Con-Way service center. With the development of the new electronic features, the company monitored usage rates and received customer feedback about its Web-based and e-business functions.

"As customers use these electronic connections it has become clear that we're dealing with two different audiences, and each is at distinctly different levels of e-business development," noted Jackie Barretta, chief information officer of Con-Way Transportation Services. "The electronically advanced firms, especially those with high shipment volumes, want a complete electronic transaction interface. Those with smaller shipment volumes and less electronic development resources want us to make our eBOL system easier to use and tailor data entry to their needs."[31]

Con-Way Transportation Services began to explore new ways to improve its line-haul operations, which involved the movement of freight over long distances from service center to service center for redistribution.[32] Each workday, Con-Way Central, Con-Way Southern, Con-Way Western, and Con-Way Canada sent out 6,500 trucks and drivers to pick up and deliver an average of more than 105,000 LTL shipments ranging from 50 pounds to 18,000 pounds. These shipments were routed through a network of more than 400 service centers throughout Canada and the United States.[33]

After a failed attempt by a University of Michigan consulting group to develop an automated route optimization model that paralleled the workings of an LTL trucking environment, Con-Way turned to someone in-house.

YaFeng Du, a technical expert who had been working at CNF Inc. for a little more than three years,

was approached to find a solution. With a doctorate in industrial engineering from the University of California at Berkeley, Du also holds a master's degree in electrical engineering and formerly worked for the Chinese Army designing rocket guidance systems.[34, 35]

After nine months, Du created an automated scheduling system that incorporated the practicalities of the LTL trucking industry. Du explained:

I figured it would take me six months, but I told them it would be a year in order to make more room.[36]

I was given one absolute operating constraint. Every shipment picked up each day must begin movement to its destination that same night. That rule drives Con-Way on-time performance and was set in any model I developed.[37]

Four IT staff members were assigned to deploy and maintain the line-haul automation system while

The *Commercial Carrier Journal* ranked Con-Way Transportation fourth in the LTL general freight category. Employees who contributed to its success included (left to right): Mike Falabella of Con-Way Western Express, Dr. YaFeng Du of CTS, Lori Blaney of Con-Way NOW, Gerald Detter, Michael Umphrey of Con-Way Southern Express, Teresa Patterson of Con-Way Central Express, Rubin Rivera of Con-Way Western Express, and Kevin Richardson of Con-Way Integrated Services.

Du diagnosed and repaired problems. The system was successfully rolled out in 2003.

The $3 million line-haul automation system improved efficiency by 1 to 3 percent over the manual route planning, saving Con-Way Central in excess of $2 million in annual operating costs.[38] Compared to the manual dispatch system, Du's automated system allowed Con-Way Central to use 111 fewer trucks and 68 fewer drivers, trimming routes by 26,530 miles annually. It boosted the average truck's load by 370 pounds.[39]

In January 2003, Con-Way Transportation received *CIO* magazine's Enterprise Value Award for Du's system that reduced routing process time from several hours to seven minutes. By 2003, Con-Way estimated the system was saving between $4 million and $5 million annually, while improving on-time delivery performance.[40]

In September 2003, *InformationWeek* magazine ranked Con-Way Transportation first in the transportation industry as one of the most innovative IT users, ahead of many of its larger rivals including FedEx, Roadway, Yellow, and UPS. Overall, Con-Way ranked 15th in the listings among *FORTUNE*® 500 companies such as General Motors, Dell, and J.P. Morgan Chase & Company.[41]

HOS RULES

In 2003, the U.S. Department of Transportation revised the hours-of-service (HOS) rules for truck drivers to combat driver fatigue and improve safety. The new rules reduced the total time a driver could be on duty from 15 to 14 consecutive hours, and it increased the mandatory off-duty rest period from eight to 10 hours.[42, 43]

Drivers and companies violating the HOS rules could face fines of $550 to $11,000 per infraction.[44] The new rules seemed to be working, and within two years of implementing the new regulations, many companies saw their DOT-reportable accidents fall by 10 to 15 percent.[45]

Also in 2003, CTS earned the International Organization for Standardization (ISO) 9001 and 14001 quality certifications for all of its Con-Way companies and facilities. The ISO 9001 certification recognized CTS for its excellence in operational compliance with processes and procedures that measure up to other leading companies. CTS also earned the

Andy Cheek (left), vice president of operations at AQSR International, and Con-Way Transportation Services President and CEO Jerry Detter hold ISO certificates in 2003, the first year that all of the Con-Way companies became certified. For 42 days, auditors from AQSR examined Con-Way's operations and found a group of highly motivated, thoroughly trained individuals who consistently exceeded the customer's expectations.

ISO 14001 certification for compliance with processes and procedures that protect the environment.[46] Bryan Millican, CTS executive vice president, sales and marketing, at the time, explained:

A number of our customers asked us to become ISO certified. It's part of the business process and commitment they expect from their key vendors.[47]

MANAGEMENT CHANGES

At age 41, Stotlar earned a promotion to chief operating officer of CTS in June 2002.[48] About the same time, Richard V. Palazzo announced that he would retire as president and CEO of Con-Way Central, capping off a 40-year career. David S. McClimon, president and CEO of Con-Way Western, became Palazzo's replacement. John G. Labrie, then Con-Way Western's vice president of operations, took over for McClimon.[49]

In January 2004, Donald E. Moffitt, then 71, announced his retirement as chairman effective at the end of the month, capping off his nearly 50-year career at the trucking firm.[50] Kennedy became the new chairman.[51] Since joining the CNF board in 1996, Kennedy had retired from his previous position as president and CEO of the Watkins-Johnson

Company in 2000. Shortly after Moffitt's retirement, Quesnel announced his retirement as CNF's president and CEO.[52] And as the board searched for Quesnel's successor, it elected Kennedy as CNF's interim CEO.[53]

THE SEARCH FOR A CEO

"The board was really trying to go through a deliberative process to pick the right person, or at least what they believed were the right qualifications for where they saw the company going at that time," said Stotlar. "You've got all these dynamics happening back behind the scenes. … We wanted an internal candidate. We didn't want an external candidate."[54]

However, the board was also vetting external candidates. And behind these discussions were two additional camps with specific alliances: One for Detter and another for Williford.

Then, in an unexpected turn of events, after a December 2004 CTS board meeting, Detter and Kennedy met privately. Detter, who had finished meeting with Kennedy, approached Stotlar and told him he would be retiring from the company.

"Jerry [Detter] came in and said, 'I'm retiring, and you're going to be the new CEO of CTS.' No one was more surprised than I was," recounted Stotlar.

As part of his duties as a senior leader of Con-Way, Stotlar briefed the CNF board and strategized with Kennedy and Williford about how to better coordinate the different aspects of the company. There were discussions of making Williford the new corporate CEO and appointing Stotlar as chief operating officer of CNF.[55]

"I was never told I was in the running for the CNF CEO job," explained Stotlar.

On April 26, 2005, CNF's board of directors then named Stotlar as president and CEO, while Williford announced his retirement and became an advisor to the corporation.[56]

Other executive changes occurred during 2004 and 2005, including the retirement of Eb Schmoller as CNF's general counsel after 28 years with the corporation. He was replaced by Jennifer Pileggi, who had been an in-house attorney for Menlo. CNF Chief Financial Officer Chutta Ratnathicam retired on March 31, 2005, and was replaced by Kevin Schick, a 22-year veteran of the company.[57]

J. Edwin "Ed" Conaway, who was president and CEO of Con-Way NOW, earned a promotion to CTS vice president of sales for Con-Way Freight in November 2005.[58] Michelle D. Potter, was promoted from vice president of operations to head Con-Way NOW.[59]

THE NEW CON-WAY TRUCKLOAD

In 2004, Con-Way announced it would launch a new division called Con-Way Truckload Services that

Douglas Stotlar became CNF's president and CEO on April 26, 2005.

would begin operating in the first quarter of 2005. This division would transport freight via truckload to a limited geographic region.[60] The new service added 450 jobs.

Clayton T. "Clay" Halla was hired as president of Con-Way Truckload. Previously, he worked at Southern Cal Transport in Birmingham, Alabama, where he was vice president of operations.[61] Con-Way Truckload Services budgeted $200 million to purchase 46 new Volvo model VN670 over-the-road tractors and 115 new 53-foot trailers.

On January 18, 2005, the first of Con-Way Truckload's two-person driver teams left the company's Memphis, Tennessee, headquarters on a nearly 37-hour trip to Blythe, California. Initially, the new truckload unit had 23 driver teams, as well as managers and operating staff members.[62] After only three months in business, Con-Way Truckload became profitable. By the end of 2005,

it had 200 teams of drivers and 80 regional drivers.[63] Stotlar explained:

This time around, we had a very good understanding of the cost structure of the truckload business. The new Con-Way Truckload started very strong out of the gates.[64]

LEADERSHIP CHANGES AT CTS AND CNF

After Stotlar's appointment as CEO of CNF, he began focusing on taking CNF from serving solely as a holding company to one that would function as an operating company. He identified David S. McClimon to take over as CEO of CTS. Millican was promoted to the newly created position of CNF senior vice president of sales and marketing. Dave Miller became president of Con-Way Central, moving from his prior role as president of Con-Way Southern. Phil Worthington was appointed president of Con-Way Southern.

Con-Way Western President and CEO Labrie was named a CNF vice president and became president of Con-Way Supply Chain Solutions, overseeing Con-Way Truckload, Con-Way Truckload

In 2005, Con-Way Truckload began operations with 46 new Volvo tractors and became profitable after only three months.

Brokerage, Con-Way NOW, and Con-Way Air.[65] Other personnel changes included naming Kevin M. Hartman, Con-Way Central vice president of operations, the new Con-Way Western head; promoting Bruce H. Moss, a 15-year veteran at the company, to replace Hartman at Con-Way Central; and shifting Con-Way Logistics vice president and general manager Mike S. Bare to Con-Way Central where he replaced Moss as vice president of sales.[66]

"Everybody's been around for a long, long time because they like the culture," Stotlar commented. "The people that we have in our employ are people who personally share the corporate values. I can honestly say, when I sit around a table with all these people, every one of them I wouldn't mind having as my next-door neighbor. We like each other, we know

each other, we're comfortable with each other, and we trust each other."[67]

Robert Bianco, who had joined the corporation in 1989 before becoming logistics manager at Menlo in 1992, became a CNF vice president and president of Menlo Worldwide in 2005, and Gary Kowalski was appointed chief operating officer.[68]

INDUSTRY RANKINGS

The *Commercial Carrier Journal* began publishing an annual ranking of North America's top carriers based on gross revenues in the 1960s. Beginning in 2005, the *Journal* considered other factors including fleet size, the number of power units owned or controlled, and the number of drivers or owner-operators employed. Under this methodology, CTS was ranked as No. 11 out of 250 of the top North American carriers.[69] In the LTL general freight segment, CTS ranked No. 4, exceeded only by FedEx Freight, Roadway Express, and Yellow Transportation.

In 2005, CTS received Ford Motor Company's prestigious Q1 certification. The certification process took more than a year as Ford reviewed Con-Way's on-time delivery performance, invoicing accuracy, financial soundness, adherence to Department of Transportation regulations, and employee safety records. The company joined only a handful of Ford service suppliers who have achieved Q1 certification.[70]

GROWING SOUTH OF THE BORDER

Eager to expand its role in the cross-border manufacturing trade between the United States and Mexico, Con-Way leased new facilities in the cities of Nuevo Laredo, Monterrey, San Luis Potosi, Guadalajara, Queretaro, and Mexico City, and added 50 employees to Con-Way Mexico Express in June 2005.[71]

Since Mexican law prevented foreign companies from owning a controlling interest in domestic trucking firms, Con-Way partnered with Mexican haulers to provide transportation, warehousing,

Con-Way provides ongoing training and certification to employees on loading techniques and safety issues, including how to handle hazardous materials.

Con-Way Canada Express opened two new terminals in 2002, including one in Windsor, Ontario, which serves as the busiest international gateway between the United States and Canada. Here, a Con-Way Canada tractor made the trip across the border.

and freight assembly. As the Mexican economy became more integrated with its NAFTA (North American Free Trade Agreement) partners, namely the United States and Canada, Con-Way positioned itself for rapid expansion.

Con-Way Freight President McClimon, explained:

Building this network is the next logical step in providing Con-Way Freight service throughout all the NAFTA markets. We eventually want to provide the same service in Mexico that we currently provide in the United States and Canada.[72]

PROMOTING GOODWILL

CTS continued a number of initiatives and began new ones in communicating values and philanthropy. The company reached out to create a positive image to the public, as well as focusing on its own employees' needs.

An organization called the Texas Military Family Foundation (TMFF), received a donation of 35,000 decks of playing cards for soldiers stationed in Iraq. CTS teamed up with BNSF Railway and others to ship the cards from California to Fort Hood, where they would then be sent on to Iraq.[73]

In 2005, CTS celebrated its 15th consecutive year as a sponsor for the Red Ribbon Campaign, the largest and oldest drug prevention program in the nation. More than 900 Con-Way employees from its six U.S. companies visited more than 1,100 elementary and high schools to present the anti-drug message.[74]

CTS also focused its efforts internally. Understanding the importance of a consistent mission and corporate culture across service lines, Stotlar created the position of CNF vice president of culture and training, appointing Pat Jannausch to that office. Jannausch explained:

When Doug created my position, it was a statement. You will rarely find a communication from the top that doesn't reference culture—whether it is from Doug or any president of our many business units. ... It has been woven into the fabric of this culture that we base our decisions on our values. Our values are how we will succeed.[75]

INDUSTRY RECOGNITION

Even with all of the management changes, CNF and Con-Way executives maintained a focus on Con-Way's main mission—to deliver superior customer service and grow as market forces demanded. CTS was named one of the nation's top 100 innovative organizations in August 2005 by *CIO* magazine for its application of information technology.[76]

In May 2005, CTS launched a new program referred to as the "final-mile" delivery service for distribution-critical retail and industrial businesses

"Since late summer, we have added more than 120 dock doors to the network," McClimon announced in November 2005. By this point, CTS had 440 facilities that collectively utilized more than 15,000 dock doors.[79]

The physical expansions for CTS facilities in 2005 included:

- Service centers in West Fargo, North Dakota, and Bedford, Pennsylvania, which replaced smaller facilities and added 41 new doors.
- A 31-door service center in Woodinville, Washington, to support business growth in the Seattle region. This was the company's fourth terminal in the area.
- The addition of 50 doors to the Tonawanda facility that services the Buffalo, New York, market.
- The purchase of a former Consolidated Freightways property located next to New Jersey's Port Elizabeth and less than a mile from the Newark Airport.

The purchase of the Newark property proved especially significant because of its strategic location near a deep-water port, airport, and major four-lane ground routes, including the New Jersey Turnpike and highways 95 and 78. Stotlar commented:

We've always been very proactive in making sure we have capacity with the bricks and mortar infrastructure, because the lead times are so long.[80]

NATURAL DISASTERS

Throughout Con-Way's history, numerous storms, earthquakes, and blizzards have created situations where drivers can make a difference. For example, a CF tanker driver delivered 6,000 gallons of water to a thirsty Oregon community after Typhoon Frieda hit in 1962, blasting the Pacific Northwest and damaging the Portland terminal. In 1964, two Canadian Freightways drivers delivered relief supplies to quake-stricken Seward, Alaska. Then there were the blizzards and storms of 1975, 1976, 1978, and 1979, where drivers "bucked giant snowdrifts, zero visibility, whiteouts, and frozen fuel lines to deliver their freight."[81]

By November 2005, Con-Way Transportation Services had 440 facilities that collectively utilized more than 15,000 dock doors.

with multiple selling locations within a single urban market. Through local cross-docking, warehousing, and final delivery of freight it provided just-in-time inventory and time-specific delivery demands for its customers.[77]

The Con-Way carriers became the first in the transportation industry to offer a Web-based system that automatically sends an e-mail notification to Canadian and U.S. LTL customers on the rare occasion that a shipment is late.

Con-Way excelled financially as its operating income rose 34 percent during the third quarter of 2005, while its total operating ratio hit 87.3 percent.[78]

UNPARALLELED GROWTH

In 2005, Con-Way continued to expand its freight-handling capabilities.

The active 2005 Atlantic hurricane season tested the mettle of Con-Way drivers and personnel along the Gulf of Mexico. Five of the season's seven major hurricanes—Dennis, Emily, Katrina, Rita, and Wilma—caused heavy devastation to areas along the Gulf of Mexico Coast.

After striking Florida as a Category 1 hurricane, Katrina strengthened to a Category 5 storm in the Gulf and made landfall on August 29, devastating Louisiana and Mississippi. The city of New Orleans flooded after its levees failed. Overall, more than 1,800 people lost their lives as a result of the storm that caused an estimated $81 billion in damage, making it the costliest natural disaster in American history.[82]

In the aftermath of Hurricane Katrina, Con-Way made numerous deliveries of supplies to areas affected by the disaster. In one instance, a Con-Way tractor-trailer met a Wal-Mart truck on a bridge where employees of both companies worked together to transfer 100 electric generators to the Wal-Mart truck for final delivery.[83]

Hurricane Rita, also strengthening into a Category 5 storm, struck Texas on September 23, 2005, resulting in an estimated $11.3 billion in damage that disrupted oil and refining capacity, causing a surge in fuel prices.[84] Despite the potentially negative financial ramifications, Con-Way imposed a temporary cap on its fuel surcharge to alleviate additional financial hardship to its customers.[85] Stotlar noted:

We are an efficient yet flexible company, and that served us well during the recent Katrina and Rita hurricanes, where the financial impact was negligible because of our ability to quickly reroute our services and limit disruption of operations. The company and its employees responded to the crisis by donating more than $550,000 to the American Red Cross for hurricane relief.[86]

As 2005 came to a close, CNF continued to examine how to benefit from the company's sterling reputation and trusted Con-Way name. This would pave the way for a Herculean effort to streamline the company's image through a company-wide rebranding. In the future, the Con-Ways would make several major acquisitions and finally merge the backroom operations of its three regional LTL carriers to provide one strong, unified presence to the public.

CHAPTER TEN

Con·way®

2006 AND BEYOND

We're behaving as one company now. We can now react to the marketplace much more quickly. We're already making very rifle-shot sales and marketing approaches to individual needs [and] lane-based needs, as well as targeted sales approaches where we have the most competitive advantage.

—Douglas W. Stotlar,
president and CEO,
Con-way Inc.[1]

AS CON-WAY TRANSPORTATION SERvices (CTS) approached its 25th anniversary, CNF had grown into the market leader in the supply chain management industry.

"In a year that saw our organization accomplish a major transition in executive management, the focus of our people on service excellence and superior quality for our customers never wavered," said CNF President and CEO Douglas W. Stotlar. "These impressive results are a testament to that focus, the strength and determination of our team, and the robust nature of our business model."[2]

CTS reported a record operating income of $331.1 million for 2005, and Menlo Worldwide's profits jumped to $26.7 million, a 17.4 percent increase over the previous year. CNF also repurchased more than 3 million common shares worth $149.1 million in 2005.[3]

After its remarkable financial results, CNF achieved a BBB rating from Standard & Poor's as well as Fitch Ratings.

"These rating actions speak to the stability and strength of CNF's financial position, and the earnings growth and cash flow potential of the enterprise," said Kevin Schick, CNF's senior vice president and chief financial officer. "We're a leading player in the LTL trucking and logistics markets, and we have an excellent balance sheet, financial flexibility, and

a high-service business model that has stood the test of time."[4]

THE "NEW" CON-WAY INC.

While competing against such industry giants as FedEx and UPS, Con-Way offered superior performance while maintaining a tight-knit corporate culture that bred loyalty and pride among its employees. However, as Con-Way continued to differentiate itself from its competitors, executives recognized that continuing the myriad Con-Way names for each unit created confusion in the marketplace and would make the company's vision of migrating from a holding company to an enterprise operating model more difficult. This was a major hindrance as it competed directly with recognized name brands.

As Chairman Keith Kennedy explained:

Above: This 2006 commemorative coin, which featured Leland James on the other side (see page 187), was distributed on April 18, 2006, to celebrate the renaming of the historic CNF Corporation to Con-way Inc. *(From the collection of Raymond O'Brien.)*

Opposite: After Con-way announced its rebranding efforts, a Con-way Freight truck displaying the corporation's new logos parked in front of the NYSE on Wall Street.

Con-Way was the "Coca-Cola" of the industry, and not using that as our brand name was just wasting a key resource. ... When I see a FedEx truck, it says FedEx, but when I saw a CWX truck on the road, only I knew what it was.[5]

Doug Stotlar, president and CEO, officially rang the opening bell of the NYSE on May 12, 2006, in celebration of Con-way's stock ticker symbol changing from CNF to CNW.

At the April 18, 2006, shareholders' meeting, the CNF board proposed a name change to shareholders—from CNF Inc. to Con-way Inc. This would alleviate the confusion and place a single, recognizable brand in front of the industry and its customers. The name change was approved and officially introduced on April 19, 2006. At the same time, Con-Way Transportation changed its name to Con-way Freight.

On May 5, 2006, Con-way officially changed its stock ticker symbol from "CNF" to "CNW" and began trading on the New York Stock Exchange (NYSE) under the new CNW ticker symbol.[6] As part of the kickoff celebration, a set of Con-way double trailers displaying the new Con-way Freight logo were parked in front of the NYSE alongside Wyler Racing team's No. 60 Con-way Toyota Tundra race truck. Con-way executives hosted an analyst conference on Wall Street on May 11, 2006, and the next day Douglas Stotlar, president and CEO, rang the NYSE

opening bell on behalf of Con-way's 27,000 employees as part of the celebration.[7]

The event drew significant media interest and both the Bloomberg Business News, and the Dow Jones Newswires interviewed Stotlar. CNBC spoke to Con-way Freight President Dave McClimon.[8]

In 2006, a *Traffic World* headline announced the name change: "Goodbye CNF, Hello 'Con-way': Con-Way Regional Carriers Regroup as Con-way Freight as $4.2 Billion Trucking Giant Rebrands."[9] Con-way's rebranding efforts extended far past cosmetic changes, instead serving as the impetus for a business model renovation. Disparate business units such as Con-way Freight and Menlo Worldwide began working together far more closely than ever. Con-way Inc. also embarked on a series of key mergers and acquisitions as it sought to leverage and expand the specialized services it offered to its customers.

THE REBIRTH OF A LOGO

As part of the transition from CNF to Con-way, the 20-year-old corporate logo underwent a transformation. According to Pat Jannausch, vice president of culture and training, the boxy letters of the original logo now looked old-fashioned. At the same time, from a marketing standpoint, the corporation's hodgepodge of multiple brands and logos sent a confusing message to potential customers.

"Some people knew Con-Way Central Express as CCX, [and] some called it Con-Way Central," Jannausch said. "When Doug [Stotlar] became CEO, his desire was to turn this from a holding company into an operating company, which meant that the level at the top needed to look the same, sound the same, be the same as the whole rest of the company."[10]

As Stotlar explained, "CNF is a venerable symbol that traces its origins to the old Consolidated Freightways organization. [However,] over the past 20 years, the Con-way name has emerged as a powerful, respected brand in its own right, known for service excellence and superior shareholder value."[11]

Jannausch and Edward P. "Ned" Moritz, who retired as vice president of branding in December 2007, worked with brand consulting company Siegel+Gale, based in New York City, to develop new logos for Con-way Inc.[12] After conducting numerous interviews of the firm's employees, executives, and customers, Siegel+Gale developed Con-way's current signature blue logo—a lowercase "w" with a slanted hyphen visually connecting the "n" in "Con" with the "w" in "way." With those changes, the logo

looked more like a signature, but kept intact the hyphenated origin of the company's original name.

After the final design was chosen, Con-way began an exhaustive review of every item in its inventory in need of rebranding, including forms, signs, and uniforms. According to Moritz, "It is amazing how many pieces of equipment and other items that had a name or a logo on it."[13]

"I was dealt a good hand in that Ned and the marketing team had done very solid groundwork for the rebranding process," said Tom Nightingale, who left Schneider National to become vice president of communications and chief marketing officer in June 2006. "The marketing team that I joined had done most of the heavy lifting before I arrived at Con-way. They had a well-buttoned-down plan to tackle the technical details. My task was to harness the power embedded in our brands and leverage every marketing medium possible."[14]

Con-way budgeted $20 million spread across two to three years for the exhaustive rebranding process of applying new logos to its 35,000 units of rolling stock, signage at 440 terminals, and 15,000 new uniforms, as well as marketing and advertising efforts.[15]

Jennifer W. Pileggi, senior vice president, general counsel, and corporate secretary, handled the legal trademark issues of the name change. She began her legal career in 1990 at the law firm of Heller, Ehrman, White, and McAuliffe in San Francisco, California,

In the picture on the left, a driver reviews a bill of lading with a customer in front of a Con-Way Truckload truck in the older red-and-blue color scheme. The picture above shows the same driver sporting a new uniform with a truck bearing updated colors and logos.

RACING SPONSORSHIP

AFTER CON-WAY TRANSPORTATION Service's one-race sponsorship of Robert Pressley of HT Motorsports in 2005, the company became the primary sponsor of the No. 60 Wyler Racing team for the 2006 and 2007 seasons of the NASCAR Craftsman Truck Series. And, beginning in the 2008 season, Con-way inked a deal with Roush Fenway Racing.

It was no coincidence that the corporation became a major racing sponsor the same year that CNF Inc. officially changed its name to Con-way Inc., noted Ned Moritz, retired vice president of branding.

"We needed a platform to promote the new brand," Moritz said. "We went into the NASCAR Craftsman Truck Series [and] lined up all of the entertainment resources that we needed, and we told the NASCAR people, okay, put this old brand logo on, but in April 2006, you're going to have to change it."[1]

Driver Jack Sprague was the first to wear the Con-way white-and-blue uniform in 2006,

finishing fifth overall that season and ninth for the 2007 season, as he drove behind the wheel of a specially engineered Toyota Tundra.[2]

Alongside the racing sponsorship came a line of merchandise for fans, ranging from hats, shirts, and cups printed with the new Con-way logo. When Moritz went to the Dodge Ram Tough 200 race in St. Louis on April 29, 2006, he discovered the new logo and look was a winner.

"All of our employees who showed up at the tent for entertainment were wearing shirts, hats, everything, with the new logo," he said.[3]

For the 2008 season, Con-way Freight became the primary sponsor of the No. 6 Ford F-150, piloted by rookie driver Colin Braun of Roush Fenway Racing.[4] Braun, a rising star in American motor sports, had signed a long-term contract with the racing team the previous year to drive in the NASCAR Truck Series in 2008. Roush Fenway Racing, co-owned by automotive supplier magnate Jack Roush of Michigan, is one of the largest rac-

---

and joined Menlo in 1996, becoming part of the corporation's executive team and chief attorney in December 2004.

Pileggi and her team focused on making certain every legal aspect of the name change was accounted for.

"When we changed certain parts of the company's name, we had to get notifications out to customers," Pileggi said. "Their approval wasn't required, but we wanted to make sure that the changes were not negatively received. We also had to notify the regulatory agencies."[16]

At the same time, Pileggi and other executives helped ease the minds of drivers during Con-way's evolution.

"They had a huge amount of pride in the particular regional division that they worked for,"

Pileggi explained. "It took them a little while to get used to [being thought of as a large group rather than regional carriers], but it went very well, and all employees have really embraced it."

CONSOLIDATING THE BRAND

Instead of remaining a holding company for Con-way Freight, under the new reorganization, CTS oversaw the corporation's asset-based regional and transcontinental truckload service units, including the former Con-Way NOW and Con-Way Full Load units, which became Con-way Expedite and Brokerage, respectively. Also falling under CTS jurisdiction was Road Systems Inc., the trailer manufacturing and rebuilding unit that Consolidated Freightways purchased in 1979.[17]

Right: Sponsoring NASCAR Craftsman Truck Series driver Colin Braun proved a popular way to re-emphasize Con-way's rebranding. Braun's No. 6 Con-way truck is shown parked in front of the grandstands of the Daytona International Speedway.

Opposite: Con-way sponsored NASCAR Craftsman Truck Series rookie driver Colin Braun of Roush Fenway Racing. While still a teenager, Braun's racing accomplishments included being the youngest driver in history to stand on the podium at the Le Mans 24 Hours race, earning second place at the age of 19.

ing teams running NASCAR cars in the Sprint, Nationwide, and Craftsman Truck Series, as well as the ARCA RE/MAX Series.

Braun's professional racing career had started at the young age of 16, when he drove in the Rolex 24 Hours of Daytona in a Porsche 996 GT3 Cup car. At age 17, he had become the youngest driver in North America to win a major league motor race when he won the Brumos 250 at Daytona International Speedway. And, at age 19, Braun was the youngest driver in history to stand on the podium at the famous Le Mans 24 Hours race and accept a second-place trophy.

After signing on with Roush, Braun finished in the top 10 in the ARCA series and won three races.

"This is a dream come true," said Braun. "To be with a team like Roush Fenway Racing and to have the opportunity to drive the No. 6 Con-way Freight F-150 is really exciting."[5]

According to John G. Labrie, president of Con-way Freight: "We are excited to be joining one of the largest and most successful racing organizations in the business. This sponsorship takes our NASCAR participation to the next level. Roush Fenway and Ford Racing are a proven team, which is providing Con-way with an excellent program. We look forward to an exciting and successful season for the No. 6 Con-way Freight Ford F-150."[6]

On July 24, 2006, Con-way announced the sale of Con-way Expedite to privately held Panther Expedited Services for $6.2 million.[18] The downturn in the American automotive industry, a primary customer of expedited services, prompted the sale.[19] After assessing the future prospects for the expedited services marketplace, Con-way decided to focus on its core business lines.

Con-way Air briefly became known as Con-way Forwarding until the unit shut down in June 2006. The remaining brokerage business was renamed Con-way Truckload Services.

"We're going to invest in LTL and truckload freight transportation, [as well as] global contract logistics," Stotlar noted. "We believe these markets present the best prospects for material growth in

long-term revenues and profits, and increased shareholder returns."[20]

As Con-way's rebranding efforts continued, the corporation's regional and inter-regional LTL units unified under the Con-way Freight name on August 22, 2007. The former Con-way Central Express, Con-way Southern Express, and Con-way Western Express dropped their names, logos, and colors, consolidating under the Con-way Freight banner.[21]

Discussion arose about changing the Menlo Worldwide name to Con-way Logistics, as the rebranding continued. One of the reasons for considering the Menlo name change was that when Menlo Worldwide Forwarding was sold to UPS in 2004, some customers thought that UPS had purchased all Menlo operations. It was soon discovered, however, that the Con-way name was already trademarked in

WORLDWIDE LOGISTICS

34 countries in the European market. Lekkerland GmbH & Co. KG, a German convenience store company, owned the rights to it.

"We still wanted to reach the goal of a true masterbrand, where every company name held Con-way as the first part of the name," said Nightingale.[22]

Lekkerland ultimately refused to relinquish the Con-way name. Menlo executives and Con-way's board of directors decided to retain the Menlo name, which by now had regained all of its previous recognition. The Con-way connection would instead be noted graphically, through a redesign of the Menlo logo. The logo lost its traditional "infinite M" logo, and the older gray color was replaced with the modern "Con-way blue." The font was changed to resemble the script of the new Con-way logo. This new Menlo logo became part of the "Con-way trident," alongside the Con-way Freight and Con-way Truckload units.

REENGINEERING MENLO

As a third-party logistics company, Menlo Worldwide remained focused on creating and managing supply chain solutions. An "asset light" company, Menlo managed networks of other companies' trucks, ships, and aircraft on behalf of its customers. It contracted outside transportation companies and other suppliers, and it derived profits from the considerable cost savings passed along to its customers.

THE LEAN VISION

LEAN MANUFACTURING IS A KNOWN CONCEPT THROUGHout the manufacturing world. It embodies practices to reduce waste, increase efficiency, empower employees, and increase transparency of production so that any errors or waste can be immediately identified and corrected.

"When I started in 2003, my charter was to create a template program," explained Jeff Rivera, director of operations, Menlo Worldwide. "General Motors had been driving lean warehousing in their world, and [as our customer] wanted Menlo to replicate that for them."[1]

Lean was originally a manufacturing process—applying it to the logistics industry was quite innovative. The practices are extremely visual and transparent. An easy way to think about applying lean practices is to use a baseball game as an analogy. Everyone can see the field, scoreboard, pitch count, and what type of pitch was thrown last.

Menlo has a defined set of key performance indicators, incorporating customer input. Employees in each functional area can view information on a "Status at a Glance" board, which is amended hourly to track the progress of departmental goals. The lead manager for the area is responsible for updating the information.

"We do real-time performance measurement tracking," said Anthony Oliverio, senior director of operations strategy, Menlo Worldwide. "We also use a system called Metrics Manager, where we begin to manage our activity on a daily basis instead of monthly or weekly."[2]

Menlo's innovative use of lean practices includes participation in all departments. Even human resources is reducing the number of steps in processing a new hire or a promotion.

"We're trying to eliminate time waste and inefficient use of resources," Rivera added. "In our industry, there are so many strong companies out there. We are asset light. We lease our warehouses. We have people and computers. If you don't have processes better than your competitors, and if you don't have people better than your competitors, you will lose. The lean operating system helped us empower and engage our people."[3]

"We integrate our systems, and then we drive the solutions through other suppliers," explained Robert L. Bianco Jr., president of Menlo Worldwide. "We manage large scale projects and long-term engagements for our customers."[23]

Throughout the 1990s, customers demanded that logistics companies provide warehouse capacity, transportation, and project management services throughout North America. Menlo offered those services and more, combining many functions once handled separately.[24] By 2000, companies expected logistics firms to extend these services globally, providing speed and flexibility alongside cost savings.[25]

"More and more companies continue to outsource supply chain functions, as we saw through the 1990s," Bianco explained. "This is a global market, worth over a quarter trillion dollars that's growing at a double digit pace. ... There are lots of runways for

companies like Menlo that have the experience, the systems, the people, and the expertise to deliver value-added solutions to growing customers."[26]

In 2006, the third-party logistics industry reached $390 billion worldwide, with the U.S. market alone growing 9.5 percent.[27] Retaining customers in a crowded marketplace took foresight and flexibility.

Menlo was competing with an increasing number of companies specializing in logistics execution software, consulting firms that provide supply chain redesign work, freight forwarders and integrators, and regional niche logistics companies. However, by providing more complete logistics solutions, Menlo differentiated itself from the competition.

"We had to change our business model, [since] our customers were emphatic that if we didn't change to meet their demands, they were going to find a partner that did," said Robert Bassett, vice presi-

Menlo Worldwide has incorporated lean practices into its workflow, including this Status at a Glance board.

explained Oliverio. "In 2007, we had some 378 kaizen events across the company, which yielded savings of $5.74 million."[4]

Customer satisfaction has increased, and employee turnover has decreased, reflecting that employee morale has improved. Teams are recognized according to five levels: bronze, silver, gold, platinum, and diamond. Each facility has a celebration when a team is recognized—there is also a bonus program tied to performance. Teams that have achieved or exceeded performance goals also increase the size of their bonuses.

"More than 70 Menlo sites are using lean," said Rivera. "A key piece to the success of lean is management acceptance of lean concepts. What I have seen with Doug Stotlar [CEO of Con-way Inc.] and the Con-way team is that they are truly passionate about the lean approach. Management is completely behind it. It is a huge contributor in how quickly we've seen the benefits."[5]

Although the program is in its early stages, having been implemented in 2005, there are signs that it is successful.

"We sit down with managers every month and look at their continuous improvement road map, which reports what they have done in the last 30 days and what they will be doing in the next 30 days, including kaizen events [a small project whose main goal is to improve a process],"

Menlo's use of lean is also influencing Con-way. Lean consultants are working with Con-way Enterprise Services, a group that supports Menlo Worldwide and all Con-way companies from a backroom finance and technology operational standpoint.

dent of sales for Menlo Worldwide. "And, we've been very successful at changing our model to respond to market and customer needs."

"We don't just hand our clients software and leave, or give them a solution and leave, like consultants or software providers," Bianco said. "We design the solution. We integrate the software. We stay there, operate it, and provide the value that we sold you."[28]

At the same time, executives realized that Menlo had much to gain from working more closely with its sister companies at Con-way Freight and Con-way Truckload.

"We've now migrated to a mindset that considers Con-way a sister company," said Bassett. "If Con-way can be competitive, and contracts permit, it has as good a chance at winning the business as any other carrier out there."

INTERNATIONAL GROWTH

Menlo Worldwide's international operations grew rapidly in the early to mid-2000s. Menlo's European business expanded at a 24.5 percent year-over-year rate, as many customers established manufacturing operations in Eastern Europe. In Asia, Menlo experienced a 24.8 percent rise in business, year over year. Latin American business grew at a 10 percent rate.

In 2007, combined revenues from the Con-way Truckload division approached $500 million. CTS continued to invest in its successful LTL and truckload operations, merging the brokerage operations into Con-way Truckload in 2006.

"It's a sign of the globalization of the world's economy," Bianco observed. "Asia has become the workshop of the world. Manufacturing has gone to Asia, and if you're in the supply chain business, you have to be at the point of manufacturing. North America has become a consumer market, and [so] our solutions became more centered around final-mile delivery."[29]

In March 2006, Menlo launched a new subsidiary to serve the Malaysian cities of Kuala Lumpur and Penang. Officially named Menlo Worldwide (Malaysia) Sdn. Bhd., but more commonly known as Menlo Malaysia, the subsidiary provided local and global freight transportation management, distribution, warehousing, and inventory management. Menlo Malaysia shared its Kuala Lumpur operations with MLH Logistics, a Malaysian firm with a long-standing partnership with Menlo.[30]

In August 2006, Menlo announced a major expansion of its multi-client logistics center in Eersel, Holland. The completion of the addition increased the size of the facility to a total of 350,000 square feet and gave Menlo 30 percent more space for inventory management, warehousing, distribution, and supply-chain management services.[31] That same month, Menlo won a contract to provide Siemens AG's Communications Group with warehousing and logistics services in Australia, including inventory control and shipping services. Menlo also opened a new multi-client logistics center in Sydney, Australia, to serve the South Pacific region.[32]

GENERAL MOTORS BUYS VECTOR

General Motors Corporation notified Con-way of its intention to purchase Vector SCM in June 2006. A joint venture between Menlo Worldwide and General Motors, Vector was formed in Decem-

ber 2000 to provide logistics services for the automaker's supply chain. The contract permitted General Motors to purchase Menlo's membership interest in Vector.[33]

On December 11, 2006, Con-way and the automaker announced that they had set Vector's fair market value at $96.4 million. For its share of the joint venture, Con-way received $84.8 million. Menlo retained all non-GM related commercial contracts providing it with another platform for growth.[34]

"We were surprised that GM decided to buy Vector, although it was well within the commitments of the contract," noted Gary D. Kowalski, Menlo Worldwide's chief operating officer. "At the end of the day, GM gained great people and the great processes that we put in place, [while] the sale helped with Con-way's overall cash flow."[35]

SPIN® SELLING

SINCE THEIR INCEPTION, THE ORIGINAL CON-WAY regional LTL carriers offered unheard of next-day and second-day delivery service, surpassing their goals of 95 percent on-time delivery. That reputation of high-quality, dependable service has allowed Con-way to grow at an unprecedented rate.

By the 2000s, however, competitors began approaching Con-way's level of on-time deliveries at a comparable service cost. This led Con-way to take a different approach to sales, as Ed Conaway, vice president of sales for Con-Way Freight, explained:

In the past, we told customers how good we were; they told us how good the competition was. Our goal now is don't talk about the competition. Don't talk about Con-way. Don't talk about price.

What do you talk about? You talk about the customer and their business and what's going on with their business. Before long, they begin to understand why they need Con-way. Once you get there and they like you, they'll agree that Con-way is the best in the business. ... The customer wants to convince you that the price

is the price. But once you understand explicit needs, it's a whole different conversation.[1]

Con-way has begun using a process called SPIN® (Situation, Problem, Implication, Need-pay-off) Selling, which was developed in the 1970s by Neil Rackham and a team of 30 researchers working on a sales study for a group of multinational companies that included IBM and the Xerox Corporation.[2] It is a scientific, measurable sales process that can be used to track sales calls.

"The most important part is we can identify customers' explicit needs and that there is an additional cost for a customer using a less service-oriented trucking company," Conaway added. "That's the key, because once you get explicit needs on the table, you can talk about how less service-oriented companies have more failures, which adds to customer service costs. Those with low service levels lose customers and can't negotiate as good a price. Once you lay out the hidden costs to the customers, they are willing to pay a fair price and are able to understand why that price difference exists."[3]

HONORING THOSE WHO SERVE

In 2006, Con-way was honored by both the Indiana National Guard and Reserve and the Michigan National Guard and Reserve with the prestigious Above and Beyond award for its support of employees called to active duty.

According to National Guard officials, the awards recognize employers for exceptional support of their employees who serve in Reserve components. Criteria for the awards included company support of the employee's family, compensation, and benefits, as well as recognition of the employee while on active duty.

Con-way President and CEO Doug Stotlar, second from left, and Con-way Freight Chief Operating Officer Dave Miller, right, accepted the 2007 Secretary of Defense Employer Support Freedom Award. Con-way was nominated for the award by Alan Haskew, left, a driver trainer from Salt Lake City, and Michael McAllister, second from right, a freight operations supervisor from Indianapolis. *(Photo courtesy of Employer Support of the Guard and Reserve [ESGR].)*

Con-way offers its employees who are enlisted pay differentials and uninterrupted health benefits for their families. Human resources representatives maintain contact with families to ensure they understand all available benefits, while employee volunteers assist them with everyday challenges such as home maintenance, auto repairs, and snow removal. For employees on active duty, Con-way Freight also sends care packages full of items such as soap, shampoo, and magazines.[36]

"Our commitment to employees in the Guard and Reserve is a responsibility we take very seriously," said David L. Miller, chief operating officer of Con-way Freight. "They are risking their lives to defend and protect our way of life. That we honor them with as much support to them and their families as we can reasonably provide is the least we can do."[37]

In 2007, Miller testified before the U.S. Commission on the National Guard and Reserves, urging Congress to pass legislation providing tax incentives and other assistance for companies that offer full financial support to employees on reserve duty.

"These employees and their families are making a tremendous sacrifice," Miller said. "We are committed to supporting our deployed employees, their families, and the nation. … There are costs involved when reservists are deployed, both in hiring, training, and paying replacement staff, and the continuing support of that employee and the family while that employee is on active duty. It would be appropriate for Congress to consider some form of relief for those companies that demonstrate this level of commitment."[38]

In September 2007, Con-way Inc. won the Secretary of Defense Employer Support Freedom Award, the highest recognition bestowed by the National Committee for Employer Support of the Guard and Reserve (ESGR), a Department of Defense organization promoting cooperation between the Guard and reserves and civilian employers. Con-way was one of 15 organizations to receive the honor, out of 1,000 nominees across the United States.[39]

Alan Haskew, a Con-way Freight driver–sales representative from Salt Lake City who served in Kuwait, and Michael McAllister, a Con-way Freight operations supervisor from Indianapolis who served in Iraq with the Indiana National Guard, nominated their company to receive the honor.[40]

Former Secretary of Defense William Perry created the Freedom Award in 1996. Winners are chosen on the basis of multiple criteria, including pay, benefits, and leave policies; supervisor training; service member recognition; family and deployed member support; and previous ESGR awards. Conway was in good company as previous winners have included Starbucks, Harley-Davidson, and The Home Depot.[41]

OPENING GLOBAL MARKETS TO LTL

To examine the conditions in the transportation industry, Con-way commissioned MergeGlobal, a research and consulting firm, to study shipping patterns, outsourcing practices, business economics, and customer supply chain issues. The study revealed a clear opportunity for premium services offering faster transit coupled with greater consistency and reliability.

In September 2006, Con-way Freight executives formed a partnership with APL Logistics, a subsidiary of Singapore-based Neptune Orient Lines. This partnership led to the development of OceanGuaranteed,

In September 2006, Con-way Freight and APL Logistics introduced OceanGuaranteed, a timely, less-than–container load cargo service, which provided overseas freight transportation capabilities to customers seeking port-to-door delivery from originating ports in China to destinations within the United States.

a new service initially specializing in delivering less-than–container load shipments from China to the United States, providing "port-to-door" guaranteed service from the Chinese cities of Hong Kong, Shanghai, and Shenzhen to the port of Los Angeles. Once cargo was delivered to an American port, Con-way Freight would take over shipping duties, serving as the domestic LTL truck transport service to ensure faster transit times and day-definite, cost-effective delivery options when compared to airfreight services.[42]

Dave McClimon, then president of Con-way Freight, described the rationale behind the partnership:

In today's global marketplace, the majority of our customers are sourcing some aspect of their business to China. They are managing longer supply chains, yet they still remain under pressure to accelerate products through their domestic distribution networks as rapidly and cost efficiently as possible. Combining our network with APL Logistics creates a new service that directly addresses this critical requirement.[43]

For Customs-Trade Partnership Against Terrorism (C-TPAT) certified customers, shipments tendered under OceanGuaranteed were segregated in dedicated C-TPAT-only containers, minimizing potential delays and allowing these cargoes to pass through customs quickly. APL Logistics and Con-way Freight established a simplified pricing structure for the program. OceanGuaranteed shipments received expedited handling, including late-gate privileges at origin, "last on, first off" loading/unloading, and priority shipboard stowage for rapid discharge at the destination port.[44]

OceanGuaranteed allows customers to track shipments via the Internet, receiving shipment details, transit times, and customs' status 24-

hours-a-day, 7-days-a-week. Shipments that fail to meet the delivery-day commitment receive a 20 percent discount, subject to the terms of the service guarantee. By January 2007, APL and Con-way expanded OceanGuaranteed service, allowing customers to ship from four ports at Kaoshiung, Taiwan; Yokohama, Japan; Busan, South Korea; and Singapore.[45]

TEAMING UP WITH TROPICAL SHIPPING

In April 2007, Con-way Freight formalized its product offering with Tropical Shipping, an ocean carrier that served more than 30 ports from New Jersey and South Florida to the Bahamas and the Caribbean. Similar to Con-way's arrangements with APL, the partnership with Tropical Shipping provided service for less-than–container load shipments, serving ports in the Bahamas, the Eastern Caribbean, the British and U.S. Virgin Islands, the Turks and Caicos Islands, the Cayman Islands, and the Dominican Republic.[46]

Con-way's partnership with APL led to the development of OceanGuaranteed, offering faster transit times and day-definite, cost-effective, less-than–container load shipping solutions between Asia and the United States.

RECOGNIZING CON-WAY'S EMPLOYEES

In April 2007, the Lam Research Corporation of Fremont, California, a major supplier of wafer fabrication equipment to the semiconductor industry, awarded Menlo Worldwide its supplier excellence award for providing 99.9 percent on-time delivery. It was the first time Lam had ever bestowed such an honor on a logistics company, which was usually reserved for semiconductor and technology firms.[47]

Menlo also received the Award of Excellence from the Global Institute of Logistics in 2007 for applying lean manufacturing principles to the logistics industry. The institute, founded in 2001, acted as a bridge between academics and business leaders to improve the global logistics community.[48]

As Con-way Freight approached its 25th anniversary, and its parent corporation its 79th anniversary, FORTUNE® magazine ranked it as No. 1 in transportation and logistics on its 2007 list of "America's Most Admired Companies."[49]

Kurt Pederson, a driver–sales representative from Con-way Freight–Western, Phoenix, was called the "goodwill ambassador of the Phoenix Service Center" by fellow employees and named Con-way CEO Constellation Award Winner.

"This is an exceptional honor for our enterprise," Stotlar said. "Being recognized as FORTUNE® [magazine's] most admired company in these industries is a true testament to the integrity and dedication of Con-way people and their daily commitment to and demonstration of our core values, in North America and around the world."[50]

In March 2007, the American Trucking Associations honored Con-way Freight driver Dennis Day from Lawrenceville, Georgia, as one of 16 captains of "America's Road Team," a select group of drivers from different companies that are chosen to represent the trucking industry on various goodwill tours or other public events.

SAFETY: A CORE VALUE

OVER THE YEARS, CON-WAY INC. AND ITS COMPO-nent companies have been honored for their safety, customer service, dependability, and employee relations. Safety continues to be a main focus for everyone, according to Marshall Fulbright, a driver–sales representative since 1987.

Con-way provides training and recertification to ensure that employees remain current on all safety measures, Fulbright noted. Part of that training includes hazardous materials (hazmat) recertification.

"They really try to promote safety above anything," Fulbright added.[1]

"Con-way also has a program called ICE, for Improved Customer Experience," he continued. "It's going to put a customer in a bind if the shipment is damaged in transit or if they don't get all of the shipment due to damage. Con-way [promotes] this program to keep customers' freight safe and exception-free. They do everything to train us on how to tie things, block and brace things properly. [The shipment] is going to get to the customer in 100 percent great shape."

In October 2006, Con-way and its members received numerous awards at the annual American Trucking Associations' (ATA) Management Conference and Exhibition held in Dallas, Texas.

They are representative of the types of awards Con-way has won throughout the decades.[2]

Con-way Freight–Southern received the ATA's President's Trophy in the Over 100 Million Miles Driven category for its five-year safety record, recognizing the company as having the safest trucking fleet of its size in America. The company had previously won the same honor in 2002. Con-way Freight–Southern also won a first place safety award in the Less-than-Truckload Local Over 100 Million Miles Driven category.

The ATA Executive Committee recognized Con-way President and CEO Douglas Stotlar, and all of Con-way Inc., for contributing to an educational meeting for the Department of Transportation's Pipeline and Hazardous Materials Safety Administration at a Con-way Freight facility.

Con-way Freight was recognized by the ATA for its participation in the Highway Watch program, the national safety and security program that trains America's transportation workers to help prevent terrorists from using large vehicles or hazardous cargoes as weapons and to protect America's critical highway transportation infrastructure. Highway Watch is administered by the ATA under an agreement with the U.S. Department of Homeland Security. Con-way

---

Day attained an extraordinary safety record in his 27 years of driving, achieving two million accident-free miles along with numerous safety honors. He joined a distinguished list of Con-way drivers who had previously served on "America's Road Team," including Bob Diaz, Bruce Andrews, Mark Stamper, Linda Nodland, Al Gerber, Darren Beard, Ina Daly, David May, and Jeff Vermillion.[51]

Two months after Day became a Road Team captain, the Federal Motor Carrier Safety Administration picked former Road Team Captain David May of Con-way Freight–Central to participate in the Commercial Driver's License Advisory Com-

mittee. A resident of West Seneca, New York, May had more than 1.4 million accident-free miles and had been a three-time winner of the New York State Truck Driving Championships. May also served as one of four professional drivers on the panel that examined driver training requirements.[52]

CONTRACT FREIGHTERS INC.

Throughout its history, Con-way had grown organically. In 2006, executives determined that a large truckload business would serve as the linchpin

Freight started a corporate-wide effort to provide extra training to 10,000 of its employees.

Robert Petrancosta, Con-way Freight vice president of safety and environmental compliance, received two awards. He won the 2006 Leadership Award for his contributions to the ATA's Safety and Loss Prevention Management Council, as well as a special recognition award from the Hazardous Materials Policy Committee for a special one-day education initiative he created for the benefit of the U.S. Department of

Transportation's Hazardous Materials Safety Administration.

In addition to that honor, in 2007, the Federal Motor Carrier Safety Administration picked Petrancosta to join its 20-member safety advisory panel. The group advised the agency's administrator on policy issues and rule development, as well as regulation interpretation and implementation.[3]

Three Con-way driver–sales representatives were also recognized. Dale Duncan, a Con-way driver from Chula Vista, California, was recognized as being the best truck driver in America. Duncan won the ATA's 2006 grand champion title at the national truck driving championships held in August. Con-way drivers David May from Cheektowaga, New York, and Jeff Vermillion from Denver, Colorado, were honored for their contributions as ATA's Road Team Captains during the previous two years.

Curt J. Shewchuk, Con-way director of corporate protective services, who had been named the ATA's Security Professional of the Year, was elected National Chairman of the ATA's Safety, Security, and Loss Prevention Management Council. A 32-year law enforcement and security veteran, Shewchuk was responsible for the management of worldwide security initiatives for all Con-way companies.

Also in 2006, Con-way Freight sent 58 drivers to the ATA National Driving Competition held in New Orleans. As it had several times in the past, Con-way sent the largest contingent of drivers for any single LTL company at the event.[4]

Maintenance and safety standards are strictly enforced at Con-way. Here, a driver was conducting a routine oil check on his vehicle.

between Con-way's LTL freight and logistics businesses. Stotlar explained:

Menlo was contracting $700 million on truckload services, so there was a lot of opportunity to leverage a truckload platform, not so much to drive more synergy with Menlo, but to leverage the assets of Con-way Truckload. We also had the asset network of our Con-way LTL companies to leverage for the truckload company, including secure Con-way locations where loads could be dropped off over the weekend before final deliveries were made on Monday.[53]

Con-way had already spent nine years working with Contract Freighters Inc. (CFI) to move LTL linehaul with CFI's contract truckload service. Con-way Freight leaders had an excellent working relationship with CFI President Herb Schmidt, as well as the rest of the professionally managed company. As early as September 2006, Conway and CFI began considering the possibility of an acquisition.

"Herb [Schmidt] and I knew that our companies shared the same philosophy from a service orientation standpoint," Stotlar said. "We shared the same philosophies on integrity, commitment, excellence, safety, the core values."[54]

CFI was founded in 1951 and had since grown to include more than 2,600 tractors and 7,000 trailers, as well as nearly 3,000 employees, including approximately 2,500 drivers.[55]

The Griot family had a long-standing business philosophy of remaining engaged in the business, but letting professional management get the best results possible. Under Glenn Brown's day-to-day leadership and the Griots' oversight, CFI flourished. When Brown turned over the reins to Schmidt in 2005, the company was a perfect complement to Con-way.

Right: Former CFI President Herb Schmidt (second from left) worked alongside Con-way Truckload employees and CFI employees at the CFI headquarters in Joplin, Missouri. After Con-way acquired CFI, it merged into Con-way Truckload.

Below: Con-way had spent almost 10 years working with CFI's contract truckload service before it purchased CFI for $750 million on July 16, 2007.

The acquisition talks came to fruition on July 16, 2007, when Con-way announced it was purchasing Contract Freighters for $750 million. Contract Freighters would be merged with Con-way Truckload, creating a business unit that had more than $500 million in annual revenues. By combining its efforts with the Missouri-based carrier, Con-way hoped to diversify its LTL and truckload mix to moderate the cyclical nature of its business units, while requiring a platform for growth and synergy with a strong leadership team.[56]

"CFI was a much more sophisticated truckload operator than we were, and we could leverage their customer base to eliminate empty miles and operate at higher efficiency," Stotlar explained.[57]

Schmidt, who officially became president of Con-way Truckload in January 2008, added:

I'm very excited about the prospect of being part of the Con-way organization, giving us more leverage with the customers, giving us more services to sell, cer-

Con-way is committed to environmentally friendly policies for its vehicle standards. Recent modifications have included synthetic lubricants and clutch-type fans, as well as a strict policy on idling.

tainly giving us more capital to grow. There are a lot of synergies to be gained, [including] serving Menlo. We have the assets to back them up, so it's just a real good marriage.[58]

Schmidt began working part-time in the freight transportation industry, loading trucks during his last year of college. After graduating, he became a UPS driver for eight months before becoming a manager. One day, Schmidt's father happened to run across the president of CFI and spoke to him at length about his son's career at UPS. That chance conversation led to a job interview, and Schmidt soon went to work as a director of safety at CFI.

"At the time [1984], it wasn't that large," Schmidt said. "It was about 425 trucks and about a thousand trailers. I felt like I was going back into the Dark Ages, having come from UPS."[59]

The "marriage" of Con-way and CFI provided a number of obvious benefits. CFI had been Con-way Freight's largest provider of contract service for long-haul transcontinental truckload transportation. At the same time, Con-way had been CFI's largest customer. CFI had operations in Mexico for nearly 20 years and was one of the largest cross-border truckload carriers. Its capabilities could be combined with Con-way Freight's Mexico network and Menlo's border-based logistics operations.[60]

The merger was completed on August 23, 2007, and structured so Con-way acquired CFI's parent holding company, Transportation Resources Inc., as well as CFI and all other subsidiaries of the parent holding company. Following the acquisition, CFI underwent a rebranding process, becoming Con-way Truckload.

HELPING THE ENVIRONMENT

On the environmental side, Con-way has invested heavily in meeting the EPA's guidelines to reduce heavy truck emissions, especially the reduction of nitrogen oxides and particulate matter pollutants. These changes, however, cause diesel engines to burn more fuel, producing more carbon dioxide than previous generations of motors. In addition, a lack of highway infrastructure improvements in recent decades has led to increased traffic congestion around many metropolitan areas, which in turn reduces productivity and forces trucking firms such as Con-way to burn even more fuel.

"We want to be good stewards of the environment," Stotlar explained. "I want the [world] to be a clean place for my children. We keep meeting all the regulations and doing the right things and adding more aerodynamics, and we're already extremely efficient with how we run our networks."[61]

Con-way's fleet travels more than 825 million miles annually, consuming approximately 140 million gallons of diesel fuel. To reduce the environmental effects of its fleet, Con-way Freight joined the SmartWay™ Transport Partnership in July 2006.

The Environmental Protection Agency (EPA) and the motor freight industry created the SmartWay™ partnership to improve energy efficiency and significantly reduce air pollution and the emission of greenhouse gases such as carbon dioxide and nitrogen oxide.[62] As a member of SmartWay™, Con-way pledged to purchase environmentally friendly engines that produce lower emissions and tested fuel-efficient tires, external aerodynamic improvements, and reduced air drag mirrors.[63]

"We also have a strict idling policy in place with an automatic shut off," McClimon said, adding that

Con-way's environmentally friendly modifications included switching to synthetic lubricants and clutch-type fans, which increase engine efficiency while lowering emissions.[64]

Each year, the EPA distributes SmartWay™ Excellence Awards based on several criteria, including the overall impact of an organization on the environment. In 2006, CFI won the award for its use of fuel-saving, single-wide tires; idling control equipment; and aerodynamic devices, which helped reduce carbon dioxide emissions by 27 percent. CFI also won the SmartWay™ Excellence Award in 2007, giving it the right to display the SmartWay™ Transport Partner logo on company materials.

Emblematic of Con-way's commitment to sustainability, both Con-way Freight and Con-way Truckload reduced the speed governors on their trucks to a maximum speed of 62 miles per hour in 2007.

By 2012, the SmartWay™ partnership expects to reach its goal of reducing yearly emissions of carbon dioxide by 33 million to 66 million metric tons and nitrogen oxide by 200,000 tons.[65]

MENLO'S STRATEGY IN ASIA

Expanding its reach into Southeast Asia, Menlo Worldwide announced on June 7, 2007, that it was acquiring Cougar Holdings for $33.9 million—$28.2 million in cash, plus the assumption of $5.7 million of Cougar's debts. Based in Singapore,

---

With the 2007 acquisitions of Cougar Logistics and Chic Logistics, Menlo increased its presence in the Asia–Pacific region, growing from 13 operating sites to 155.

Cougar Holdings owned Cougar Express Logistics, which had 320 employees and managed 2.4 million square feet of warehouse space. With 12 locations in the region and 200 Asian and global clients, Cougar expanded Menlo's reach.[66]

"The strategy behind the acquisition is to capitalize on the globalization of the economy, with Asia [serving as] a high growth area for the supply chain," Bianco said. "Our existing customer base was pleading with us to accelerate the build out of our capabilities in Asia. We moved from an organic strategy to an acquisition strategy in Asia and acquired what we considered the best logistics company out there—Cougar Logistics."[67]

Four days after closing the Cougar acquisition on September 5, 2007, Menlo announced it had signed a $60 million agreement to purchase Chic Holdings Ltd., owner of Chic Logistics based in Shanghai, China.[68] Chic was a profitable and established 3PL (third-party logistics) company with a network of 130 sites in 78 cities. It had revenues of $55.2 million in 2006.

The Chic purchase gave Menlo a strong foothold in the world's most populous country, as well as access to an increased variety of available options for current and prospective customers.[69]

"Chic Logistics has a compounded annual growth rate close to 40 percent year over year," Bianco said.[70]

With the purchases of Cougar and Chic, Menlo increased its presence in the Asia–Pacific region, growing from 13 operating sites to 155. Its number of employees grew from 350 to more than 2,300, and its warehouse capacity expanded from 300,000 to 3.5 million square feet.[71] Menlo also established two new facilities in Singapore, and upgraded two facilities in Thailand and Malaysia. Stotlar described the rationale behind the acquisitions:

We're entering the Asia and China markets at about the right time because they're recognizing that their supply chain systems and transportation provider networks are very fragmented. We're buying in when that fragmentation is starting to consolidate, and they don't have the sophisticated systems that the more mature companies like Menlo have.

We bought platforms in Asia that allow us to bring our systems and our multinational client networks and tie them together with their

Robert L. Bianco Jr., who became president of Menlo Worldwide in 2004, led the strategic expansion into Asia and drove the acquisitions of Chic Logistics and Cougar Logistics in 2007.

regional distribution and regional supply chain capabilities. We'll be able to give them higher-level sophistication, better visibility, better IT tools, and a new account base with which to grow them relatively quickly.[72]

THE LEADERSHIP ACADEMY

To improve employee training and the development of professional skills, the corporation launched the Con-way Leadership Academy at five sites across the globe in June 2007. An enhancement of Con-way's already well-known education programs, the Academy featured a curriculum designed to teach the fundamentals of leadership as well as strategic and advanced leadership preparation. The programs were precisely calibrated for employees at specific stages of their careers to help Con-way's employees succeed.[73]

In 2007, 950 employees were selected to complete their first courses in Ann Arbor, Michigan; Portland, Oregon; Buena Park, California; Aurora, Illinois; and Dallas, Texas. Overseas, the Leadership Academy set up training locations in Amsterdam and Singapore.

A DIFFICULT MARKET

The transportation industry frequently serves as a bellwether for the nation's economy and business cycles.

"Trucking does well as a recession ends, but it does very poorly before a recession begins," explained Donald Moffitt, former chairman of the board. "That's when people quit stocking, quit ordering from the warehouse."[74]

Throughout 2007 and into 2008, economists predicted a recession on the horizon.[75] Goldman Sachs, Wall Street's biggest investment bank, predicted in January 2008 that the housing slump of 2007 and the troubles in the subprime mortgage market had already started the world on a path toward global recession. At the same time, domestic automakers, including GM, Ford, and Chrysler, predicted falling new car sales, another traditional harbinger of an economic downturn.[76] As a result, Con-way Freight and Menlo Worldwide experienced falling gross revenues, profits, and tonnage.

The market became increasingly competitive in 2007, and in June, Stotlar announced that Con-way was "doing what is necessary to defend our core business and to protect our market share in what continues to be a soft freight environment."

Although the future may be uncertain, Con-way may experience an increase nonetheless.

"We would expect to see a flight to quality in times like these, as small companies feel the pinch and go bankrupt," explained Nightingale. "We would expect [new customers] to come to a large, high-quality carrier such as ourselves, to search for solutions at a company that has stability and longevity like Con-way."[77]

Despite the downturn, Con-way Freight marched forward with more infrastructure expansions, building for the future.[78]

COMBINING THE COMPONENTS

Shortly after Con-way announced it would purchase CFI, Con-way Freight President McClimon left the corporation to pursue other interests. On July 17, 2007, John G. Labrie, who had been Con-way's senior vice president of strategy and enterprise operations, was named as McClimon's replacement.[79]

A month after Labrie's promotion, the corporation announced that it was combining its three regional companies—Con-way Freight–Central, Con-way Freight–Southern, and Con-way Freight–

Just after John G. Labrie was appointed president of Con-way Freight in July 2007, the company combined its three regional companies into one centralized organization headquartered in Ann Arbor, Michigan.

Western—into one centralized organization head-quartered in Ann Arbor, Michigan.[80]

"We had been talking for quite some time about the need to streamline the Freight organization because we had three semi-autonomous business units and then a holding company over those three units that reported to the corporate entity," Stotlar explained. "Any time we wanted to make changes, there was wrangling back and forth between business units. With the realignment, we're behaving like one company now and can react to the marketplace much quicker."[81]

Following the reorganization, Labrie said that Con-way Freight would be the only nationwide LTL carrier that could, through a single network, provide regional, inter-regional, and long-haul service capability.[82]

"We have always been differentiated on transit time performance against transit time and coverage, but for the last couple of years, we hadn't marketed those points," Labrie said. "We are refocusing our sales and marketing efforts around the fact that we provide more direct coverage than any other carrier in the market. We are the carrier that has the fastest transit times in the country and the highest performance against those transit times. We are going back to emphasizing the basics."[83]

Con-way Freight adopted uniform processes and streamlined its organization, which meant the closing of the former Southern and Western companies' headquarters and trimming the executive staffs. Joining Labrie's new Con-way Freight executive management team were Miller, chief operating officer; Michael D. Yuenger, vice president of finance; J. Edwin Conaway, executive vice president of sales; Sean M. Devine, vice president of engineering; Manoj Chopra, vice president of pricing; and Scott J. Engers, vice president of employee relations.[84]

Yuenger had been Con-way Freight's controller since 2005 and joined Con-Way Central Express in 1991 as its controller. Devine, formerly vice president of consulting services for the management software company Emptoris Inc., joined Con-way Inc. in 2007 as vice president of engineering and supply management.

The former director of pricing for RadioShack Corporation, Chopra had joined Con-way earlier that August. His executive experience included stints at FedEx Services and i2 Technologies.

Engers had joined Consolidated Freightways Inc. in 1984. In 1988, Engers was promoted to vice president and corporate counsel for CTS. In 2005, he was promoted to vice president and deputy general counsel for Con-way.

In 2007, Miller, president of Con-way Central since 2005, was elected to a two-year term on the U.S. Chamber Board of Directors, where he continues to advise senior chamber staff members and speak on issues facing state and local chambers, associations, and other business groups in an effort to promote pro-growth government policies and programs.[85]

Reorganization included combining and eliminating redundant administration positions, and moving more than 150 positions to Ann Arbor, where Con-way Freight is headquartered, while maintaining small area offices in Los Angeles, California, and Fort Worth, Texas, as well as creating a new area office in Philadelphia.[86]

MENLO LANDS MAJOR U.S. DEFENSE CONTRACT

Menlo pursued and won a contract with the Department of Defense (DOD) U.S. Transportation Command (USTRANSCOM) to streamline and improve domestic transportation and distribution operations for all four U.S. military branches. Under the $1.6 billion logistics contract, Menlo will improve the performance and efficiency of the military's domestic transportation network, synchronizing up to 260 independent shipping sites and hundreds of transportation service providers in the 48 contiguous states.[87]

Known as the Defense Transportation Coordination Initiative (DTCI), Air Force General Norton A. Schwartz, commander of USTRANSCOM, described the program as a team effort "to increase the effectiveness and efficiency of [defense] freight movements in the continental United States. Menlo will utilize best commercial practices to enable load consolidation and optimization, use of more efficient intermodal means of transportation, and tailored scheduling."[88]

According to Bianco, "The Defense Department … deal will almost double the size of our company."[89]

The Defense Department had been considering outsourcing its domestic transportation for five years, Stotlar said.

"In addition to the efficiencies and expected cost savings we'll gain, this long-term partnership with Menlo Worldwide Government Service allows us to implement several commercial best practices into our transportation operations," said Air Force Col. James Lovell, director, DTCI Program Management Office.[90]

"The Defense Logistics Agency [DLA] and USTRANSCOM have worked closely on the Defense Transportation Coordination Initiative for several years. This award represents a significant accomplishment in our collective efforts to streamline distribution processes and provide better and more cost-effective support to our nation's warfighters," said Army Lt. Gen. Robert Dail, DLA director.[91]

"This is a milestone win for Menlo and our partners," said Bianco. "USTRANSCOM is to be commended for their foresight, vision, and commitment to a best-in-class solution for improving distribution and logistics for our nation's warfighters. This is a tremendous opportunity to leverage and apply our experience with some of the nation's largest commercial businesses into a highly efficient logistics solution for the military. We look forward to a successful, long-term partnership with USTRANSCOM, DLA, and the DOD that delivers new efficiencies and superior performance for our military's domestic transportation operations."[92]

Con-way tapped into its resources when preparing its bid for the DTCI, mainly due to extensive federal government contracting regulations. Menlo competed against logistics industry titans, including IBM, UPS, Raytheon, and Lockheed Martin.[93]

Menlo worked with three principal subcontractors:

- Computer Sciences Corp. provided IT infrastructure hosting, network management, and integration services.
- One Networks Enterprises Inc. supplied the transportation management software for shipment planning, optimization, and execution.
- Olgoonik Logistics offered professional services supporting the participation of minority-owned and small business firms as service contractors.[94]

UPCOMING CHALLENGES

Con-way's major challenges in the coming year include the full and complete integration of Con-way Freight from its former component structure, integrating CFI into the corporation, and folding the Chic and Cougar acquisitions into Menlo Worldwide operations. At the same time, both Con-way and the industry at large face many unknowns, as Stotlar explained:

President and CEO Douglas W. Stotlar looks toward the future while building on Con-way's legacy of values, innovation, and committed employees.

Getting the three companies to work outside of their silos and work together will be tough ... but so far, the spirit of cooperation has been very high.

While there will always be questions as to what the future may bring, one thing is certain—the entrepreneurial spirit and the innovation that brought Con-way to this point will continue. With generations of experience competing in one of the toughest industries, Con-way's employees have consistently risen to meet the challenge and find new ways to create value and succeed.[95]

FUTURE OPPORTUNITIES

In 2008, Con-way Freight celebrated its 25th anniversary. Originally conceived as disparate, independent, regional LTL trucking companies, Con-way Freight was now a unified entity, working to provide its customers with the most efficient and reliable transportation services in the industry.

Con-way Inc. remained the heir to the rich traditions and ideals of the historic Consolidated Freightways. Built on the goal of providing unprecedented next-day delivery service, Con-way had inherited the mantle of innovation that Leland James had pioneered, growing into a well-recognized and esteemed member of the freight transportation industry.

Con-way continues to strive for and achieve superior performance while maintaining a corporate culture that breeds loyalty and pride among its employees. Combined with Con-way's business formula of delivering the highest levels of service, the company has proved stunningly successful in a crowded marketplace. Con-way's ability to adapt and evolve to fluctuating market conditions, ever-changing technology, and evolving customer needs has allowed Con-way to maintain a place at the top of the transportation industry.

NOTES TO SOURCES

CHAPTER ONE

1. *Consolidated Freightways Inc.: The First 50 Years, 1929–1979,* Consolidated Freightways Inc., San Francisco, 1979, page 10.
2. Kenneth D. Durr and Philip L. Cantelon, *Never Stand Still: A History of CNF Transportation Inc.,* (Rockville, Maryland: Montrose Press, 1999), pages 20–21.
3. *Consolidated Freightways Inc.,* 10.
4. John L. Butler, "From Molasses to Macadam: The Building of America's Highways, Part 1," *Antique Automobile,* March/April 1991, pages 33–34.
5. Brian Butko, *Greetings from the Lincoln Highway: America's First Coast-to-Coast Road,* (Mechanicsburg, Pennsylvania: Stackpole Books, 2005), page 6.
6. *Never Stand Still,* 15.
7. *Consolidated Freightways Inc.,* 4.
8. Ibid, 11.
9. *Never Stand Still,* 43–44.
10. *Consolidated Freightways Inc.,* 11.
11. Frank J. Taylor, "Battle of the Hotshot," *Saturday Evening Post,* 16 November 1940, pages 18–19, 102, 104–105.
12. *Consolidated Freightways Inc.,* 11.
13. Ibid, 11–12.
14. Ibid, 12.
15. Ibid.
16. Ibid, 12–13.
17. Ibid, 13.
18. *Never Stand Still,* 30.
19. *Consolidated Freightways Inc.,* 6.
20. Ibid, 6.
21. Ibid, 13.
22. *Never Stand Still,* 40.
23. "Battle of the Hotshot," 18–19, 102, 104–105.
24. *Never Stand Still,* 15–16.
25. *Consolidated Freightways Inc.,* 4–5.
26. *Never Stand Still,* 37.
27. *Consolidated Freightways Inc.,* 16.
28. "Letters to the Editor: Truckers Make Reply," *Marshfield Times,* 4 February 1937.
29. "Letters to the Editor: Truckers Make Reply."
30. "Battle of the Hotshot," 18–19, 102, 104–105.
31. *Consolidated Freightways Inc.,* 21.
32. *Never Stand Still,* 42–43.
33. Ibid, 52–53.
34. Ibid, 55.
35. "Consolidated Freight Lines Advertises Itself Out of a Winter Slump," *Western Advertising,* February 1937.
36. Phil Cogswell, "Consolidated Standardizes on Diesel Engine Equipment," *Motor Transportation,* November 1936, pages 9, 36.
37. "Proponents of Highway Transportation Present Views: Trucking Heads Back Increases: Expansion Weight and Size Program Explained," *Oregonian,* 18 February 1937.
38. S. M. Blair, "Consolidated Cuts Accidents with Help of Employees: Safety Consciousness Cuts Year's Toll Sixty Per Cent," *Motor Transportation,* December 1936.
39. "Consolidated Standardizes on Diesel Engine Equipment," 9, 36.
40. *Consolidated Freightways Inc.,* 16–17.
41. "Consolidated Freight's Payload Drive Begins," *Morning Oregonian,* 7 November 1936.
42. "Consolidated Freight Lines, Inc.," *Klamath Falls Free Press,* 28 January 1937.
43. "Consolidated Adds Cab-over-Engine Fageol," *Trade Lanes,* 16 April 1937.
44. "Howdja Like to Drive A Truck: 22 Levers to Pull or Push, 15 Forward Speeds, on Big Freighter," *Wenatchee World,* 18 March 1937.
45. "Freight Service is Observing Birthday: Motor Carrier Operating in Bismarck Established Just 10 Years Ago," *Mandan Daily Pioneer,* 1939.
46. "Cars Cross Bridge 100 Per Minute," *Chico Enterprise,* 12 November 1936.
47. "Freightways First Truck Over Unique Bridge," *Traffic Manager,* July 1940.
48. "Ten Years and a Hundred Million Miles from Scratch," *Trade Lanes,* 7 April 1939, pages 4–9, 18–19.
49. "Super-System Formed by Six Long-Distance Lines," *Pacific Truckman,* 9 November 1939.
50. "Ten Years and a Hundred Million Miles from Scratch," pages 4–9, 18–19.
51. "Battle of the Hotshot," 18–19, 102, 104–105.
52. *Never Stand Still,* 104.
53. "200 Horsepower, 22 Balloons!" *Automotive News,* October 1940.
54. *Never Stand Still,* 152–153.
55. *Consolidated Freightways Inc.,* 29.
56. "Consolidated of Oregon Receives Authority to Buy Volk Bros. Inc.," *Transport Topics,* 11 August 1941, page 6.
57. *Never Stand Still,* 120–121.
58. *Consolidated Freightways Inc.,* 31.

59. *Never Stand Still*, 142.
60. *Consolidated Freightways Inc.*, 34.
61. *Never Stand Still*, 144.

CHAPTER TWO

1. Kenneth D. Durr and Philip L. Cantelon, *Never Stand Still: A History of CNF Transportation Inc.*, (Rockville, Maryland: Montrose Press, 1999), page 198.
2. *Consolidated Freightways Inc.: The First 50 Years, 1929–1979*, Consolidated Freightways Inc., San Francisco, 1979, page 41.
3. "New Heavy Duty Reefers Roll Northwest Highways," *Western Motor Transport*, October 1939, page 26.
4. *Never Stand Still*, 133.
5. *Consolidated Freightways Inc.*, 34.
6. *Never Stand Still*, 136–137.
7. *Consolidated Freightways Inc.*, 33.
8. Ibid.
9. *Never Stand Still*, 139.
10. Ibid, 140.
11. *Consolidated Freightways Inc.*, 36.
12. Ibid, 32.
13. *Never Stand Still*, 143.
14. *Consolidated Freightways Inc.*, 37.
15. Bob Cosgrove, "Making Tracks … Railroads, though They've Declined, Were Essential Lifelines to Industry's Development," *Technology Century*, Engineering Technology Publishing, Inc., 1995, page 151.
16. *Never Stand Still*, 158–159.
17. Ibid, 181.
18. Ibid, 147.
19. Ibid.
20. "A Synopsis of the History of Freightliner Corporation," Freightliner Corporation, 1 September 1986.
21. Kristin Todd, "Ken Self: A Legend at Freightliner," *Overdrive*, July 1996, page 59.
22. *Never Stand Still*, 120.
23. "Ken Self," 59.
24. *Never Stand Still*, 120.
25. "Ken Self," 60.
26. "A Synopsis of the History of Freightliner Corporation."
27. Ibid.
28. Ibid.
29. *Never Stand Still*, 156.
30. "A Synopsis of the History of Freightliner Corporation."
31. *Never Stand Still*, 155–156.
32. *Consolidated Freightways Inc.*, 34.
33. Ibid.
34. "Ken Self," 60.
35. Caption from a photograph, Freightliner Corporation, circa 1953.
36. *Consolidated Freightways Inc.*, 35.
37. "Ken Self," 60.
38. *Consolidated Freightways Inc.*, 34.

39. *Never Stand Still*, 137.
40. Ibid, 166–169.
41. *Consolidated Freightways Inc.*, 36.
42. *Never Stand Still*, 169.
43. *Consolidated Freightways Inc.*, 37.
44. *Never Stand Still*, 173.
45. *Consolidated Freightways Inc.*, 36.
46. *Never Stand Still*, 180.
47. *Consolidated Freightways Inc.*, 35–38.
48. *Never Stand Still*, 193–194.
49. *Consolidated Freightways Inc.*, 41–42.
50. *Never Stand Still*, 192.
51. Ed Cray, *Chrome Colossus: General Motors and its Times*, (New York: McGraw-Hill, 1980), pages 191–192.
52. "Ken Self," 60.
53. *Never Stand Still*, 194.
54. Ibid, 196.
55. Raymond F. O'Brien, interview by Jeffrey L. Rodengen, digital recording, 23 May 2007, Write Stuff Enterprises, Inc.
56. Ibid.
57. *Never Stand Still*, 212.
58. O'Brien interview.
59. *Never Stand Still*, 216.
60. *Consolidated Freightways Inc.*, 42–43.
61. *Never Stand Still*, 202.
62. *Consolidated Freightways Inc.*, 44.
63. *Never Stand Still*, 199.
64. *Consolidated Freightways Inc.*, 44.
65. *Never Stand Still*, 204.
66. *Consolidated Freightways Inc.*, 44.
67. *Never Stand Still*, 214.
68. *Consolidated Freightways Inc.*, 46.
69. *Never Stand Still*, 199.
70. Ibid, 207.
71. Ibid, 208–209.
72. Ibid, 209.
73. Ibid.
74. Ibid, 212.
75. Ibid, 213.
76. *Consolidated Freightways Inc.*, 46–47.
77. *Never Stand Still*, 220.
78. Ibid, 218–219.
79. Ibid, 221.
80. *Consolidated Freightways Inc.*, 47.

CHAPTER TWO SIDEBAR: TRANSCONTINENTAL TRAVEL

1. A. I. Lindbeck, "Freeways on Roads Proposed: Restrictions for Owners of Property on Highways Asked; Truck Bills Filed," *Oregon Journal*, 14 January 1941.
2. "Federal-Aid Highway Act of 1956: Creating the Interstate System," National Atlas of the United States, Washington, D.C., http://www.nationalatlas.gov/.
3. Ed Cray, *Chrome Colossus: General Motors and its Times*, (New York: McGraw-Hill, 1980), page 326.

4. Louis Mleczko, "All Roads Lead to … Prosperity, If Paved with More Than Good Intentions," *Technology Century*, Engineering Technology Publishing, Inc., 1995, pages 146–147.
5. "Dwight D. Eisenhower National System of Interstate and Defense Highways," Federal Highway Administration, http://www.fhwa.dot.gov/.
6. Ken Scharnberg, *Opportunities in Trucking Careers*, (Chicago: NTC/Contemporary Publishing Group, Inc., 1999), pages 11–12.
7. "Federal-Aid Highway Act of 1956: Creating the Interstate System."
8. "National Defense Highway System," http://www.GlobalSecurity.org/.
9. "Dwight D. Eisenhower National System of Interstates and Defense Highways."
10. "National Defense Highway System."

CHAPTER TWO SIDEBAR: ON TO OREGON

1. *Consolidated Freightways Inc.: The First 50 Years, 1929–1979*, Consolidated Freightways Inc., San Francisco, 1979, page 47.

CHAPTER TWO SIDEBAR: OPERATION REINDEER

1. *Consolidated Freightways Inc.: The First 50 Years, 1929–1979*, Consolidated Freightways Inc., San Francisco, 1979, page 44.
2. "President's Park (White House)— Christmas Pageant of Peace History," U.S. National Park Service, http://www.nps.gov/.
3. *Consolidated Freightways Inc.*, 44.
4. "President's Park (White House)— Christmas Pageant of Peace History."
5. *Consolidated Freightways Inc.*, 44.

CHAPTER THREE

1. Ray Halloran, interview by Jeffrey L. Rodengen, digital recording, 22 May 2007, Write Stuff Enterprises, Inc.
2. *Consolidated Freightways Inc.: The First 50 Years, 1929–1979*, Consolidated Freightways Inc., San Francisco, 1979, page 46.
3. Kenneth D. Durr and Philip L. Cantelon, *Never Stand Still: A History of CNF Transportation Inc.*, (Rockville, Maryland: Montrose Press, 1999), page 229.
4. *Consolidated Freightways Inc.*, 47.
5. *Never Stand Still*, 227.

6. *Consolidated Freightways Inc.*, 42, 46.
7. *Never Stand Still*, 210.
8. Ibid, 228–230.
9. Ibid, 218.
10. *Consolidated Freightways Inc.*, 42.
11. *Never Stand Still*, 228.
12. *Consolidated Freightways Inc.*, 47, 49.
13. Halloran interview.
14. Ibid.
15. *Never Stand Still*, 243–245.
16. Donald Moffitt, interview by Jeffrey L. Rodengen, digital recording, 22 May 2007, Write Stuff Enterprises, Inc.
17. *Never Stand Still*, 224–225.
18. Raymond F. O'Brien, interview by Jeffrey L. Rodengen, digital recording, 23 May 2007, Write Stuff Enterprises, Inc.
19. *Consolidated Freightways Inc.*, 51.
20. *Never Stand Still*, 265.
21. *Consolidated Freightways Inc.*, 62.
22. O'Brien interview.
23. Kristin Todd, "Ken Self: A Legend at Freightliner," *Overdrive*, July 1996, pages 58–60.
24. *Never Stand Still*, 238.
25. *Consolidated Freightways Inc.*, 51.
26. Ibid, 61.
27. *Never Stand Still*, 261.
28. Ibid, 239–242.
29. *Consolidated Freightways Inc.*, 51.
30. *Never Stand Still*, 247–248.
31. *Consolidated Freightways Inc.*, 49.
32. *Never Stand Still*, 250.
33. Ibid, 252.
34. *Consolidated Freightways Inc.*, 50.
35. *Never Stand Still*, 262.
36. *Consolidated Freightways Inc.*, 50.
37. *Never Stand Still*, 263.
38. Ibid, 250, 253–255.
39. *Consolidated Freightways Inc.*, 51, 62.
40. "A Fighting Program for Teamsters, Part 3: Attacks on Teamsters," http://www.SocialistAlternative.org/.
41. *Never Stand Still*, 258–59.
42. Ibid, 279.
43. Moffitt interview.
44. *Never Stand Still*, 263–264.
45. *Consolidated Freightways Inc.*, 50.
46. *Never Stand Still*, 264.
47. *Consolidated Freightways Inc.*, 50.
48. *Never Stand Still*, 267–268.
49. Jim Schlueter, interview by Jeffrey L. Rodengen, digital recording, 27 August 2007, Write Stuff Enterprises, Inc.
50. *Never Stand Still*, 268–269.
51. Wayne Byerley, interview by Jeffrey L. Rodengen, digital recording, 21 May 2007, Write Stuff Enterprises, Inc.
52. *Consolidated Freightways Inc.*, 51.
53. O'Brien interview.
54. *Never Stand Still*, 275.
55. David Bollier, *Citizen Action and Other Big Ideas: A History of Ralph Nader and the Modern Consumer Movement*, (Washington, D.C.: Center for Study of Responsive Law, 1991), Chapter 2.
56. Thomas Gale Moore, "Trucking Deregulation," Concise Encyclopedia of Economics, http://www.econlib.org/.
57. *Never Stand Still*, 281.
58. Ibid, 304.
59. "A Synopsis of the History of the Freightliner Corporation," Freightliner Corporation, 1 September 1986.
60. *Consolidated Freightways Inc.*, 62.
61. *Never Stand Still*, 305.
62. Moffitt interview.
63. *Consolidated Freightways Inc.*, 62, 63.
64. Byerley interview.
65. O'Brien interview.
66. *Never Stand Still*, 271, 283.
67. Ibid, 284–286.
68. Ibid, 288–290.
69. Ibid, 319.
70. *Consolidated Freightways Inc.*, 52.
71. *Never Stand Still*, 294.
72. *Consolidated Freightways Inc.*, 52.
73. Ibid, 49, 53.

CHAPTER FOUR

1. Wayne Byerley, interview by Jeffrey L. Rodengen, digital recording, 21 May 2007, Write Stuff Enterprises, Inc.
2. "Consolidated Freightways Inc. 1978 Annual Report: 50 Years of Innovation and Service," page 3.
3. Ibid, 4.
4. "Employment Status of the Civilian Non-Institutional Population, 1940 to Date (2007)," U.S. Department of Labor, Bureau of Labor Statistics, http://www.bls.gov/.
5. "Teamster Test: Bending the Wage Guidelines," *Time*, 9 April 1979.
6. "Consolidated Freightways Inc. 1978 Annual Report," 5.
7. "Teamster Test."
8. Kenneth D. Durr and Philip L. Cantelon, *Never Stand Still: A History of CNF Transportation Inc.*, (Rockville, Maryland: Montrose Press, 1999), page 297.
9. "Teamster Test."
10. *Never Stand Still*, 297.
11. Raymond F. O'Brien, interview by Jeffrey L. Rodengen, digital recording, 23 May 2007, Write Stuff Enterprises, Inc.
12. Ned Moritz, interview by Jeffrey L. Rodengen, digital recording, 1 May 2007, Write Stuff Enterprises, Inc.
13. *Never Stand Still*, 299.
14. "The Last Roadblock to Decontrolled Trucking," *Business Week*, 23 May 1983.
15. Thomas Gale Moore, "Trucking Deregulation," Concise Encyclopedia of Economics, http://www.econlib.org/.
16. John Hickerson, interview by Jeffrey L. Rodengen, digital recording, 22 May 2007, Write Stuff Enterprises, Inc.
17. *Never Stand Still*, 301.
18. Donna Cottardi, interview by Jeffrey L. Rodengen, digital recording, 19 September 2007, Write Stuff Enterprises, Inc.
19. *Never Stand Still*, 297.
20. O'Brien interview.
21. Kristin Todd, "Ken Self: A Legend at Freightliner," *Overdrive*, July 1996, page 60.
22. "Consolidated Freightways Inc. 1978 Annual Report," 19–21.
23. Donald Moffitt, interview by Jeffrey L. Rodengen, digital recording, 22 May 2007, Write Stuff Enterprises, Inc.
24. "Consolidated Freightways Inc. 1978 Annual Report," 22.
25. *Never Stand Still*, 307.
26. O'Brien interview.
27. Moffitt interview.
28. O'Brien interview.
29. *Never Stand Still*, 310.
30. "Freightliner Corporation Chronology," Freightliner Corporation, 1986.
31. Moffitt interview.
32. O'Brien interview.
33. Byerley interview.
34. *Never Stand Still*, 317.
35. Ibid, 302.
36. Moffitt interview.
37. Ibid.
38. *Never Stand Still*, 319.
39. Bryan Millican, interview by Jeffrey L. Rodengen, digital recording, 2 May 2007, Write Stuff Enterprises, Inc.
40. *Never Stand Still*, 321, 322–323.
41. Moffitt interview.
42. *Never Stand Still*, 327.
43. Halloran interview.
44. Robert P. Crowner, "Con-Way Central Express," a study presented at the North American Case Research Symposium, 1988, page 2.
45. *Never Stand Still*, 325, 325–326.
46. Allan Kunigis, "Unique Vision, Solid Execution," *Transportation CEO*, Fall 2000, page 12.
47. "Con-Way Central Express," 2.
48. Ibid.
49. "Consolidated Freightways: The Motor Carrier Management—Its People and Structure," *Freighter*, March 1977, page 39.

50. Moritz interview.
51. *Never Stand Still*, 292.
52. Richard L. Madden, "Effects of Trailer Ruling Awaited," *New York Times*, 19 June 1983, late city final edition.
53. *Never Stand Still*, 314.
54. Moffit interview.
55. *Never Stand Still*, 333–334.
56. Hickerson interview.
57. *Never Stand Still*, 332.
58. O'Brien interview.
59. Eb Schmoller, interview by Jeffrey L. Rodengen, digital recording, 23 May 2007, Write Stuff Enterprises, Inc.
60. Millican interview.
61. Moritz interview.
62. Schmoller interview.
63. Moritz interview.
64. Byerley interview.
65. Dave McClimon, interview by Jeffrey L. Rodengen, digital recording, 1 May 2007, Write Stuff Enterprises, Inc.
66. Robert Bull, interview by Jeffrey L. Rodengen with Joseph Cabadas, digital recording, 2 May 2007, Write Stuff Enterprises, Inc.
67. Byerley interview.
68. Ibid.
69. Jim Gray, "We've Only Just Begun …" *Pacesetter*, Spring 2003, page 6.
70. O'Brien interview.
71. *Never Stand Still*, 344.
72. John Labrie, "Happy Birthday Team CWX: Our 20-Year Great Beginning," *Pacesetter*, Summer 2003, page 4.
73. "Con-Way Central Express," page 1.
74. Kay Beher, interview by Jeffrey L. Rodengen with Joseph Cabadas, digital recording, 1 May 2007, Write Stuff Enterprises, Inc.
75. Kevin Schick, interview by Jeffrey L. Rodengen, digital recording, 23 May 2007, Write Stuff Enterprises, Inc.
76. Schick interview.
77. Kay Beher, "3001 Gets Mothballed," *CCX Milemarker*, May/June 1992, page 3.
78. Millican interview.
79. Beher interview.
80. *Ten Years and Rolling … the Con-Way Companies*, Con-Way Transportation Services, 1993, page 12.
81. Gerald L. Detter, "The First 100 Days!" Con-Way Central Express newsletter, 8 November 1983, page 4.
82. David McClimon, "CCX's First 15 Years Are Marked by Growth, Service Excellence, and Employee Dedication," *CCX Milemarker*, Second Quarter 1998, page 4.
83. Bull interview.
84. Beher interview.
85. "The First 100 Days!" page 4.
86. O'Brien interview.
87. *Never Stand Still*, 345–346.
88. "Penn-Yan Acquisition," *The Freighter*, Third Quarter 1983, page 4.
89. Ibid.
90. *Never Stand Still*, 346–347.
91. "Penn-Yan Acquisition," 4.

CHAPTER FOUR SIDEBAR: FORCES BEHIND DEREGULATION

1. "Trucking War: Deregulating the Highways," *Time*, 5 February 1979.
2. Ibid.
3. "Employment Status of the Civilian Non-Institutional Population, 1940 to Date (2007)," U.S. Department of Labor, Bureau of Labor Statistics, http://www.bls.gov/.
4. Kenneth D. Durr and Philip L. Cantelon, *Never Stand Still: A History of CNF Transportation Inc.*, (Rockville, Maryland: Montrose Press, 1999), pages 301–302.
5. "Commercial Vehicles Still Face Bumpy Road," *Globe and Mail*, 17 January 1983.
6. *Never Stand Still*, 299.

CHAPTER FOUR SIDEBAR: AIRFREIGHT OPPORTUNITY?

1. Kenneth D. Durr and Philip L. Cantelon, *Never Stand Still: A History of CNF Transportation Inc.*, (Rockville, Maryland: Montrose Press, 1999), page 316.
2. Ibid, 315.
3. Ibid, 316.
4. Ibid, 317, 326.
5. Ibid, 317.
6. Moritz interview.
7. *Never Stand Still*, 338–339.

CHAPTER FIVE

1. *Ten Years and Rolling … the Con-Way Companies*, Con-Way Transportation Services, 1993, page 2.
2. Pat Wechsler, "Trucking: A Case Study; Trends Since Deregulation," *Dun's Business Month*, May 1984.
3. David L. Miller, interview by Jeffrey L. Rodengen, digital recording, 1 May 2007, Write Stuff Enterprises, Inc.
4. Thomas Gale Moore, "Trucking Deregulation," Concise Encyclopedia of Economics, http://www.econlib.org/.
5. "Trucking."
6. Steve Tinghitella, "Common Carriers Seen Declining, as Contract Carriage Booms," *Dun's Business Month*, January 1984.
7. Kenneth D. Durr and Philip L. Cantelon, *Never Stand Still: A History of CNF Transportation Inc.*, (Rockville, Maryland: Montrose Press, 1999), page 349.
8. "Trucking."
9. Ibid.
10. Ibid.
11. Byron Olsen and Joseph Cabadas, *The American Auto Factory*, (St. Paul, Minnesota: MBI Publishing Co., 2002), page 150.
12. *Never Stand Still*, 350, 351–352.
13. David L. Miller with Ned Mortiz, interview by Jeffrey L. Rodengen, digital recording, 2 May 2007, Write Stuff Enterprises, Inc.
14. Miller interview.
15. Ned Moritz, interview by Jeffrey L. Rodengen, digital recording, 1 May 2007, Write Stuff Enterprises, Inc.
16. Rock Magnan, interview by Jeffrey L. Rodengen, digital recording, 22 May 2007, Write Stuff Enterprises, Inc.
17. David McClimon, interview by Jeffrey L. Rodengen, digital recording, 1 May 2007, Write Stuff Enterprises, Inc.
18. Ibid.
19. Hugh "Wes" Cornett, interview by Jeffrey L. Rodengen with Joseph Cabadas, digital recording, 1 May 2007, Write Stuff Enterprises, Inc.
20. Gerald L. Detter, "The First 100 Days: Cargo Claims and Personnel," *CCX Newsletter*, 8 November 1983, page 1.
21. Ibid.
22. "First Year Reflections," *CCX Newsletter*, 16 July 1984, page 2.
23. McClimon interview.
24. Gerald L. Detter, "Performance Is Our Key to Growth," *CCX Milemarker*, July/August 1985, pages 1, 3.
25. Gerald L. Detter, "Happy Second Anniversary," *CCX Newsletter*, May/June 1985, page 1.
26. "Performance Is Our Key to Growth."
27. Bryan Millican, "CCX Opens Number 27," *CCX Milemarker*, September/October 1985, page 1.
28. "Marketing Highlights: Records … Records!" *CCX Milemarker*, September/October 1986, page 6.
29. "Trucking."
30. Raymond F. O'Brien, interview by Jeffrey L. Rodengen, digital recording, 23 May 2007, Write Stuff Enterprises, Inc.
31. Wayne Byerley, interview by Jeffrey L. Rodengen, digital recording, 21 May 2007, Write Stuff Enterprises, Inc.
32. Allan Kunigis, "Unique Vision, Solid Execution," *CEO Transportation*, Fall 2000, page 12.

33. Gerald L. Detter, "We Have Grown Together," *CCX Milemarker*, November/December 1985, page 1.
34. Miller interview.
35. Gerald L. Detter, "CCX: Union-Free," *CCX Milemarker*, July/August 1986, page 1.
36. Byerley interview.
37. "Incentive Program Supports Ongoing Success," *CCX Milemarker*, November/December 1986, page 1.
38. Gerald L. Detter, "2 Million Dollars—Wow!" *CCX Milemarker*, September/October 1987, page 1.
39. Cornett interview.
40. "Grigsby Number 1000," *CCX Milemarker*, September/October 1986, page 2.
41. Gerald L. Detter, "Focus On," *CCX Milemarker*, March/April 1986, page 2.
42. Gerald L. Detter, "CCX's Fourth Anniversary—Batting One Thousand," *CCX Milemarker*, May/June 1987, page 1.
43. Bryan Millican, "New Terminal Expansion Impacts Results," *CCX Milemarker*, May/June 1987, page 8.
44. Bryan Millican, "Marketing Highlights: Competitive Update," *CCX Milemarker*, September/October 1987, page 3.
45. "2 Million Dollars—Wow!"
46. Gerald L. Detter, "There's a Fine Line Between Confidence and Arrogance," and "CCX's 3,000,000th Shipment," *CCX Milemarker*, November/December 1987, page 1.
47. "Hats Off to Our 2-Millionth Shipment Winner," *CCX Milemarker*, March/April 1987, page 3.
48. Gerald L. Detter, "President's Message," *CCX Milemarker*, June 1988, page 3.
49. Kay Beher, "Five-Year Operational Highlights," *CCX Milemarker*, June 1988, pages 8–9.
50. Ibid.
51. "Special 5th Anniversary Edition," *Pacesetter*, 15 May 1988, page 2.
52. George C. Reid, "President's Message," *Pacesetter*, Spring 1993, page 3.
53. *Never Stand Still*, 344.
54. J. Edwin Conaway, interview by Jeffrey L. Rodengen with Joseph Cabadas, digital recording, 2 May 2007, Write Stuff Enterprises, Inc.
55. "Consolidated Freightways: The Motor Carrier Management—Its People and Structure," *Freighter*, March 1977, page 45.
56. Sam Dunbar, "Moving Freight Safely … for 20 Years," *Pacesetter*, Spring 2003, pages 14–15.

57. "Safety," *Pacesetter*, Winter 1988, page 7.
58. "Special 5th Anniversary Edition."
59. George C. Reid, "President's Message," *Pacesetter*, Spring 1993, page 2.
60. "Special 5th Anniversary Edition."
61. Ted Regner, "Marketing Highlights," *Pacesetter*, October/November/December 1985, page 2.
62. "Special 5th Anniversary Edition."
63. George C. Reid, "President's Message," *Pacesetter*, Spring 1993, page 3.
64. Conaway interview.
65. "CWX Triple Power," *Pacesetter*, Winter 1988, page 8.
66. George C. Reid, "President's Message," *Pacesetter*, Spring 1993, page 3.
67. "Special 5th Anniversary Edition."
68. George C. Reid, "President's Message," *Pacesetter*, Spring 1993, page 3.
69. "California Considers Deregulation," *Pacesetter*, Winter 1988, page 12.
70. George C. Reid, "President's Message," *Pacesetter*, Spring 1993, page 3.
71. "On Time Service," *Pacesetter*, Winter 1988, page 6.
72. George C. Reid, "President's Message," *Pacesetter*, Winter 1988, page 2.
73. *Never Stand Still*, 371.
74. "Consolidated Freightways."
75. "Con-Way Regional Carriers, the Overnight Sensation," a CF Inc. advertisement, May 1990.
76. *Never Stand Still*, 372.
77. Ibid.
78. R. T. Robertson, "A Land Services Update," *CWX Pacesetter*, Summer 1986, page 1.
79. John Hickerson, interview by Jeffrey L. Rodengen, digital recording, 22 May 2007, Write Stuff Enterprises, Inc.
80. *Ten Years and Rolling … the Con-Way Companies*, 17–19.
81. Ibid, 17.
82. Phil Worthington, interview by Jeffrey L. Rodengen, digital recording, 23 May 2007, Write Stuff Enterprises, Inc.
83. *Ten Years and Rolling … the Con-Way Companies*, 17–19.
84. Donald Moffitt, interview by Jeffrey L. Rodengen, digital recording, 22 May 2007, Write Stuff Enterprises, Inc.
85. *Never Stand Still*, 354, 355, 356, 357–8, 359.
86. "Notice of Annual Meeting of Shareholders," Consolidated Freightways Inc., 18 March 1987, page 3.
87. *Never Stand Still*, 359.

88. R. T. Robertson, "CFLS Forms International Group," *CCX Milemarker*, September/October 1986, page 1.
89. *Never Stand Still*, 361, 361–362.
90. "CF Air Freight Expands Hub," *CCX Milemarker*, September/October 1987, page 2.
91. *Never Stand Still*, 362–363.
92. Ibid, 364.
93. Ibid, 365–367.
94. O'Brien interview.
95. *Never Stand Still*, 374.
96. "Notice of Annual Meeting of Shareholders," Consolidated Freightways Inc., 14 March 1988, page 18.
97. Moffitt interview.
98. *Never Stand Still*, 375–376.

CHAPTER FIVE SIDEBAR: DETTER'S WAY

1. Doug Stotlar, interview by Jeffrey L. Rodengen, digital recording, 22 May 2007, Write Stuff Enterprises, Inc.
2. Wayne Byerley, interview by Jeffrey L. Rodengen, digital recording, 21 May 2007, Write Stuff Enterprises, Inc.

CHAPTER FIVE SIDEBAR: A DIFFERENT KIND OF COMPANY

1. Bryan Millican, interview by Jeffrey L. Rodengen, digital recording, 2 May 2007, Write Stuff Enterprises, Inc.
2. Ibid.
3. Pat Jannausch, interview by Jeffrey L. Rodengen, digital recording, 1 May 2007, Write Stuff Enterprises, Inc.
4. "Account Management Center: What Is Telemarketing?" *CCX Milemarker*, November/December 1986, pages 4–5.

CHAPTER SIX

1. David McClimon, interview by Jeffrey L. Rodengen, digital recording, 1 May 2007, Write Stuff Enterprises, Inc.
2. "Emery Air Freight Corporation with John C. Emery as President—Delaware," http://www.cripophily.net/.
3. Ibid.
4. Donald Moffitt, interview by Jeffrey L. Rodengen, digital recording, 22 May 2007, Write Stuff Enterprises, Inc.
5. "Emery Air Freight Corporation with John C. Emery as President—Delaware."
6. Moffitt interview.
7. Kenneth D. Durr and Philip L. Cantelon, *Never Stand Still: A History of CNF Transportation Inc.*,

(Rockville, Maryland: Montrose Press, 1999), page 376.
8. Moffitt interview.
9. "Emery Air Freight Corporation with John C. Emery as President—Delaware."
10. "2005 Notice of Annual Stockholders Meeting," Telltabs Inc., 17 March 2005, page 5.
11. *Never Stand Still*, 376–377.
12. Eb Schmoller, interview by Jeffrey L. Rodengen, digital recording, 23 May 2007, Write Stuff Enterprises, Inc.
13. "Consolidated Buys Emery Air Freight," *Chicago Sun-Times*, 14 February 1989.
14. *Never Stand Still*, 388.
15. Lawrence M. Fisher, "Business People: Chairman Is Named for Emery Worldwide," *New York Times*, 6 September 1990.
16. *Never Stand Still*, 379.
17. Ibid, 380.
18. "Atlantic City, N.J., Casino King with Midas Touch Dies," *Knight-Ridder/Tribune Business News*, 20 October 2000.
19. Raymond F. O'Brien, interview by Jeffrey L. Rodengen, digital recording, 23 May 2007, Write Stuff Enterprises, Inc.
20. *Never Stand Still*, 381.
21. Ibid, 382–385.
22. "Traffic Briefs: CTS Improvements to Cost $75 Million," *Journal of Commerce*, 30 October 1989.
23. "Con-Way Companies Continue National Expansion in 1989," Con-Way Transportation Services press release, 23 October 1989.
24. Ibid.
25. Gerald Detter, "CCX Charts a Quality Course for the 1990s," *CCX Milemarker*, November/December 1989, pages 1, 8.
26. "Con-Way Central Express Announces Major Expansion, Opens Six New Service Centers," CF Land Services, 15 May 1989.
27. *Ten Years and Rolling ... the Con-Way Companies*, Con-Way Transportation Services, 1993, page 12.
28. "Con-Way Western Express Expands Bay Area Operations, Opens New Freight Service Center in San Francisco," CF Land Services, 2 March 1989.
29. "Con-Way Southern Express Expands Overnight Delivery to Florida with New Jacksonville Service Center," CF Land Services, 2 August 1989.
30. Scott Price, "Con-Way Sets 13 Terminals in Four States," *Business Journal–Charlotte*, 27 March 1989.

31. *Ten Years and Rolling ... the Con-Way Companies*, 18–19.
32. John Hickerson, interview by Jeffrey L. Rodengen, digital recording, 22 May 2007, Write Stuff Enterprises, Inc.
33. Leo Abruzzese, "Consolidated Freightways Opens Texas Subsidiary; Unit Will Serve Southwest States," *Journal of Commerce*, 19 November 1989.
34. Hickerson interview.
35. Ibid.
36. Ibid.
37. Ibid.
38. *Ten Years and Rolling ... the Con-Way Companies*, 22–23.
39. *Never Stand Still*, 401.
40. "CEX Plans $6 Million Dollar Expansion," CF Land Services press release, 12 January 1988.
41. "Con-Way Eastern Express Inaugurates New Express Freight Service from Northeast U.S. to Puerto Rico," CF Land Services press release, 27 April 1989.
42. *Never Stand Still*, 402.
43. Ibid, 373.
44. Ibid, 402.
45. Ibid.
46. Ibid, 403.
47. McClimon interview.
48. *Never Stand Still*, 403.
49. "CEX Closes," *CCX Milemarker*, September/October 1990, page 3.
50. *Never Stand Still*, 403.
51. Ibid, 373, 374.
52. Ibid, 386.
53. Ibid, 387, 388.
54. Ibid, 389.
55. Ibid, 388.
56. Kevin C. Schick, interview by Jeffrey L. Rodengen, digital recording, 23 May 2007, Write Stuff Enterprises, Inc.
57. *Never Stand Still*, 389.
58. Schick interview.
59. *Never Stand Still*, 389.
60. McClimon interview.
61. "Notice of Annual Meeting of Shareholders," Consolidated Freightways Inc., March 13, 1989.
62. Kate Bohner Lewis, "Full Circle," *Forbes*, 27 March 1995, pages 56–57.
63. Moffitt interview.
64. "Consolidated Freightways Inc. (CNF)," reprint from *Wall Street Journal*, 20 February 1995.
65. "Full Circle."
66. *Never Stand Still*, 393.
67. "Full Circle."
68. *Never Stand Still*, 399–400.
69. "Full Circle."
70. Ibid.
71. "An Interview with Don Moffitt," *The Freighter*, Spring 1992, pages 9–11.
72. *Never Stand Still*, 405.

73. Gerald L. Detter, "Despite Challenges, CCX Continues to Grow," *CCX Milemarker*, November/December 1990.
74. Ibid.
75. Hickerson interview.
76. *Ten Years and Rolling ... the Con-Way Companies*, 23.
77. Ibid, 19.
78. Bryan Millican, "Marketing Highlights," *CCX Milemarker*, November/December 1991.
79. *Never Stand Still*, 412.
80. Ibid, 412–413.
81. Ibid, 431.

CHAPTER SIX SIDEBAR: CON-WAY INTERMODAL

1. *Ten Years and Rolling ... the Con-Way Companies*, Con-Way Transportation Services, 1993, page 24.
2. Ibid.
3. *Ten Years and Rolling ... the Con-Way Companies*, 24–27.
4. Ibid.
5. "CF Makes Importing and Exporting as Easy as L-T-L," *Chilton's Distribution*, October 1989.
6. Perry A. Trunick, "Distribution Information Management Gains Importance," *Transportation & Distribution*, October 1989.

CHAPTER SEVEN

1. Gerald Detter, "We Are in the Game to Win," *CCX Milemarker*, Third Quarter 1993, page 1.
2. Gary Kowalski, interview by Jeffrey L. Rodengen, digital recording, 28 August 2007, Write Stuff Enterprises, Inc.
3. Kenneth D. Durr and Philip L. Cantelon, *Never Stand Still: A History of CNF Transportation Inc.*, (Rockville, Maryland: Montrose Press, 1999), page 420.
4. *Never Stand Still*, 420–422.
5. Kowalski interview.
6. Robert L. Bianco, executive biography, Con-way Inc., http://www.con-way.com/.
7. Robert L. Bianco, interview by Jeffrey L. Rodengen, digital recording, 22 May 2007, Write Stuff Enterprises, Inc.
8. Rock Magnan, interview by Jeffrey L. Rodengen, digital recording, 22 May 2007, Write Stuff Enterprises, Inc.
9. *Never Stand Still*, 421.
10. Magnan interview.
11. *Never Stand Still*, 421–422.
12. "Con-Way Transportation Services Qualifies 100 Percent of Drivers for New Commercial Driver's License,"

Con-Way Transportation Services, PR Newswire, 31 March 1992.

13. Ibid.

14. "CSE Adds Puerto Rico to Its Destination List," *Commercial Appeal*, 28 September 1992.

15. Dane Hamilton, "Con-Way Southwest Gets Green Light to Join 2 Texas Operating Authorities," *Journal of Commerce*, 8 October 1992.

16. "Con-Way Western Express Opens New Service to Hawaii," Con-Way Transportation Services, Business Wire, 22 December 1992.

17. *Never Stand Still*, 423–429.

18. Magnan interview.

19. Ibid.

20. Dane Hamilton, "Con-Way Central Labor Dispute Could Come to Boil at Friday Rally," *Journal of Commerce*, 22 October 1992.

21. *Journal of Commerce* staff, "Teamsters Planning National Campaign Against Con-Way," *Buffalo News*, 7 December 1992.

22. Joseph P. Ritz, "Court Halts Con-Way Picketing," *Buffalo News*, 26 November 1992.

23. Robert W. Coon, interview by Jeffrey L. Rodengen, digital recording, 22 May 2007, Write Stuff Enterprises, Inc.

24. "Court Halts Con-Way Picketing."

25. "Teamsters Planning National Campaign Against Con-Way."

26. Dane Hamilton, "Board Decision on Hiring Non-Union Drivers Appealed," *Journal of Commerce*, 18 December 1992.

27. Dane Hamilton, "Teamsters Aim to Force Union Pacts on Less-than-Truckload Carriers," *Journal of Commerce*, 9 December 1992.

28. David M. Cawthorne, "CF Dividing Up Operating Rights Based on Government Regulation," *Traffic World*, 14 December 1992.

29. Bryan Millican, "Expansion Update," *CCX Milemarker*, November/December 1992.

30. Gary Vianueva, interview by Jeffrey L. Rodengen, digital recording, 2 May 2007, Write Stuff Enterprises, Inc.

31. Ibid.

32. Ibid.

33. Dane Hamilton, "Teamsters Use CF Meeting to Combat Non-Union Operation," *Journal of Commerce*, 15 April 1993.

34. John D. Schulz, "CF's Moffitt Cites Solid Progress as Teamsters Step Up Reform Effort," *Traffic World*, 3 May 1993.

35. Ibid.

36. Donald Moffitt, interview by Jeffrey L. Rodengen, digital recording,

22 May 2007, Write Stuff Enterprises, Inc.

37. "Consolidated Freightways Climbs Back into Black," *Journal of Commerce*, 2 February 1994.

38. "CF's Moffitt Cites Solid Progress as Teamsters Step Up Reform Effort."

39. Ibid.

40. Joe Gose, "Red Hot Regionals: Non-Union Subsidiaries Mean Big Bucks to Big Trucking Firms," *Kansas City Business Journal*, 26 November 1993.

41. *Ten Years and Rolling … the Con-Way Companies*, Con-Way Transportation Services, 1993, page 2.

42. Ron Lietzke, "Trucker Keys in on Service, Innovation," *Columbus Dispatch*, 19 July 1993.

43. Bradford Wernle, "Trucking Firm Finds Its Route to Success," *Crain's Detroit Business*, 16 August 1993.

44. "Trucker Keys in on Service, Innovation."

45. "Trucking Firm Finds Its Route to Success."

46. "Con-Way Southwest Expands Dallas–Fort Worth Operations," *Traffic World*, 9 August 1993.

47. J. Edwin Conaway, interview by Jeffrey L. Rodengen with Joseph Cabadas, digital recording, 2 May 2007.

48. Ibid.

49. John Hickerson, interview by Jeffrey L. Rodengen, digital recording, 22 May 2007, Write Stuff Enterprises, Inc.

50. Ibid.

51. Ibid.

52. Ibid.

53. Wayne Byerley, interview by Jeffrey L. Rodengen, digital recording, 21 May 2007, Write Stuff Enterprises, Inc.

54. "Consolidated Freightways Climbs Back into Black," *Journal of Commerce*, 2 February 1994.

55. *Never Stand Still*, 434–435.

56. Ibid, 434.

57. Ibid, 435.

58. Ibid, 435–437.

59. Perry A. Trunick, "LTL Faces Clouds of Doubt," *Transportation & Distribution*, July 1994.

60. Ibid.

61. Robert Bull, interview by Jeffrey L. Rodengen with Joseph Cabadas, digital recording, 2 May 2007, Write Stuff Enterprises, Inc.

62. Dave McClimon, interview by Jeffrey L. Rodengen, digital recording, 1 May 2007, Write Stuff Enterprises, Inc.

63. Ibid.

64. Bull interview.

65. McClimon interview.

66. Ned Moritz, interview by Jeffrey L. Rodengen, digital recording, 1 May 2007, Write Stuff Enterprises, Inc.

67. David L. Miller, interview by Jeffrey L. Rodengen, digital recording, 1 May 2007, Write Stuff Enterprises, Inc.

68. Kay Beher, interview by Jeffrey L. Rodengen with Joseph Cabadas, digital recording, 1 May 2007, Write Stuff Enterprises, Inc.

69. Pat Jannausch, interview by Jeffrey L. Rodengen, digital recording, 1 May 2007, Write Stuff Enterprises, Inc.

70. Daryl LaFitte, interview by Jeffrey L. Rodengen with Joseph Cabadas, digital recording, 2 May 2007, Write Stuff Enterprises, Inc.

71. Miller interview.

72. Beher interview.

73. "LTL Faces Clouds of Doubt."

74. Perry A. Trunick, "A Constant State of Change; Changes in the Less-than-Truckload Industry for 1995," *Transportation & Distribution*, January 1995.

75. Lisa H. Harrington, "Motor Carrier Productivity: Improvements Make a Difference," *Transportation & Distribution*, September 1994.

76. Moritz interview.

77. *Never Stand Still*, 438.

78. Ibid.

79. Ibid, 444.

80. Moffitt interview.

81. Ibid.

82. Perry A. Trunick, "Stretching the Limits of Regional Trucking," *Transportation & Distribution*, January 1996.

83. "A Constant State of Change; Changes in the Less-than-Truckload Industry for 1995."

84. Ibid.

85. *Never Stand Still*, 440.

86. Ibid, 444–445.

87. Hickerson interview.

88. Phil Worthington, interview by Jeffrey L. Rodengen, digital recording, 23 May 2007, Write Stuff Enterprises, Inc.

89. Rip Watson, "Con-Way Is Merging Two Operating Units," *Journal of Commerce*, November 23, 1994.

90. Conaway interview.

91. Ibid.

92. Robert W. Coon, interview by Jeffrey L. Rodengen, digital recording, 22 May 2007, Write Stuff Enterprises, Inc.

93. Steve Wilhelm, "Deregulation Forces Truckers to Shift Gears," *Puget Sound Business Journal*, 11 November 1994.

94. Ibid.

95. Steve Wilhelm, "Truckers Caught in Headlights of Deregulation,"

Puget Sound Business Journal, 16 June 1995.

96. "Con-Way Western Express Introduces New Service to Alaska," Con-Way Transportation Services, Business Wire, 1 June 1995.

97. "Charles E. Boone Names President of Con-Way Western Express," CNF Transportation Inc., 6 November 1995.

98. "Con-Way Central Express Begins Construction of $9.5 million, 100,000-square-foot Service Center in Plainfield, Ind.," Con-Way Transportation Services, Business Wire, 15 September 1994.

99. "Con-Way Central Express Opens $12 Million, State-of-the-Art Service Center in Plainfield, Ind.," Con-Way Transportation Services, Business Wire, 28 July 1995.

100. "Con-Way Central Express Expands Its Regional Trucking Network," Con-Way Transportation Services, Business Wire, 12 July 1995

101. "Con-Way Central Express Expands into Quebec," CNF Transportation Inc., 6 February 1996.

102. John D. Schulz, "Con-Way Service 'Pushes the Envelope,' Extends Next-Day Lanes to 625 Miles," *Traffic World*, 16 June 1996.

103. "Con-Way Central Express Launches New Puerto Rico Service," CNF Transportation Inc., 31 July 1996.

104. "Con-Way Western Express Wins Major Freight Transportation Contract from The Home Depot," Con-Way Transportation Services, Business Wire, 7 October 1996.

105. "Con-Way Intermodal Steps Up Use of Image-Processing Technology," *Traffic World*, 20 January 1992.

106. Ibid.

107. "Con-Way Transportation Services Opens Outpost in Cyberspace," Con-Way Transportation Services, Business Wire, 22 August 1995.

108. Jackie Barretta, interview by Jeffrey L. Rodengen, digital recording, 27 August 2007, Write Stuff Enterprises, Inc.

109. Jacquelyn A. Barretta, executive biography, Con-way Inc., http://www.con-way.com/.

110. Barretta interview.

111. Ibid.

112. "Con-Way NOW Set to Begin Operations in August," *CCX Milemarker*, Second Quarter 1996, page 7.

113. Ibid.

114. Marsha Stopa, "Con-Way Transportation Starts Emergency-Freight Unit," *Crain's Detroit Business*, 7 October 1996.

115. Doug Stotlar, interview by Jeffrey L. Rodengen, digital recording, 22 May 2007, Write Stuff Enterprises, Inc.

116. "Con-Way Transportation Starts Emergency-Freight Unit."

117. Stotlar interview, 22 May 2007.

118. Mark Mensheha, "Con-Way Southwest Express Unveils New Freight Service Here," *San Antonio Business Journal*, 18 November 1994.

119. Kenneth Howe, "Con Freight Headed for a Split; Transport Company to Break into 2 Firms," *San Francisco Chronicle*, 15 November 1996.

120. Dave Anderson, interview by Jeffrey L. Rodengen, digital recording, 30 August 2007, Write Stuff Enterprises, Inc.

121. *Never Stand Still*, 447.

122. "Con Freight Headed for a Split; Transport Company to Break into 2 Firms."

CHAPTER SEVEN SIDEBAR: A CHILLY BUSINESS

1. John D. Schulz, "Con-Way Signs Exclusive Five-Year Deal with Louis Saia III for Pallet Reefers," *Traffic World*, 27 September 1993.

2. Ron Lietzke, "Trucker Keys in on Service, Innovation," *Columbus Dispatch*, 19 July 1993.

3. "Con-Way Signs Exclusive Five-Year Deal with Louis Saia III for Pallet Reefers."

4. John Labrie, interview by Jeffrey L. Rodengen, digital recording, 12 November 2007, Write Stuff Enterprises, Inc.

5. "Con-Way Signs Exclusive Five-Year Deal with Louis Saia III for Pallet Reefers."

6. "The Pallet Reefer Service," *CCX Milemarker*, First Quarter 1994, page 12.

7. Jerry Jackson, "Shipping Small Loads No Big Deal for Company; Trucking Business Provides Special Refrigerated Containers," *Orlando Sentinel*, 18 October 1993.

8. Labrie interview.

CHAPTER SEVEN SIDEBAR: CON-WAY INTERMODAL

1. John D. Schultz, "Con-Way Intermodal Sets Strategy in Europe Markets East and West," *Traffic World*, 29 June 1992.

2. Ibid.

3. "Con-Way Intermodal Introduces Con-Quest," Con-Way Transportation Services, Business Wire, 13 April 1992.

4. Brian Johns, "Con-Way Sets Intermodal Expansion," *Journal of Commerce*, 19 April 1993.

5. "Con-Way Plans to Invest $4.6 Million in Equipment," *Journal of Commerce*, 21 April 1994.

6. Kevin McKenzie, "Trucking: Con-Way Provides Link to Railroads," *Commerce Appeal*, Memphis, 3 May 1993.

7. "Con-Way Expands Latin America Service," *Journal of Commerce*, 21 June 1993.

8. "Con-Way Truckload Services Expands Multi-Modal Capabilities with Addition of Dedicated Fleet for Over-the-Road Operations," Con-Way Transportation Services, Business Wire, 25 April 1995.

CHAPTER EIGHT

1. John D. Schulz, "Sailing into Retirement," *Traffic World*, 4 May 1998, page 22.

2. Kenneth D. Durr and Philip L. Cantelon, *Never Stand Still: A History of CNF Transportation Inc.*, (Rockville, Maryland: Montrose Press, 1999), 450–451.

3. Ibid.

4. John D. Schulz, "Trucking's 'Rolls Royce'; Con-Way Leads the Way in Service, Profitability, While Avoiding Low-Pricing Traps with Shippers," *Traffic World*, 2 June 1997.

5. Keith Kennedy Jr., interview by Jeffrey L. Rodengen, digital recording, 22 May 2007, Write Stuff Enterprises, Inc.

6. *Never Stand Still*, 454–455.

7. Ibid, 455.

8. Ibid, 410, 452, 455–456.

9. "Con-Way Transportation Names Richard V. Palazzo as President and Chief Executive of Con-Way Central Unit," CNF Transportation Inc., 24 July 1997.

10. "Con-Way Transportation Moves Headquarters to Ann Arbor; Relocation Enables One of North America's Premier Trucking Companies to Strengthen Ties to Its Customer Base and Operations," CNF Transportation Inc., 20 October 1998.

11. Terry Kosdrosky, "Con-Way HQ Now Near Ann Arbor," *Crain's Detroit Business*, 9 November 1998, page 6.

12. "Trucking's 'Rolls Royce'; Con-Way Leads the Way in Service, Profitability, While Avoiding Low-Pricing Traps with Shippers."

13. Ibid.

14. Ibid.

15. Ibid.

16. "Ten-Year Anniversary Distinguishes Con-Way Southern

Express as a Driving Success,"
Con-Way Transportation Services,
1 April 1997.

17. "First President of Con-Way
Southern Express Dies At Home;
Thomas C. Smith Remembered as
Trucking Industry Leader," Con-
Way Transportation Services,
30 October 1997.

18. "CNF Transportation Posts Net
Income Increase for Third Quarter,"
CNF Transportation Inc., 1999.

19. *Never Stand Still*, 464.

20. Gary Kowalski, interview by Jeffrey
L. Rodengen, digital recording,
29 August 2007, Write Stuff
Enterprises, Inc.

21. "Fortune Survey Singles Out CNF's
Trucking Services as No. 1 in
North America," CNF
Transportation Inc., 17 February
1999.

22. "CNF Transportation Posts Net
Income Increase for Third Quarter."

23. *Never Stand Still*, 464.

24. "CNF Transportation Posts Net
Income Increase for Third Quarter."

25. Ibid.

26. *Never Stand Still*, 465.

27. "CNF Transportation Posts Net
Income Increase for Third Quarter."

28. Gregory S. Johnson, "Con-Way
NOW on the Move," *Journal of
Commerce*, 2 June 1997.

29. "Con-Way NOW Expands
Expedited Services Network into
Minnesota, West Virginia, New
York," Con-Way Transportation
Services, 6 February 1997.

30. Christopher D. Parker, "Nashville Is
Latest Stop for Shipper," *Nashville
Business Journal*, 30 June 1997.

31. "Con-Way NOW Launches
Southern U.S. Expansion," Con-
Way Transportation Services,
28 May 1997.

32. "Nashville Is Latest Stop for
Shipper."

33. "Con-Way NOW Launches
Southern U.S. Expansion."

34. "Con-Way Names Three Executives
to New Positions," Con-Way
Transportation Services,
11 November 1997.

35. "Con-Way NOW Expands into
Northeast United States," Con-Way
Transportation Services,
13 January 1998.

36. "Con-Way NOW Expands into
Southwest; Staging Areas in
Dallas/Fort Worth and Little Rock
Added to Pickup Network," CNF
Transportation Services, 26 August
1999.

37. Pat Jannausch, interview by
Jeffrey L. Rodengen, digital
recording, 1 May 2007, Write Stuff
Enterprises, Inc.

38. Ibid.

39. Julia P. Jannausch, "Journey to
the Dream," Con-way Inc.

40. Jannausch interview.

41. Ibid.

42. "Journey to the Dream."

43. *Never Stand Still*, 466.

44. 1998 Annual Report, CNF
Transportation Inc., page 15.

45. Ibid, 17.

46. Ibid, 16.

47. Robert Bassett, interview by Jeffrey
L. Rodengen, digital recording,
23 May 2007, Write Stuff
Enterprises, Inc.

48. John D. Schulz, "Stretching Out:
Con-Way Western, Southern Units
Expand to Full Interregional
Coverage," *Traffic World*,
22 December 1997.

49. "Con-Way Offering Three-Day
Service," *Journal of Commerce*,
12 July 1999.

50. "Stretching Out: Con-Way Western,
Southern Units Expand to Full
Interregional Coverage."

51. Ibid.

52. "Trucking's 'Rolls Royce'; Con-Way
Leads the Way in Service,
Profitability, While Avoiding Low-
Pricing Traps with Shippers."

53. John D. Schulz, "A National
Viking? FDX has many options in
deciding whether to create 'Con-
Way II,'" *Traffic World*, 13 October
1997.

54. "Intermodal Broadening Its Role as
Shippers Demand Greater Service
Capabilities; Con-Way Truckload
Hosts Lively Discussion on Key
Industry Issues at Atlanta Event,"
CNF Transportation Inc., 7 May
1997.

55. Ned Moritz, interview by Joseph
Cabadas, 24 October 2007.

56. Ibid.

57. Ned Moritz and Pat Jannausch
with Thomas Nightingale, interview
by Joseph Cabadas, 17 December
2007.

58. 2001 Annual Report, CNF Inc.,
page 7.

59. "Con-Way Western Express Makes
Heavy Investment in Operations
and Infrastructure," CNF Inc.,
14 February 2000.

60. "Con-Way Central Express Opens
New High-Volume Freight Handling
Facility," CNF Inc., 3 August 2000.

61. "Con-Way Central Express to Open
New High-Volume Freight
Assembly Center in Fremont,
Indiana," CNF Inc., 21 May 2001.

62. "CON-WAY Central Express to
Open Two New Service Centers;
78 New Next-Day Lanes Created
and Service Levels Improved," CNF
Inc., 22 October 2001.

63. "Con-Way Southern Express Opens
New Freight Assembly Center;

Chester, Virginia Facility Will
Reduce 300 Transit Times for
Shippers," CNF Inc., 9 November
2000.

64. "Con-Way Southern Express Opens
New High-Volume Freight Handling
Center; Birmingham, AL, Facility
Will Increase Next-Day Delivery
Points," CNF Inc., 11 December
2000.

65. "Con-Way Southern Express
Breaks Ground for New Freight
Assembly Center Near Tulsa,
Oklahoma," CNF Inc., 22 October
2001.

66. John D. Schulz, "Recovery Indeed;
National, Regional LTL Carriers
Enjoy Fiscal Fruits of Cost-Saving
Moves, Improved Pricing,
Efficiencies," *Traffic World*,
February 1998.

67. Ibid.

68. "Con-Way Timeline: Milestones in
Setting New Industry Standards,"
Con-way Inc.

69. "Con-Way Adds 1,500th Canadian-
Made Sterling Truck to Fleet in
Canada," CNF Inc., 1 May 2000.

70. "Con-Way Canada Express
Expands Operations to Five More
Provinces," CNF Inc., 1 May 2000.

71. Ibid.

72. Rick Smith, interview by Jeffrey L.
Rodengen, digital recording,
29 August 2007, Write Stuff
Enterprises, Inc.

73. Ibid.

74. "Con-Way Canada Opens Service
Connections to British Columbia,"
CNF Inc., 4 September 2001.

75. "CON-WAY Launches New Kind of
Logistics Service With a 'Shared
Network' Approach to Solutions,"
CNF Inc., 20 October 1998.

76. "New Con-Way Business Targets
Smaller Companies," *Logistics
Management*, 30 November 1998.

77. "Con-Way Integrated Services
Secures Multi-Year Logistics
Contract with Safelite Glass
Corporation," CNF Inc.,
15 February 2000.

78. Peter Bradley, "The Service Is
Great. Now What?" *Logistics
Management*, 31 March 1998.

79. "CON-WAY Changes Business Unit
Name to Logistics," CNF Inc.,
24 July 2001.

80. Ibid.

81. Ibid.

82. Gregory S. Johnson, "Moving into
Fast Lane," *Journal of Commerce*,
15 April 1998.

83. Ibid.

84. Ibid.

85. "CON-WAY Announces New Priority
Handling Service—CON-WAY
Guaranteed! To Launch February
1," CNF Inc., 18 January 1999.

86. Ibid.
87. "Wal-Mart Names CON-WAY as Key Carrier for Inbound Logistics," CNF Inc., 11 March 1999.
88. Ibid.
89. "United States: Three Die as Emery Worldwide Jet Crashes," *Lloyd's List*, 18 February 2000.
90. "Loss of Pitch Control on Takeoff; Emery World Airlines, Flight 17, McDonnell Douglas DC-8-71-F, N8079U; Rancho Cordova, California; February 16, 2000," Aircraft Accident Report, National Transportation Safety Board, 15 August 2005, page 37.
91. "Emery Crash Not History Just Yet; Emery Crash Exposes Cargo Planes Maintenance Woes," news editorial, *Dayton Daily News*, 15 May 2002.
92. "Emery Pilots Warned of Safety Problems," *Dayton Daily News*, 17 February 2000.
93. "Emery DC-8 Cargo Plane Crashes Near Sacramento, California," http://www.CNN.com/, 17 February 2000.
94. "Loss of Pitch Control on Takeoff; Emery World Airlines, Flight 17, McDonnell Douglas DC-8-71-F, N8079U; Rancho Cordova, California; February 16, 2000," 16.
95. "Emery Pilots Warned of Safety Problems."
96. Chris Isidore, "FAA Charges Air Carrier Lacks Ability and Willingness to Fix Safety Flaws," CNN/Money.com, http://money.CNN.com/, 13 August 2001.
97. Kennedy interview.
98. Emery Worldwide Airlines Inc. v. United States and Federal Express Corporation, United States Court of Appeals for the Federal Circuit, decided 31 August 2001.
99. Ibid.
100. Ibid.
101. "FAA Charges Air Carrier Lacks Ability and Willingness to Fix Safety Flaws."
102. Ibid.
103. "Con-Way NOW Expands Expedite Operations by Adding Air Service," CNF Inc., 3 April 2000.
104. "Con-Way NOW Expands Air Express Coverage: Service Now Offered to 176 Additional Cities," CNF Inc., 14 July 2000.
105. "Con-Way NOW Announces New Service Product; Offers Expedited Service Levels for Dedicated Truckload Shipments," CNF Inc., 27 February 2001.
106. Richard Armstrong, "Vector SCM," Armstrong & Associates Inc., http://www.3plogistics.com/vectorscm.htm/, 23 August 2001.

107. Rock Magnan, interview by Jeffrey L. Rodengen, digital recording, 22 May 2007, Write Stuff Enterprises, Inc.
108. Kowalski interview.
109. "CON-WAY Adds More E-Commerce Features to Web Site; Customer Specific Rate Quotes and Listings of Frequent Vendors and Customers Now Provided to Registered Users," CNF Inc., 8 August 2000.
110. "XML Bill of Lading Added to CON-WAY's E-Business Offerings; New Data Transfer Tool Offers Speed and Flexibility to Customers," CNF Inc., 5 June 2001.
111. "E-Commerce Productivity Creates New CON-WAY Consulting Business," CNF Inc., 16 November 2000.
112. Ibid.
113. "Con-Way Business Solutions Closed; Consulting Services Focused on Supply Chain Analysis Retained Under New Con-Way Logistics Name," CNF Inc., 9 August 2001.
114. "CON-WAY Makes Commitment of Over $1 Million to Safety; New Tractors Being Equipped With High Tech Collision Avoidance System," CNF Inc., 9 April 2001.
115. Ibid.
116. "CON-WAY Participates in World Trade Center Support Mission," CNF Inc., 19 September 2001.
117. "CON-WAY Employees and Company Donate $305,821.46 to Red Cross Disaster Relief Effort," CNF Inc., 9 October 2001.
118. Chris Isidore, "CNF Grounds Emery for Good; Freight Company Will Use Other Cargo Carriers, Take $200M 4Q Charge," CNN/Money.com, http://money.CNN.com/, 5 December 2001.
119. CNF 2001 Annual Report, page 8.
120. Angela Greiling Keane, "But for a Bolt: Missing Part Faulted for Fatal Crash in 2000 of Emery Freighter; NTSB Blames Maintenance," *Traffic World*, 11 August 2003.
121. "CNF Inc. Form 10-K, Year Ended December 31, 2001," CNF Inc., 22 March 2002.

CHAPTER EIGHT SIDEBAR: THE "13 THINGS" LIST

1. Pat Jannausch, interview by Jeffrey L. Rodengen, digital recording, 1 May 2007, Write Stuff Enterprises, Inc.

CHAPTER EIGHT SIDEBAR: AIDING A SILVER SLUGGER

1. "CNF Transportation's Air Freight and Trucking Companies Team Up to Provide 'The Lift' for 'Silver Slugger' Sammy Sosa," CNF Inc., 27 October 1998.

CHAPTER EIGHT SIDEBAR: CHAMPIONSHIP DREAMS

1. "Fortune Survey Singles Out CNF's Trucking Services as No. 1 in North America," CNF Inc., 17 February 1999.
2. "Drivers Named to America's Road Team," *Traffic World*, 2 February 1998.
3. "CON-WAY Driver Appointed to ATA Road Team for 1999: Al Gerber to Serve as Captain on Prestigious Industry Program," CNF Inc., 26 January 1999.
4. "CON-WAY Canadian Driver Wins National Champion Title in 3-Axle Class; First Champion for CON-WAY at Canadian Competition," CNF Inc., 4 October 1999.
5. Ibid.
6. "Con-Way Central Express Driver Appointed to ATA Road Team for 2000," CNF Inc., 24 January 2000.
7. "Con-Way Sends Record Number of State Champions to National Truck Driving Championships in New Orleans: 49 Drivers to Represent Company," CNF Inc., 24 July 2000.
8. "CON-WAY Drivers Win Captain Spots on 2001 America's Road Team; Will Serve as Industry Ambassadors for Two Years," CNF Inc., 6 June 2001.
9. Ibid.
10. "CON-WAY Breaks All-Time Record in Number of State Champions Attending National Truck Driving Championships in Minneapolis; 60 Drivers to Represent Company," CNF Inc., 23 July 2001.
11. "Fortune Survey Singles Out CNF's Trucking Services as No. 1 in North America."
12. "Con-Ways Receive Performance Awards from Four Major Shippers," CNF Inc., 23 May 2000.

CHAPTER NINE

1. Doug Stotlar, interview by Jeffrey L. Rodengen, digital recording, 22 May 2007, Write Stuff Enterprises, Inc.
2. "Con-Way Adds Truckload Brokerage Service," CNF Inc., 2 January 2002.
3. John D. Schultz, "Undisputed No. 1: Con-Way Formula of High Service,

Full Rates, Diversification Captures Shippers, Profits," *Traffic World*, 24 June 2002.

4. Ibid.

5. Ibid.

6. Keith Kennedy, interview by Jeffrey L. Rodengen, digital recording, 22 May 2007, Write Stuff Enterprises, Inc.

7. James Cooke, "UPS Snaps Up Menlo's Forwarding Unit," *Logistics Management*, 1 November 2004.

8. CNF Inc., 8-K, EX-99, SEC File 1-05046, dated 30 September 2004, filed on 6 October 2004.

9. Holli E. Estridge, "Trucking Company Buys Land at Alliance; Con-way Freight to Build Service Center," *Dallas Business Journal*, 11 September 2006.

10. "Con-Way Central Express to Open New, Larger Greencastle, Pennsylvania Service Center; Capacity Added Due to Increased Business Volumes," CNF Inc., 4 November 2004.

11. "Con-Way Sees Triple Business in Move to Larger Space," *Memphis Business Journal*, 26 July 2004.

12. "Con-Way Southern Express Opens New, Larger Memphis Facility; Business Growth Drives Investment to Triple Capacity," CNF Inc., 26 July 2004.

13. "Con-Way Southern Express Breaks Ground for New Service Center in Newnan, Georgia," CNF Inc., 28 March 2003.

14. "Con-Way Canada Express to Open Two New Service Centers; Freight Handling and Service Capabilities to Increase," CNF Inc., 4 February 2002.

15. Ibid.

16. "Con-Way Expands Next-Day and Second-Day L-T-L Service Lanes," CNF Inc., 5 July 2002.

17. Ibid.

18. "Con-Way to Implement Homeland Security Surcharge for All Cross-Border U.S. and Canada Shipments," CNF Inc., 11 November 2002.

19. "Con-Way Signs On to U.S. and Canada Security Initiatives," CNF Inc., 21 November 2002.

20. "Con-Way Carriers Approved for Customs Self Assessment Program; Program Will Improve U.S. to Canada Freight Security and Crossing Times," CNF Inc., 8 January 2003.

21. "Con-Way Appoints Curtis Shewchuk Director of Corporate Protective Services," CNF Inc., 27 March 2003.

22. "Con-Way Launches 'Slower and Lower' Intermodal Service," *Logistics Management*, 1 October 2002.

23. Dave Anderson, interview by Jeffrey L. Rodengen, digital recording, 30 August 2007, Write Stuff Enterprises, Inc.

24. Ibid.

25. Robert W. Coon, interview by Jeffrey L. Rodengen, digital recording, 22 May 2007, Write Stuff Enterprises, Inc.

26. "Con-Way Helps Levy Home Entertainment Control Delivery of Latest Harry Potter Book," CNF Inc., 21 June 2003.

27. "New Potter Book Goes Public June 21; Three Years after 'Goblet,' Here Comes 'Phoenix,'" http://www.CNN.com/, 16 January 2003.

28. "Con-Way Helps Levy Home Entertainment Control Delivery of Latest Harry Potter Book," CNF Inc., 21 June 2003.

29. Ibid.

30. "Precision Delivery of New Harry Potter Book Given by Con-Way; Levy Home Entertainment's Guidelines Could Not Be Missed; Potter Parties Can't Be Disappointed," CNF Inc., 16 July 2005.

31. "CON-WAY Announces Major Web Site Enhancement; Electronic Bill of Lading Template Makes EBOL Easier, Faster to Use," CNF Inc., 12 February 2002.

32. Richard Pastore, "Cruise Control," *CIO Magazine*, 1 February 2003.

33. "Draft: Con-Way Linehaul Automation System," CNF Inc., 26 April 2002.

34. "Cruise Control."

35. "Draft: Con-Way Linehaul Automation System."

36. "Cruise Control."

37. John D. Schulz, "Con-Way 'Buys Time'; Ex-Chinese Rocket Scientist Concludes 5-Year Project for Line-Haul Automation to Ensure Top LTL Service," *Traffic World*, 24 June 2002.

38. Ibid.

39. "Cruise Control."

40. "Con-Way Receives Prestigious Information Technology Award; Automated Linehaul System Among Nation's Top Five Applications; System Receives Enterprise Value Award," CNF Inc., 19 February 2003.

41. "Con-Way IT Efforts Ranked First in Transportation Industry; Company Cited as Leader in National Survey," CNF Inc., 29 September 2003.

42. Sean Kilcarr, "HOS: New Rules, Same Problems; The Impact of New Hours-of-Service Regs on Trucking Will Be Widespread and Varied, but in the End May Not Address the Fundamental Factors That

Contribute to Driver Fatigue," *Fleet Owner*, August 2003, pages 24–25, 28, 30.

43. Deborah Whistler, "HOS Safety Improvements," *Newport's Heavy Duty Trucking*, February 2005, pages 6, 8.

44. "HOS."

45. "HOS Safety Improvements."

46. "Con-Way Awarded Certification for ISO 9001 and 14001; Quality Certification Applies to All Con-Way Companies and Facilities," CNF Inc., 28 May 2003.

47. Ibid.

48. "Doug Stotlar Appointed CON-WAY Chief Operating Officer," CNF Inc., 20 June 2002.

49. "Richard Palazzo to Retire from Con-Way Central Express; David S. McClimon Named Con-Way Central Express President and Chief Executive Officer; John G. Labrie Named President and Chief Executive Officer of Con-Way Western Express," CNF Inc., 20 June 2002.

50. "CNF Profits up 22 Percent in 4Q," *Trailer Body Builders*, 27 January 2004.

51. *Never Stand Still*, 526.

52. "Next CEO at CNF?" *Traffic World*, 1 March 2004.

53. "CNF Board Elects Interim CEO," http://www.TruckingInfo.com/.

54. Stotlar interview, 22 May 2007.

55. Ibid.

56. "CNF Board Elects Douglas Stotlar President and CEO," CNF Inc., 26 April 2005.

57. "CNF Inc. 2004 Annual Report," 14 March 2005.

58. "New Vice President of Sales Named at Con-Way; J. Edwin 'Ed' Conaway Named to Top Sales Position," CNF Inc., 18 November 2005.

59. "Michelle D. Potter Named President of Con-Way NOW," CNF Inc., November 29, 2005.

60. "Con-Way to Launch New Truckload Company," CNF Inc., 3 June 2004.

61. "Clayton Halla Appointed President of Con-Way Truckload," CNF Inc., 13 July 2004.

62. "Con-Way Truckload Begins Operations; First Driver Teams to Leave Memphis on Transcontinental Runs," CNF Inc., 17 January 2005.

63. "Con-way: Our Beginning," Con-way Inc., PowerPoint presentation, pages 30–31.

64. Stotlar interview, 22 May 2007.

65. "CNF Names New Executives," CNF Inc., 6 June 2005.

66. "Con-Way Announces Senior Management Organization

Changes," CNF Inc., 10 January 2005.

67. Bill Carey, "CNF's New Vision," *Traffic World*, 19 September 2005.

68. "CNF Names New Executives."

69. Avery Vise, "The Top 100. The Big Picture: *CCJ*'s The Top 100 Now Considers Fleet Size, Driver Force," *Commercial Carrier Journal*, 1 August 2005.

70. "Con-Way LTL Carriers Receive Ford Motor Company's Q1 Certification; Quality Certification Puts Con-Way in Select Group of Service Providers to Automaker," CNF Inc., 23 March 2005.

71. Bruce G. Hoffman, "Con-Way Transportation Expands in Mexico," *Ann Arbor News*, 22 June 2005.

72. Ibid.

73. "BSNF Teams Up to Ship Playing Cards Destined for Soldiers in Iraq," *BNSF Railway*, 22 July 2005.

74. "Con-Way Employees to Visit Schools Nationwide with Anti-Drug Message; Company Supports Red Ribbon Campaign for 15th Consecutive Year," CNF Inc., 11 October 2005.

75. Pat Jannausch, interview by Jeffrey L. Rodengen, digital recording, 1 May 2007, Write Stuff Enterprises, Inc.

76. "Con-Way Recognized for Technology Advances; High Risk Information Technology Changes Pay Business Dividends," CNF Inc., 16 August 2005.

77. "Con-Way Adds New, 'Final Mile' Local Delivery Service; Specialized Service to Offer Cross-Docking, Electronic Confirmation of Shipments and Time-Specific Store Delivery," CNF Inc., 16 May 2005.

78. "CNF Inc. Net Income from Continuing Operations Climbs 57 Percent in Third Quarter 2005," CNF Inc., 19 October 2005.

79. "Con-Way LTL Companies Expand Freight Handling Capacity," CNF Inc., 15 November 2005.

80. "CNF's New Vision."

81. *Consolidated Freightways, Inc.*, 52–53.

82. "November 2005 Atlantic Tropical Weather Summary," National Hurricane Center, 23 January 2007.

83. "Con-way Named LTL Carrier of the Year by Wal-Mart; Company Also Honored for Leadership During Katrina Disaster," Con-way Inc., 25 May 2006.

84. Richard D. Knabb with Daniel P. Brown, Jamie R. Rhome, "Tropical Cyclone Report:

Hurricane Rita 18–26 September 2005," National Hurricane Center, 17 March 2006.

85. "CNF Inc. 2005 Annual Report," 13 March 2006.

86. "CNF Inc. Net Income from Continuing Operations Climbs 57 Percent in Third-Quarter 2005."

CHAPTER NINE SIDEBAR: CONSOLIDATED FREIGHTWAYS' DEMISE

1. Kenneth Howe, "Con Freight Headed for a Split; Transport Company to Break into 2 Firms," *San Francisco Chronicle*, 15 November 1996.

2. Ibid.

3. John D. Schulz, "CF's New Generation," *Traffic World*, 13 September 1999.

4. Ibid.

5. "Consolidated Freightways Announces New Financial Resources to Support Turnaround Plan and Fourth Quarter 2001 Results," Business Wire, 20 February 2002.

6. Kathleen Pender, "CNF Inc. Keeps on Truckin,'" *San Francisco Chronicle*, 5 September 2002.

CHAPTER TEN

1. Doug Stotlar, interview by Jeff Rodengen, digital recording, 2 November 2007, Write Stuff Enterprises, Inc.

2. "CNF Inc. Reports Record Net Income; Full-Year Revenues, Operating Income Also Reach New Milestone," CNF Inc., 24 January 2006.

3. Ibid.

4. "S&P Raises Ratings on CNF to BBB; Fitch Initiates Coverage with BBB Rating and Stable Outlook; Agency Actions Cite Strong Liquidity, Sustained Improvement in Operating Performance, Profitability," CNF Inc., 6 February 2005.

5. Keith Kennedy, interview by Jeffrey L. Rodengen, digital recording, 22 May 2007, Write Stuff Enterprises, Inc.

6. "CNF to Adopt Con-way as Corporate Brand; Con-way to Succeed CNF as Corporate Name, CNW to Become New Stock Ticker Symbol in Launch of Global Branding Initiative," CNF Inc., 20 February 2006.

7. "Con-way to Host Analyst Day at NYSE," Con-way Inc., 8 May 2006.

8. "Con-way President and CEO Douglas Stotlar to Ring NYSE Opening Bell," Con-way Inc., 10 May 2006.

9. Bill Carey, "Goodbye CNF, Hello 'Con-way'; Con-Way Regional Carriers Regroup as Con-way Freight as $4.2 Billion Trucking Giant Rebrands," *Traffic World*, 24 April 1996.

10. Pat Jannausch, interview by Jeffrey L. Rodengen, digital recording, 1 May 2007, Write Stuff Enterprises, Inc.

11. Mike Ramsey, "Con-Way Says Parent Firm Taking Its Name," *Ann Arbor News*, 20 February 2006.

12. Ned Moritz, interview by Jeffrey L. Rodengen, digital recording, 30 August 2007, Write Stuff Enterprises, Inc.

13. Ibid.

14. Thomas Nightingale, interview by Jeffrey L. Rodengen, digital recording, 17 March 2007, Write Stuff Enterprises, Inc.

15. "Goodbye CNF, Hello 'Con-way'; Con-Way Regional Carriers Regroup as Con-way Freight as $4.2 Billion Trucking Giant Rebrands."

16. Jennifer Pileggi, interview by Jeffrey L. Rodengen, digital recording, 22 May 2007, Write Stuff Enterprises, Inc.

17. "CNF Shareholders Approve Name Change to Con-way; Venerable CNF Symbol Retired, Stock Trading on NYSE as CNW Starts Tomorrow," Con-way Inc., 18 April 2006.

18. "Con-way Sells Expedited Transportation Unit to Panther," Con-way Inc., 24 July 2006.

19. Thomas Nightingale, e-mail message to Joseph Cabadas, dated 9 January 2008.

20. "Con-way Sells Expedited Transportation Unit to Panther."

21. "CNF Shareholders Approve Name Change to Con-way; Venerable CNF Symbol Retired, Stock Trading on NYSE as CNW Starts Tomorrow."

22. Nightingale interview.

23. Robert L. Bianco, interview by Jeffrey L. Rodengen, digital recording, 31 October 2007, Write Stuff Enterprises, Inc.

24. Ibid.

25. Rock Magnan, interview by Jeffrey L. Rodengen, digital recording, 22 May 2007, Write Stuff Enterprises, Inc.

26. Bianco interview.

27. John Paul Quinn, "Global 3PL Growth Taking Off; With the U.S. Economy Hitting a Sluggish Spell; 3PLs Are Finding That Offshore Markets Are Where the Real Action Is—as Long as the Risks Are Understood," *Logistics Management*, 1 June 2007.

28. Bianco interview.
29. Ibid.
30. "Menlo Worldwide Launches New Malaysia Entry; Operations in Kuala Lumpur and Penang Focus on Global Transportation and Management Services for High-Tech and Consumer Product Clients," CNF Inc., 2 March 2006.
31. "Menlo Worldwide Expands in the Netherlands; New Capacity at Eersel Logistics Centre Supports Substantial Growth in Brabant Region," Con-way Inc., 17 August 2006.
32. "Menlo Worldwide Wins Contract from Siemens Ltd. Communications; 3PL Launches New Operation in Sydney to Provide Global Telecommunications Firm with Warehousing, Product Configuration, and Direct Fulfillment for the South Pacific Market," Con-way Inc., 24 August 2006.
33. "Con-way and General Motors to Enter Discussions Regarding Purchase of Vector SCM," Con-way Inc., 29 June 2006.
34. "Con-way and General Motors Agree on Valuation for Vector SCM, LLC; Vector's Value Set at $96.4 Million; Con-way to Receive Proceeds of $84.8 Million for Its Membership Interest," Con-way Inc., 11 December 2006.
35. Gary Kowalski, interview by Jeffrey L. Rodengen, digital recording, 28 August 2007, Write Stuff Enterprises, Inc.
36. "Con-way Wins Top Government Honor for Support of Employees in National Guard and Reserves," Con-way Inc., 13 September 2007.
37. "Con-Way Central Express Honored by Michigan and Indiana National Guard for Support of Employees Who Serve in Units," CNF Inc., 12 April 2006.
38. "Con-way Freight Executive Testifies on Employer Support of National Guard and Reserves; David L. Miller Urges Government to Ease Strain of Deployment on Business," Con-way Inc., 31 May 2007.
39. "Con-way Wins Top Government Honor for Support of Employees in National Guard and Reserves."
40. Ibid.
41. Ibid.
42. "APL Logistics and Con-way Freight Launch 'OceanGuaranteed' Service; Companies Create New Service Category Combining Premium Ocean Cartage with High-Performance LTL Transportation for Fast, Guaranteed Port-to-Door Delivery from China to the U.S.," Con-way Inc., 14 August 2006.

43. Ibid.
44. Ibid.
45. "APL Logistics and Con-way Freight Expand 'OceanGuaranteed' Service; Singapore, Japan, Korea, and Taiwan Added, Simplified Price Structure Remains," Con-way Inc. and APL Logistics, 17 January 2007.
46. "Con-way Freight and Tropical Shipping Launch TropicalDirect Service to the Bahamas and the Caribbean; New Solution Offers Quick and Easy Door-to-Port Shipping with One Call," Con-way Inc. and Tropical Shipping, 2 April 2007.
47. "Menlo Worldwide Wins Supplier Excellence Award from Lam Research," Con-way Inc., 3 April 2007.
48. "Menlo Worldwide Receives Award of Excellence from Global Institute of Logistics; Company Cited for Innovation, Successful Application of 'Lean' Manufacturing Principals in the Provision of Logistics Service in Europe," Con-way Inc., 14 May 2007.
49. "Con-way Ranked No. 1 in Transportation and Logistics on FORTUNE®'s 2007 List of 'America's Most Admired Companies,'" Con-way Inc., 8 March 2007.
50. Ibid.
51. "Con-way Freight Driver Named to ATA's 'America's Road Team;' Dennis Day One of Only 16 Drivers Selected to Represent the Industry," Con-way Inc., 15 March 2007.
52. "Con-way Freight Driver Represents Trucking Industry for Federal Motor Carrier Safety Administration (FMCSA) Advisory Committee; David May Recommends Training, Testing Improvements for CDL program," Con-way Inc., 7 May 2007.
53. Stotlar interview, 2 November 2007.
54. Ibid.
55. "Con-way Acquires Contract Freighters, Inc. to Accelerate Growth and Expand Service Offerings; $750 Million Acquisition Creates Unique Transportation and Logistics Enterprise with More Diversified Revenue, Broader Capabilities," Con-way Inc. and Transportation Resources Inc., 16 July 2007.
56. Ibid.
57. Stotlar interview, 2 November 2007.
58. Herb Schmidt, interview by Jeffrey L. Rodengen, digital recording, 2 November 2007, Write Stuff Enterprises, Inc.

59. Ibid.
60. "Con-way Acquires Contract Freighters, Inc. to Accelerate Growth and Expand Service Offerings; $750 Million Acquisition Creates Unique Transportation and Logistics Enterprise with More Diversified Revenue, Broader Capabilities."
61. "How It Works: Cap-and-Trade Systems," Catalyst: The Magazine of the Union of Concerned Scientists, Spring 2005.
62. "Con-way Freight Joins U.S. EPA SmartWay Environmental Partnership," Traffic World, 10 July 2006.
63. Ibid.
64. Ibid.
65. Ibid.
66. "Menlo Worldwide LLC to Acquire Southeast Asia 3PL Cougar Holdings Pte Ltd and its Primary Subsidiary Cougar Express Logistics Pte Ltd; Companies Sign Purchase Agreement, US$33.9 Million Deal to Close 90 Days Pending Regulatory Clearance, Shareholder Approval," Con-way Inc., 7 June 2007.
67. Bianco interview.
68. "Menlo Worldwide Announces Major Expansion in China with Acquisition of Shanghai-Based 3PL Chic Holdings Ltd.; US$60 Million Deal Makes Menlo a Leading Provider of Intra-China Logistics," Con-way Inc., 9 September 2007.
69. Ibid.
70. Bianco interview.
71. "Asia–Pacific Expansion Strategy Underscores Growth Prospects for Menlo Worldwide as Leading Third Party Logistics Provider," Con-way Inc., 10 October 2007.
72. Stotlar interview, 2 November 2007.
73. "Con-way Inc. Advances Employee Professional Growth and Development with the Con-way Leadership Academy; New Program Builds on Company's Traditional Emphasis on Employee Training, Launches Tailored Curriculum, Expert Trainers at 10 Sites Worldwide," Con-way Inc., 26 June 2007.
74. Donald Moffitt, interview by Jeffrey L. Rodengen, digital recording, 22 May 2007, Write Stuff Enterprises, Inc.
75. Mark J. Perry, "Is Recession Looming on Horizon in 2008?" Philadelphia Inquirer, 2 January 2008.
76. "Goldman Forecast: 'Recession-Lite;' Investment Bank Expects the First Recession Since 2001; Predicts Only a Mild Slowdown, as

Economy Could Recover by 2009," CNN/Money.com, http://money.cnn.com/, 9 January 2008.

77. Nightingale interview.

78. "Con-way Freight Announces Expansion of Freight Assembly Center in Fremont, Ind.; Major Infrastructure Investments Adds Capacity for Future Growth," Con-way Inc., 14 March 2007.

79. "John G. Labrie Named President of Con-way Freight; 17-Year Con-way Veteran Leads Less-than-Truckload Company," Con-way Inc., 27 July 2007.

80. "Con-way Freight Unveils Unified Operating Model; Less-than-Truckload Carrier Aligns Under New Management Team and Organizational Model to Improve Customer Experience," Con-way Inc., 22 August 2007.

81. Stotlar interview, 2 November 2007.

82. John Labrie, interview by Jeffrey L. Rodengen, digital recording, 12 November 2007, Write Stuff Enterprises, Inc.

83. Ibid.

84. "Con-way Freight Unveils Unified Operating Model; Less-than-Truckload Carrier Aligns Under New Management Team and Organizational Model to Improve Customer Experience."

85. "David L. Miller Elected to U.S. Chamber Board of Directors; Con-Freight Inc. Chief Operating Officer Tapped for Board Service," Con-way Inc., November 2007.

86. Moritz interview.

87. "Menlo Worldwide Selected as Prime Contractor for U.S. Transportation Command's Defense Transportation Coordination Initiative (DTCI)," Con-way Inc., 17 August 2007.

88. Ibid.

89. Bianco interview.

90. "Menlo Worldwide Selected as Prime Contractor for U.S. Transportation Command's Defense Transportation Coordination Initiative (DTCI)."

91. Ibid.

92. Ibid.

93. Stotlar interview, 2 November 2007.

94. "Menlo Worldwide Selected as Prime Contractor for U.S. Transportation Command's Defense Transportation Coordination Initiative (DTCI)."

95. Stotlar interview, 2 November 2007.

CHAPTER TEN SIDEBAR: RACING SPONSORSHIP

1. Ned Moritz, interview by Jeffrey L. Rodengen, digital recording, 30 August 2007, Write Stuff Enterprises, Inc.

2. "Jack Sprague—No. 60 Con-way Freight Toyota Tundra Chevy Silverado HD 250 Race Preview," http://www.jacksprague.com/, 13 February 2007; "Jack Sprague's Successful Run with Wyler Racing Ends with Top Twenty in South Florida," http://www.jacksprague.com/, 19 November 2007.

3. Moritz interview.

4. "Colin Braun to Drive No. 6 Con-way Freight F-150 in 2008," Con-way Inc., 16 November 2007.

5. Ibid.

6. Ibid.

CHAPTER TEN SIDEBAR: THE LEAN VISION

1. Jeff Rivera, interview by Jeffrey L. Rodengen, digital recording,
24 March 2008, Write Stuff Enterprises, Inc.

2. Anthony Oliverio, interview by Jeffrey L. Rodengen, digital recording, 26 March 2008, Write Stuff Enterprises, Inc.

3. Rivera interview.

4. Oliverio interview.

5. Rivera interview.

CHAPTER TEN SIDEBAR: SPIN® SELLING

1. J. Edwin Conaway, interview by Jeffrey L. Rodengen with Joseph Cabadas, digital recording, 2 May 2007, Write Stuff Enterprises, Inc.

2. "Neil Rackham," http://www.neilrackham.com/.

3. Conaway interview.

CHAPTER TEN SIDEBAR: SAFETY: A CORE VALUE

1. Marshall Fulbright, interview by Jeffrey L. Rodengen with Joseph Cabadas, digital recording 1 May 2007, Write Stuff Enterprises, Inc.

2. "Con-way Freight Receives Multiple Honors at American Trucking Associations Management Conference," *Traffic World*, 31 October 2006.

3. "Con-way Executive Chosen for the Federal Motor Carrier Safety Administration's National Motor Carrier Safety Advisory Committee; Robert Petrancosta Brings More Than 30 Years of Industry Experience," Con-way Inc., 26 March 2007.

4. "Con-way Freight Sends 58 Drivers to National Driving Competition; More Than Any Single LTL Company at New Orleans Competition," Con-way Inc., 26 July 2006.

INDEX

Page numbers in italics indicate photographs.

202